What Kind of Island in What Kind of Sea

Franz Fühmann

Elizabeth C. Hamilton, Translator

Dietmar Riemann, Photographer

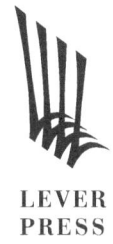

LEVER
PRESS

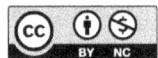
DOI: https://doi.org/10.3998/mpub.12467134
Print ISBN: 978-1-64315-027-7
Open access ISBN: 978-1-64315-028-4

Published in the United States of America by Lever Press, in partnership with Amherst College Press and Michigan Publishing

Contents

Member Institution Acknowledgments

Lever Press is a joint venture. This work was made possible by the generous support of Lever Press member libraries from the following institutions:

Adrian College

Agnes Scott College

Allegheny College

Amherst College

Bard College

Berea College

Bowdoin College

Carleton College

Claremont Graduate University

Claremont McKenna College

Clark Atlanta University

Coe College

College of Saint Benedict / Saint John's University

The College of Wooster

Denison University

DePauw University

Earlham College

Furman University

Grinnell College

Hamilton College

Harvey Mudd College

Haverford College

Hollins University

Keck Graduate Institute

Kenyon College

Knox College

Lafayette College Library

Lake Forest College

Macalester College

Middlebury College

Morehouse College

Oberlin College

Pitzer College

Pomona College

Rollins College

Santa Clara University

Scripps College

Sewanee: The University of the South

Skidmore College

Smith College

Spelman College

St. Lawrence University

St. Olaf College

Susquehanna University

Swarthmore College

Trinity University

Union College

University of Puget Sound

Ursinus College

Vassar College

Washington and Lee University

Whitman College

Willamette University

Williams College

Acknowledgments

This is a book about a book, but more so a book about human relationships to and through words and images, about what we learn about ourselves when we learn about others. It has been a privilege to bring *Was für eine Insel in was für einem Meer* to an English-speaking audience, to meet so many people involved in the original work's creation, and to learn from and with others who were as profoundly moved as I by its witness to humanity.

I am indebted to Dietmar Riemann for permitting me to reprint his extraordinary photographs in this volume and for offering a comprehensive account and detailed documentation of the making of the original book. I thank him and Marga Riemann for their generous hospitality and for shedding light on social, cultural, and political dynamics during its creation. I thank the Hinstorff Verlag GmbH in Rostock for permission to reprint Franz Fühmann's original German essay, "Photographien von geistig Behinderten," and to publish my English translation of it.

Paul-Gerhard Voget enlarged my approach to this project through his welcome and wisdom. Formerly the theological (or clerical) director of the Samaritans' Institution, he fostered conversation with residents and staff members there and with colleagues in the surrounding region, each of whom deepened my thinking about care, respect, and love for our neighbors. Renate Frost aided my understanding of the professional and personal dimensions of this work through warm conversation and generous listening. Ulrike Menzel, the Samariteranstalten's current Theologischer Vorstand, offered extraordinary support in documenting permission to include several residents' oral histories in this volume. I am grateful for her engagement and warm correspondence even during the COVID-19 pandemic.

Present and former colleagues and residents of the Samariteranstalten gave generously of their time during my visits in 2015 and 2017 and via correspondence. I thank Klaus Gubener for his rich responses to my questions, including copies of handwritten notes from his personal collection as well as insights into the collaborations and relationships at the Samariteranstalten in the 1980s. I thank Fritz Müller for sharing his memories along with writings, songs, and artwork that the residents created and enjoyed with Fühmann and Riemann. I thank Volkmar Bley and residents of Lindenhof for their gracious welcome and permission to hear and write about their stories, and remember with gratitude the late Heike Bley for her insights into living and working at the Samariteranstalten. My thanks are due to Christa M., Gerda S., Christine Z., Thomas K., Charlotte M., Margarethe R., Klaus-Dieter S., Gerd F., and Wolfgang F. for their hospitality and kind conversation. I am grateful to Rotraud S., Christel O., Kornelia B., and Heinz S. for their warm reception and chance to talk about the past and the present together with Diane Krüger, Dana Tiedge, and Jenny Baumgärtel at aufwind. I thank Christine Dormann for her kind facilitation of my stay in Fürstenwalde.

Travel for this project was supported by a Powers Travel Grant from Oberlin College in 2015. At Oberlin College my research was aided tremendously by Barbara Prior, art librarian. Megan Mitchell, academic engagement and digital initiatives coordinator, opened my thinking about what forms this project could take. I thank her for truly outstanding guidance.

The Max Kade German Writer-in-Residence program at Oberlin College brings distinguished authors to our campus every year, and guest authors Uwe Kolbe and Peter Wawerzinek each enriched my understanding of the Insel book immeasurably, along with the wider world of German literature and art. It would have been an honor simply to have heard one live reading from either of these very different, yet equally powerful and deservedly eminent authors; I have had the great good fortune to know them personally over time and to absorb the often disquieting, always illuminating insights of their thinking and writing.

My deep appreciation is due to Finn Miller, Maya Rogers, and Miriam Cory, Oberlin College student research assistants, for their excellent collaboration on alt-text descriptions of the photographs in this volume. They helped to render immensely rich images from, for them, a very distant time and place in concise language for contemporary readers. They often saw what I hadn't seen. I thank them for their sensitivity to cultural changes and for their principled commitments to respecting all human beings.

David Kamitsuka, dean of the College of Arts and Sciences at Oberlin College, encouraged my scholarship while supporting my administrative work as associate dean through extraordinary years. I thank him for keeping the highest ideals of education ever in our vision in the midst of disruption and change.

Beth Bouloukos at Lever Press merits my deep gratitude for shepherding this multifaceted project to completion. I thank her for her succinct, substantive advice and for her patience when my progress was slow. Hannah Brooks-Motl provided thoughtful editorial guidance. Reviewers of the manuscript offered critical insights from disability studies and German literary and historical scholarly perspectives that made this work better. I thank them for their expertise and for professional generosity in offering sound and constructive advice. Susan Burch writes and teaches with the highest ethical standards of any person I know; her contributions to the present work and to my overall approach to academia cannot be overstated.

Christine Mohr, Ester Riehl, and Nicole Wandersmann offered insights into the German language that aided my understanding tremendously as I began this project. Their friendship across miles, years, and languages has meant even more. Jerry Malone's insatiable curiosity propels my own. His eagle eye and precise vocabulary aided me in this project and continuously impact my thinking. I thank Laura Dunn for her steady support in caring for my cats and for her beautiful photographs.

My family's unwavering love fuels me. The present work reflects just one example of the importance of education in our lives. As a teacher and a learner I am blessed to pursue the life of the mind as well as the heart.

And who is my neighbor?
Luke 10:29

"HERE, THEN, AWE OF HUMAN DIGNITY"

Franz Fühmann and Dietmar Riemann's Photo-Essay Collection,
Was für eine Insel in was für einem Meer

Elizabeth C. Hamilton

The dignity of cognitively disabled, institutionalized people and the ethics of representing their lives are at the heart of an extraordinary, yet little-known book published in 1986 in the German Democratic Republic (GDR). *Was für eine Insel in was für einem Meer,*[1] or *What Kind of Island in What Kind of Sea*, depicts residents of an institution for people with cognitive disabilities in astonishingly beautiful black-and-white photographs by then up-and-coming photographer Dietmar Riemann and in probing, poignant essays by the esteemed literary author Franz Fühmann. The subjects of their photographs and texts lived in care of the Samariteranstalten, or Samaritans' Institution, a multi-faceted Protestant Church-run diaconal establishment, now with a secondary school for social services, about thirty-five miles east of Berlin. Both artists were in conversation with the residents of the Samariteranstalten over a long period of time, first independently of each other and then in collaboration on this book. Its title comes from a passage in which Fühmann walks toward the grounds and describes the (then) ninety-year-old institution and its forest setting. He asks as he approaches it—not for the first time but when he first considers writing about it—what kind of island is this, in what kind of sea? While this suggests that he will explore the institution as an island within the surrounding sea of Fürstenwalde and East Germany, his essay and Riemann's photographs explore the more immense seas of those beliefs, capacities, doctrines, and laws that govern care for individuals who cannot live on their own.

These were bold inquiries in the East Germany of the 1980s and are still relevant today across miles, decades, languages, and cultures. This collection of prose and photography deserves to be read anew, for it has had a significant impact in Fürstenwalde and impels the discovery of untold stories from institutions elsewhere. Then as now, representations of disability are rare that reject an othering or therapeutic imperative in favor of exploring disability as a truly human condition. Rarer still are invitations for cognitively disabled people to tell their stories to people who are willing to listen. The present study takes up this relational model of inquiry and strives as well for comparable self-awareness of the generic and professional conventions in which I write. My insights are informed by literary scholarship and cultural and oral history, including visits to Fürstenwalde. I conducted personal interviews and correspondence with Dietmar Riemann there and at his home in Mosbach; with residents of the Samariteranstalten, some whose photographs appear in the book; with Paul-Gerhard Voget, former Theologischer Vorstand, or executive theological director,[2] and Ulrike Menzel, the current Theologischer Vorstand of the Samariteranstalten; and with several current and former employees who generously gave of their time. From my faculty position at Oberlin College I conversed and corresponded with 2007 Max Kade German Writer-in-Residence Uwe Kolbe, a leading poet from the former East Germany with personal connections to both Führmann and Riemann, and also with 2014 Max Kade German Writer-in-Residence Peter Wawerzinek, a leading literary author also from the former East Germany with personal insights into many strands of this topic. My understanding of the role that the arts can play in establishing empathic relationships grew considerably through these conversations and also through the act of translating Führmann's titular essay from German to English.

The following discussion explores how Führmann and Riemann eschew learned postures of rejection, segregation, or pity to bear witness to the human dignity of the residents of the Samariteranstalten. Their dissident ethos functioned on two major levels: first, in questioning inherited Western cultural and aesthetic notions that shape and reinforce societal practices regarding disability, and second, in challenging censorship in the GDR by means of disability-affirming narrative and imagery. Führmann and Riemann's efforts to publish writing and photographs about disability and diaconal service in the GDR required courage and conviction and came, particularly for Riemann, at serious personal cost. Credit is due them for speaking truth to the powerful stereotypes that have historically discredited disabled people and put their very lives at risk. Führmann and Riemann's overarching lessons are profound: they teach that learning to know people with cognitive disabilities requires nearness, respect, and trust, not distance, superiority, or fear. They affirm that people with cognitive disabilities belong to and contribute to a humane society. They demonstrate the power of the arts to hone our capacity to perceive and appreciate human difference. And as part of the first public discourse in either East or West Germany on the crimes of Nazi "euthanasia"—a practice not new in human history, though enacted on a terrifying, state-sanctioned scale—Fühmann and Riemann asserted that the abuse and murder of people with disabilities during the Nazi era yet needed to be studied, taught, grieved, and atoned.

DISABILITY STUDIES AVANT LA LETTRE

Fühmann and Riemann began and completed their collaborative work over thirty years ago, before disability studies was firmly established in the United States and still virtually non-existent in either Germany. They explored the very nature of disability as a lived experience, cognizant of the role of words and images in informing earlier German and international historical practices of custodial care and the extreme alternate, medicalized killing. They examined the built world and the access to it that the social institutions of religion and politics both afford and restrict. They questioned the presumption that life with disability is a life of suffering, and they did not subscribe to the imperative of cure or necessity of overcoming disability. Thus, without using the contemporary vocabulary of this scholarly field, Fühmann and Riemann effectively moved from a medical model of disability to a historical and cultural view of disability as an aspect of human identity and experience. Their work explores and chips away at the contours of ableism, also without using the term, proffering interdependence and mutual regard as pathways to truer understanding. Fühmann and Riemann were not always in agreement with each other, yet they worked in concert to examine historical and cultural forces that bear on disabled human beings and impact the degree to which they are enabled to be and be seen as active participants in society. As fuller, global histories of disability are now being written, *Was für eine Insel in was für einem Meer* opens an essential window onto a formerly shuttered world.

Although there is no evidence that Fühmann or Riemann approached this project with an overtly political agenda, they were both clearly aware that their book would illuminate the degree to which the affirmative portrayal of cognitive disability and a church-run institution transgressed the official guidelines of the Sozialistische Einheitspartei Deutschlands (SED), or Socialist Unity Party, for artistic representation. The aesthetics of Socialist Realism originated in Russia and derived from the idealism of socialist values developed in nineteenth-century movements to liberate workers from poverty. Exploitative practices of capitalism such as overwork and unsafe labor conditions were held to be the primary sources of injury and disease that a fully realized socialism would alleviate. Art and literature were engaged in promoting this goal in the founding years of the GDR, and artists and writers both volunteered for and were actively sought by the emergent state for the project of building the "better Germany" after World War II. Internationally regarded writers such as Bertolt Brecht, Anna Seghers, and Ernst Bloch had returned from exile to the eastern sector where they could contribute to constructing socialism. Carol Poore notes in her definitive study, *Disability in Twentieth-Century German Culture*, that "in the works they created, these intellectuals were not only complying with SED censorship requirements but were also trying to realize an ideology in which they genuinely believed."[3] Although many works of prose, poetry, drama, film, and painting had already cast a critical view of capitalist exploitation and nationalism, the state-sanctioned literary program outlined in the Bitterfeld Conferences of 1959 and 1964 increasingly required more unified imagery to create a socialist consciousness and develop the "socialist personality." Scientific and technical revolution and centralized economic planning were to be portrayed with positive heroes, strong bodies, workers and farmers devoted to building socialism. Many writers and artists became disillusioned by the increasingly prescribed nature of cultural production as their more nuanced work was disparaged and even banned in favor of the rigid Socialist Realism. They were not categorically opposed to socialism yet saw the state's instrumentalized rationality as inadequate to explain many real and adverse dimensions of human life, as within its conceptual framework, physical weakness, exhaustion, pain, restricted mobility, or emotional emptiness are ideologically impossible.[4] Within this program, incurable impairment is an affront. A purely technological, economic reckoning of human value and purpose in the GDR could not adequately account for disability, and Fühmann and Riemann's work delivers a case in point. Through its reflections on engaging with cognitively disabled people, the book exposed the concept of the narrowly defined, production-oriented "socialist personality" to be dehumanizing, unattainable, and incompatible with a satisfying life. As the following discussion will show, Fühmann's essay notably argues that socialist ideology had the capacity to be inclusive, writing that "[g]erade an diesen Persönlichkeiten erweist sich das berühmte Marx-Wort, daß die freie Entfaltung eines Jeden die Voraussetzung der freien Entfaltung Aller sei" (It is precisely these personalities who manifest the famous Marxist axiom that the free development of the one is the condition for the free development of all) (22). He presses throughout the text that socialism afforded conceptual room to take up and live out the teaching of the Biblical question "Who is my neighbor?" inherent in the Samariteranstalten's foundational story.[5] The hurdles in publication detailed ahead point to political forces at play that were not motivated by its higher ideals.

Was für eine Insel in was für einem Meer shines light on the significant role of the church in East Germany in supporting people with disabilities. Fühmann engages openly with Christian traditions and Bible verses that seek to explain bodily and intellectual impairment, and Riemann's photographs display the visible religious markers—the deaconesses' habits, the crosses on the walls—that testify to the institution's connections to a still active church. Though Christian theology was disparaged by the SED, the services of the diaconal Samariteranstalten and others like it were accepted for pragmatic reasons and officially rationalized in geopolitical terms. Historian Gisela Helwig notes that "[c]hurch hospitals and facilities for the handicapped were initially allowed to continue their work because the state had no substitute for them, and because many religious facilities had resisted the fascist policy of euthanasia, a stance honored by the Soviet Military Administration and later by the GDR state."[6] The church-run institution provided a range of health, education, and social services that the government was unable to provide. The leadership and staff of the institution were better prepared to work with cognitively disabled residents, even if the material conditions and resources were wanting. Fühmann observes, "man weiß in Fürstenwalde um die eigenen Mängel, so um den nicht (oder kaum?) behebbaren des fehlenden Pflegepersonals—dabei hat die Samariteranstalt, von der Kirche getragen, ein weit größeres Reservoir selbstlos hilfswilliger junger Menschen als jede staatliche Schwesteranstalt" (the people in Fürstenwalde are aware of their own deficiencies, of the never- (or hardly-?) resolved dearth of caregiving personnel—though the Samaritans' Institution, supported by the Church, has a far greater reservoir of selfless young people who are willing to help than every state-run institution") (18). Paul-Gerhard Voget, then executive theological director at the Samariteranstalten, told me more directly, "die Kirche konnte mit behinderten Menschen umgehen; die SED nicht" (the church could deal with disabled people, the SED [Socialist Unity Party] could not).[7]

MAKING THE BOOK: AFFINITIES OF PURPOSE AND ROADBLOCKS TO COLLABORATION

Fühmann and Riemann may have had enough in common to be called kindred spirits, though their stark differences as artists did not make them natural collaborators. At the time of their meeting in 1980, Fühmann had already played a significant role in postwar German literature. Highly respected by his fellow writers and beloved by readers, Fühmann was the author of a wide range of literary works, including poetry, short stories, essays, children's books, film scripts, a ballet, and the collection of essays and photographs under consideration here. During his sixty-two years, he cultivated a unique literary voice, using fairy tales, classical mythology, and the Bible as sources of inspiration. Fühmann received the Heinrich-Mann-Preis in 1956; the Nationalpreis der Deutschen Demokratischen Republik in 1957 and 1974; the Deutscher Kritikerpreis in 1977; and the Geschwister-Scholl-Preis in 1982. He was widely recognized as the conscience of a new generation of writers. Contemporary German poet Uwe Kolbe, himself one of the leading lyrical voices writing in German today, appreciates that "Fühmann helped those who came after him to communicate joy in writing, in art, and in independent thinking."[8] Kolbe's own work was deeply impacted by Fühmann and provides historical and artistic insight into Fühmann's literary legacy. His essay about Fühmann in Fürstenwalde, *Rübezahl in der Garage: Franz Fühmann in Märkisch-Buchholz und Fürstenwalde 1958–1984*, weaves his personal knowledge of Fühmann into a reflective literary portrait. Kolbe's text offers the most comprehensive source of information on Fühmann's thinking and work surrounding the Samariteranstalten.[9]

Fühmann came by his wisdom both through direct instruction and by learning from his own failures. He was raised in a strict Catholic home and attended a Jesuit school near Vienna and then a Gymnasium, or academic high school, in Bohemia. The son of a committed Nazi, Fühmann volunteered at age sixteen for the Sturmabteilung, the paramilitary wing of the Nazi party, and remained obedient to Hitler until the end of the war. His imprisonment in the Soviet Union and re-education to oppose fascism led him to become a dedicated socialist. The admission of personal guilt and responsibility for his own participation in the Third Reich was a constant theme in his writing. Upon learning in the mid-1950s of Stalin's crimes, Fühmann began to view the socialist government more critically; the Prague Spring and political unrest in Czechoslovakia in 1968 further contributed to his skepticism. Alcoholism and near death from it in 1968 were the impetus for another major turnaround in Fühmann's life. Though he remained convinced his life-long of the virtues of socialism, he publicly deplored the corruption and totalitarian control that he could no longer deny. Despite periodic and short-lived thaws, East Germans were subjected to constant surveillance and faced severe penalties for non-conformity or dissent. Paranoid about its image at home and abroad, the governing SED routinely censored authors and artists who were deemed critical of the regime by prohibiting their publications, intimidating them and their families, imprisoning them, or forcing them to leave the country and forfeit their right to return. By the mid-1970s, Fühmann was a leader among cultural and literary dissidents, particularly following the forced expatriation of singer-songwriter Wolf Biermann from the GDR.[10] Fühmann died with cancer in 1984, two years before the book was published. Kolbe delivered the eulogy at Fühmann's funeral under heavy surveillance by the Staatssicherheitsdienst

(Ministry for State Security), or Stasi. In a later essay, "Der Stoff des Lebens" ("The Substance of Life"), he meditates on Riemann's photograph of Fühmann's death mask:

Andererseits läßt sich Riemanns Photographie ganz direkt verstehen als Beleuchtung der Bemühungen Fühmanns im Bereich der Kirche, wo er Gespräche führte, die anderswo in der geschlossenen Gesellschaft nicht zu führen waren—ob nun um die allgegenwärtige Zensur oder um den Begriff Freiheit insgesamt, um den grotesken, reglementierten Alltag oder um Wert und Schönheit von Literatur und Kunst, die in jenem Staat auf dem Index standen—, und wo er Menschen entgegenging, sie ernst nahm, für sie schrieb, wo er denen in freundschaftlicher Zuneigung begegnete, die anderswo ausgegrenzt wurden. Das meint seine Arbeit mit Behinderten in kirchlichen Einrichtungen, denen ein beträchtlicher Teil seines schriftstellerischen wie lebenspraktischen Engagements der letzten Lebensjahre galt.[11]

At the same time, Riemann's photograph can be directly understood as an illumination of Fühmann's efforts in the realm of the church, where he carried out conversations that were not possible elsewhere in that closed society, whether about the ever-present censor or the concept of freedom or the grotesque, regimented daily routine, about the value and beauty of literature and art that was banned in that state—, and where he went on to meet human beings, took them seriously, wrote for them, where he met in friendly affection those people who were excluded elsewhere. That was his work with disabled people in church-based institutions, to which he dedicated a considerable portion of his literary and everyday-practical engagement in his final years.

Dietmar Riemann was born in Saxony in 1950 and raised as a Christian.[12] As a young adult, Riemann was invigorated by Erich Honecker's ascent to chairmanship of the SED in 1971 and by the prospect of "socialism as it really existed," or "real existierender Sozialismus." He was proud—at first—to have been hired to photograph the brown coal generating station at Boxberg in 1972 and then to take pictures at the World Festival of Youth and Students in 1973. Riemann was approached by the Stasi to become an "Inoffizieller Mitarbeiter," or "unofficial cooperative agent," but resolutely rejected the overtures and felt betrayed by his country. Riemann went so far as to stage an outing of himself as siding with dissidents in order to dissuade the Stasi from seeking his services. From that point on, he began to question the GDR in earnest. Still, he managed to study photography at the Leipzig Hochschule für Grafik und Buchkunst Leipzig and to earn a living as a photographer. His special interest was in social documentary.

Both independently and together, Fühmann and Riemann formed relationships with the residents and staff members of the Samariteranstalten. Klaus Gubener, an educator there with abiding and deep knowledge of art and literature, connected them. He heard Fühmann give a reading in 1979 at the Evangelische Akademie in Berlin-Brandenburg and invited him to read in Fürstenwalde, which Fühmann initially declined for reasons of time.[13] In that same year, Riemann was deciding upon the topic for his graduate thesis. He had long been interested in the education of people with cognitive disabilities elsewhere in northeastern Germany and was welcomed in Fürstenwalde, where he got to know residents and staff members over an extended period of time. Riemann notes that "in den Samariteranstalten wurde ich von ausnahmslos allen Mitarbeitern und den Behinderten selbst gern gesehen—und in meiner Arbeit ohne jedes Tabu vorbehaltlos unterstützt" (in the Samaritans' Institutions I was welcomed without exception by all co-workers and by the disabled people themselves—and supported in my work without reservation, without any taboo).[14] He requested permission from Gubener to take photographs of the residents who would be traveling for a vacation by the Baltic Sea. Gubener was initially cautious but relaxed upon seeing Riemann's working methods:

> Er brach meinen anfänglichen Widerstand gegen das Ansinnen, uns während unseres Ostseeurlaubs mit der Kamera zu begleiten. Er ordnete sich völlig in das Gruppenleben ein, so daß er mit seinem Apparat kein Fremdkörper war, im Gegenteil: er wurde zu einem beliebten Gesprächspartner.[15]

> He broke my initial resistance to the suggestion that he and his camera accompany us during our Baltic Sea vacation. He integrated himself completely into the life of the group, so that he and his camera were not foreign bodies, to the contrary: he became a beloved conversation partner.

Riemann completed his thesis in 1981 with the photographs that became the basis for the Insel book. His thesis earned a 2, or "gut" (good), but not a 1, or "sehr gut" (very good), because his portrayals of the church and of disability were deemed to be too positive. Riemann himself had not originally conceived of the photos as leading to a publishable book, sensing that publishers would not see the value.[16]

It was Gubener's idea to bring Fühmann and Riemann together to collaborate on a book after having worked with each artist independently. Both men initially rejected the idea. In addition to being somewhat intimated by Fühmann's talent and social and moral stature,[17] Riemann was convinced that the GDR would simply not publish photographs of a religious institution. Fühmann, for his part, had misgivings about the capacity of photography itself to do justice to the residents of the home. He reflected upon his initial doubts in writing that eventually appeared in the book:

Photographien von geistig Behinderten: Wie werden sie auf den Betrachter wirken? Wer sich dieser Welt nur aus Schaulust naht, mit Touristenblick und Touristenbewußtsein, der erreicht nur ihre Oberfläche, in ihren Wesensbereich wird er erst dringen, wenn er ernsthaft Anteil zu nehmen versucht, aber das setzt Verstehen voraus, und das wieder Einfühlungskraft. Aber befriedigen Photographien nicht gerade die Schaulust? Verführen sie nicht zu der Hoffart des Pharisäers, wie sie Lukas berichtet: Herr, ich danke dir, daß ich nicht bin wie diese da? Es käme aber, fürs erste, alles drauf an, sich vorstellen zu können, wie diese zu sein. (11)

Photographs of people with cognitive disabilities: How will they affect the viewer? Whoever approaches this world only out of curiosity, with a tourist's point of view and a tourist's mindset, will only scratch the surface, will only enter into the essence of this world when he makes a sincere effort to share in it, but that presumes understanding, and understanding presumes empathy. Yet don't photographs in fact satisfy our curiosity? Don't they seduce us into the haughtiness of the Pharisees, who pray, as Luke reports: Lord, I thank you that I am not like these here . . . ? It would really depend on being able to imagine oneself just like these here.

Gubener, in a friendly nudge to encourage Fühmann's further collaboration, sent him a Jahrweiser,[18] a reusable calendar illustrated by the residents of the institution (see Figure 1). Its design was the project of Fritz Müller, a pastor at the institution who coordinated much singing and the making and viewing of art throughout the Samariteranstalten and greater community.

Fühmann was moved by the calendar and the engagement with and through art that it represented and agreed to hold readings at the Samariteranstalten. Riemann notes in his history of the collaboration:

Der Jahrweiser, ein immerwährender Kalender, muss Fühmann beeindruckt, regelrecht bewegt haben. Der Schriftsteller bedankte sich bei Gubener mit einem handschriftlichen Brief am 12. Januar 1980, dem Anfang eines intensiven Briefwechsels. Und schließlich sagte er zu, in Fürstenwalde zu lesen.[19]

The calendar, a perennial calendar, must have impressed Fühmann, really moved him. The writer thanked Gubener with a hand-written letter on January 12, 1980, the beginning of an intensive correspondence. And finally, he agreed to read from his works in Fürstenwalde.

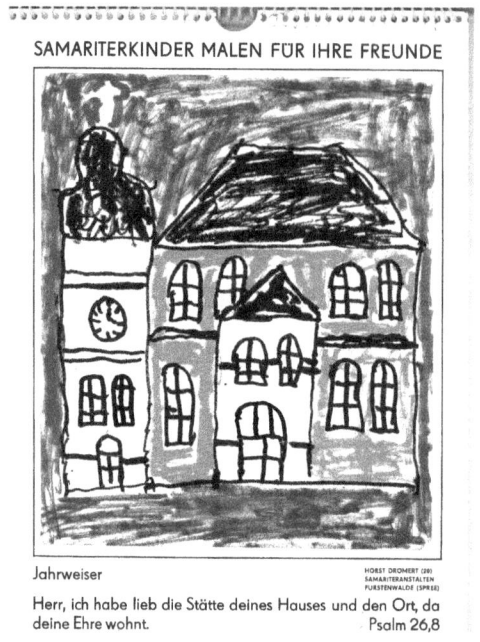

Figure 1. The Jahrweiser, or calendar, illustrated
by residents of the Samariteranstalten.

Fühmann's first reading was in April of 1980, after which he and Gubener started the "Literaturkreis," or literary circle, at the Samariteranstalten. During these gatherings, Fühmann wrote "Märchen auf Bestellung" (Fairy tales made-to-order), a number of which were published. During this time, Fühmann took it upon himself to learn more about photography, and he and Riemann began to collaborate through narrative and visual arts together with the residents of the Samariteranstalten. One had particular impact: on Easter Monday of 1981, they viewed an exhibit in the Jugendheim, or youth center, of woodcut prints on the theme of the Baseler Totentanz, or dance of death, by the West German artist Helmut Andreas Paul (HAP) Grieshaber.[20] Grieshaber's woodcuts meditate upon the theme that death comes to all. Death is personified as a skeleton on a church wall in Basel in a series of paintings on the interior wall of the cemetery. The residents, Fühmann, Riemann, Gubener, and others immersed themselves in intense and imaginative conversation about it for days. Riemann took photographs of the residents as they viewed and discussed the woodcuts. Their long conversations, transcribed by Fühmann to present to Grieshaber,[21] reveal that many residents did not share the common interpretation of Death as an adversary or figure of terror. The transcriptions show how Fühmann sought the residents' perspective on the images and engaged them in substantive conversation about the woodcuts and about death:

F.F.: Gefallen dir die Farben?

Heinz: Ja - weil der Tod noch hierher guckt - zu uns –

F.F.: Der guckt auch zu uns, nicht?

Heinz: Ja –

F.F.: Kannst du ihn anschaun?

Heinz: Ja, der guckt ja hierher (große Aufmerksamkeit der Gruppe)

F.F.: Wenn du ihm ins Gesicht siehst - hast du Angst vor dem Tod?

Frank: neee –

F.F.: Du sagst: nein?

Frank: Nein! (ganz breit, selbstsicher) n-e-i-n!

F.F.: Ist jemand unter euch, der Angst hat vor ihm?

Hi.grund: Nee - nee –

Heinz: Na vorm Tod braucht man doch keine Angst haben.

Hi.grund Widerspruch: Doch - Nein –

F.F.: Nein? Du hast keine Angst. Warum nicht?

Heinz: Na wenn wir doch wissen daß wir dann sterben - da bereitet sich der Mensch doch vor aufs Tod - daß der ihn dann holen kann –

(Lange Pause)

F.F.: Wie machst du das, vorbereiten?

Heinz: Na ins Bett gehen - hinlegen, ins Bett - wenn man krank ist und da - und kann –

(sehr große Pause, Nachdenken, er will sich nicht mehr äußern).

F.F.: Ich finde, ihr habt wunderbar recht - es ist nämlich genau das. Wer hat denn noch ein Lieblingsbild?

F.F.: Do you like the colors?

Heinz: Yes, because Death is still looking over here at us.

F.F.: He's also looking at us, isn't he?

Heinz: Yes—

F.F.: Can you look at him?

Heinz: Yeah, he's looking over here (great attentiveness of the group)

F.F.: When you look him in the eye, are you afraid of Death?

Frank: Naw—

F.F.: You're saying: no?

Frank: No! (really broadly, self confident) no-o!

F.F.: Is there someone here among you who is afraid of him?

B.[ack]ground: Nope—nope—

Heinz: Well you don't have to be afraid of Death.

B.[ack]ground Contradiction: Yes—no

F.F.: No? You aren't afraid? Why not?

Heinz: Well if we just know that we are dying—then a person just prepares himself for death—that he can come for him—

(Long pause)

F.F.: How do you do that, prepare?

Heinz: Well, you go to bed, lie down, in the bed, if you're sick, and then, and can—

(very long pause, contemplation, he doesn't want to say more).

F.F.: I think you are wonderfully right—it is as a matter of fact just that. Who else has a favorite picture?

Conversations on how to interpret the woodcuts grew among an art-loving community that now included the residents of the Samariteranstalten.

Neither the book nor the relationship between Fühmann and Riemann progressed without conflict. Political and artistic differences twice threatened to end the collaboration. They disagreed vehemently about the GDR itself. Riemann saw and expressed similarities between National Socialism and GDR Socialism, which infuriated Fühmann. Fühmann attributed the GDR's problems to human shortcomings but not necessarily to a flawed political system. Riemann had graver doubts. He acknowledges that he lived well in the GDR, earned well, and had an above-average income and owned property through an inheritance. Yet he hated the songs and military displays that his young daughter was subjected to in school, and he and his wife did not want her to have to grow up in this environment. He was already especially troubled by restrictions on his freedom of movement and speech, and his collaboration with Fühmann on this book was beginning to have punitive consequences. Riemann suffered a de facto ban on exhibitions when the gallery where his work was to be displayed was closed without further explanation.[22]

Riemann objected to two additional texts that Fühmann insisted be published in the volume: "Der freundliche Tod" and "Canto ami et non mourier" ("Ein Lied der Freundschaft und nicht des Sterbens"). Fühmann saw no other possibility for their publication in the GDR and so insisted that they appear in the Insel volume. Riemann also objected to Fühmann's (albeit favorable) comparison of his photographs with those of the internationally famous photographer Diane Arbus. Riemann pointed out the inequity that Fühmann would permit no commentary on or intervention into his essays.[23] Yet he acknowledges that "ohne Fühmann wäre das Buch nicht zustande gekommen" (without Fühmann the book would never have materialized).[24]

Publication of the book was frequently postponed because it appeared to cast the government in an unfavorable light. Fühmann, undaunted, suggested that he would use his influence to have it published in the West. The production manager, concerned about the image of the GDR abroad, countered to Riemann that it really wasn't "desirable" to produce a book about "whackos" in a church institution.[25] An especially cruel entry in a secret surveillance report from this time casts aspersions on Fühmann's own intellect, speculating that because he is spending so much time with people with cognitive disabilities, he will likely soon be committed to an asylum.[26] The book was finally published in both East and West Germany in 1986, nearly two years after Fühmann's death. The quality of the printing by the East German Rostock publisher Hinstorff was poor "selbst für DDR Verhältnisse" (even by GDR standards), according to Riemann, and he wondered whether the poor quality was an intentional effort on the part of the publisher to discredit the work.[27] The press apologized to Riemann, explaining that the printers in Magdeburg had recently installed new machinery from the West and were still learning how to use it. Nonetheless, the first run sold out. A second edition was published by Hinstorff and also by the West German publisher Büchergilde Gutenberg. It garnered positive attention in the press, including a radio interview on the Kulturmagazin program of Radio DDR 2,[28] and earned favorable attention in an East German literary journal, Weimarer Beiträge.[29] That article characterized Fühmann's writing as the confessions of a dying man who wished to contribute to public healing from fascism.

In the year of the book's publication, Riemann applied for a visa to leave the GDR. This request, if granted, would also be punished with forfeiture of citizenship and permanent separation from family members who stayed. He began to keep a secret diary to document the arduous and adversarial process, knowing that leaving had cost others dearly and for some had even ended in suicide. Shortly before the opening of the German-German border in 1989, Riemann and his wife and daughter were granted permission to leave the GDR. His diary, rich with documentation, was published with the title *Laufzettel: Tagebuch einer Ausreise* (*Routing slip: Diary of an exit*) in 2005.[30] He is still living and working in Mosbach, near Heidelberg.

NEARNESS, RESPECT, AND TRUST: FÜHMANN AND RIEMANN'S WORK WITH THE RESIDENTS

Looking outwardly and inwardly are for Fühmann and Riemann first principles in the more complicated process of understanding. The essay and photographs reveal intersubjective moments and the artists' sustained effort to get to know the residents, both as individuals and as a community. Fühmann's essay invites readers to accompany him as he explores how disability manifests itself in language, in perspectives, and in concepts that change over time and across political and cultural borders. Finding himself changed by meeting the residents, Fühmann set upon a new course of thinking and writing about people who were gradually becoming friends: "Ich werde einfach von meinen Freunden erzählen, die ich hier in Fürstenwalde gewann" (I will simply tell about my friends, those I made here in Fürstenwalde) (7). Fühmann took steps to act as a friend—for example, keeping touch with the Falcons through postcards.

Fühmann's essay unfolds without apparent foregone conclusions, chronicling the very acts of observing, engaging with, listening to, and walking alongside the people he meets. His understanding is not simple or fixed but emerges in relationships over time:

> Beim ersten Mal, drei Jahre sind's her, hatte ich vor den Pfleglingen gelesen, Märchen erzählt und Sprachspiele getrieben, die Veranstaltung hatte Anklang gefunden, Wünsche nach Wiederholung wurden geäußert, dann hatten sich Partnerschaften ergeben, und nun bin ich das fünfte Mal hier, doch jetzt wird die Freude des Wiederkommens durch ein Unbehagen gebrochen, das mir nur zu gut bekannt ist, jenes Peingefühl, das sich immer heranschleicht, wenn ich jemand, den ich als Partner schätze, zum Objekt degradieren muß. Ich werde meine Freunde und ihre Gefährten beobachten müssen, anstarren, belauern, ihre Mienen festhalten, ihre Gefühls- und Begreifensprozesse gedanklich zerstücken und Bild für Bild davon fixieren, um die Sequenz schließlich in eine Metapher umsetzen oder als Summe ziehen zu können: die leidige crux meines Berufs; genug. (8)

> The first time I held a reading for the fosterlings—it's been three years since then—I told fairy tales and led language games; the event struck a chord, wishes were voiced for doing this again, then partnerships resulted, and now I'm here for the fifth time, but now the joy of return is being broken by an unease that I know all too well, this feeling of anguish that sneaks up whenever someone I respect as a partner becomes someone whom I must degrade to an object. I will have to observe my friends and their companions, stare at them, eavesdrop, take hold of their countenances, mentally take apart their emotional and cognitive processes and fixate upon them, scene by scene, image by image, in order finally to be able to transform the sequence into a metaphor or to draw an overarching picture: the vexing crux of my profession; enough.

Fühmann's essay feels at once poetic, a product of its rich imagery, sensory evocation, and landscape, yet formally it is also raw and unedited. The rough mechanics of the text should be read as subtle authorial repositioning that mirrors Fühmann's process of taking in his environment and taking stock of his relationship with his subjects. When Fühmann asks "Wie wird man eine solche Herausforderung aufnehmen?" (How will a person take on such a challenge?), he is of course questioning his own approach as well as that of readers whom he addresses (7). The many possible English translations of the German "man" in this sentence—"one" or "a person," "you," or even "we"—can give some insight into the multiple perspectives that Fühmann holds open at once. His frequent dashes and semicolons interrupt and suspend, complicating his observations and meditations. Noun-heavy sentences suggest a search for concrete anchors. Much passive voice and the substitute passive probe and stretch perspective itself, the author's self-awareness stationing him temporarily on a porous border between objectivity and subjectivity.

Fühmann often uses the term "Pfleglinge," or "fosterlings," to identify the residents, an antiquated term connoting children in custodial care. While Fühmann's use of the word typically expresses affection, the word can also carry a note of condescension. This is one example of how the essay itself problematizes representation of the residents and opts in every case for humanizing language, however laden. As Riemann's photos attest, however, the residents were not all children. Some maintained strong connections with their families, many did not, and some were wards of the state. Their vulnerability and the question of consent to be photographed and written about were obvious considerations in the making of the book. The residents' full names do not appear in the essay, and the photographs have no captions or identifying information. Still, unique stories emerge. Fühmann pays close attention to individual residents' desires, motivations, and efforts. The slow pace of his descriptions allows their personalities and intentions to come into view. Long passages about individuals allow the presumably non-disabled reader to get to know them a bit and also to be aware of Fühmann's process of getting to know them. Here, he writes about thirteen-year-old Heike, yet still questions the validity of his own understanding:

–Dreizehn Jahre, und Falten um Mund und Augen. –Doch sie kann nicht fliehen, und die Freude ist stärker; sie gibt mir das Recht, sie sacht zu umarmen und mich neben sie zu setzen. –Noch einmal ihr Jauchzen, nun schon ganz ein Stück Alltag, dann senkt sie die Hände und schließt den Mund und arbeitet unvermittelt weiter, als wolle sie mir zeigen, was sie kann. –Ich schreibe das im Konjunktiv; ich hüte mich vor übereilten Schlüssen. (10)

–Thirteen years old, and wrinkles around her mouth and eyes. –But she cannot flee, and the joy is stronger; she gives me permission to hug her gently and to sit down next to her. –Once again, her squeal, by now just a part of everyday life, then she lowers her hands and closes her mouth and abruptly picks up her work again, as though she wanted to show me what she can do. –I write that in the subjunctive; I guard against drawing conclusions too quickly.

Fühmann examines and reframes the definition of disability frequently, drawing attention to his own limitations and those of others without cognitive disabilities. He posits that communication barriers that he and others experience with Heike are not her deficiency but theirs or, more pointedly, ours: "Sie versteht viel von unserer Sprache, wir fast nichts von der ihren, und so muß sie zu groben Mitteln greifen, um zu uns Grobsinnigen zu reden" (She understands much of our language, we almost nothing of hers, and so she has to reach for blunt means to talk to us, the coarse-minded) (10). The effect of this writing that is both documentary and meditative is an opening of critical insight into the discursive traditions that perpetuate disability's definition in absolute or oppositional terms, definitions that in turn shape human interaction. Healthy/sick, whole/deficient, and able-bodied/disabled are for Fühmann incomplete. His focus is on the range between these conceptual poles, and he explicitly seeks perspective other than his own in a text that not only thematizes but also reflects the exploration: "Er kann ihr Lachen nicht hören, hat er es gefühlt?" (He cannot hear her laughing, did he feel it?) (8). Less an examination of particular East German or European cultural context than an exploration of human nature and habits of human social organization, Fühmann asks, in essence, what disables? While he draws no simple conclusions, he begins to locate the answers outside of the human body itself, for example shining a light on cultural norms for productivity that are not universally achievable. He decries their reification in art, referring in the following passage to a poem by Theodor Fontane (1819–1898), "Wer schaffen will, muß fröhlich sein!":

Wem von uns ist es gegeben, sich so zu freuen wie Willi oder Jürgen, sich so offen zu seinem Gefühl zu bekennen, so arglos sein freies Gesicht zu zeigen? Man sage nicht, das sei eben die Einfalt der Armen im Geiste, man frage vielmehr, ob ein Geist nicht beschränkt sei, der solche Beschränkung vom Menschentum fordert, wie es etwa der Geist des "keep smiling" verlangt: alle Mienen uniformiert zu der einen, und ihr Konfektionsoptimismus löscht mit der Vielfalt der Emotionen auch alle Bekundung von Zuversicht aus. –Jede Gesellschaft macht da ihre eigene Erfahrung, und offenbar lernt keine aus ihr. –"Wer schaffen will, muß fröhlich sein!" –mir schaudert vor diesem Imperativ. (21)

Who among us is allowed to be as happy as Willi or Jürgen, to make no secret of his feelings, to show his true face without guile? Please, let's not say that this is only the simplicity of the poor in spirit, let us rather ask whether a spirit isn't itself limited when humanity requires so much constraint, like that spirit that demands we "keep smiling," that all of our faces show the same uniform expression; sugary optimism snuffs out the variety of our emotions right along with every manifestation of trust. –Every society has its own experience of that, and apparently no one learns from it. –"You have to be happy if you want to get something done!" I shudder at this imperative.

Fühmann's deep questioning and reflection about self and society pervade the essay. He delves into disability not only as an experience that is socially and historically contingent but also to explore its meaning in philosophical and metaphysical terms, attentive to the language we inherit largely through narrative and imagery: "All diese Fragen verknäulen sich, mühsam entwirrbar, ihre Aspekte gehn inein-ander über, ohne je ganz identisch zu werden" (All of these questions are knotted up, unraveled only with painstaking effort, their contours interlocking without ever being exactly identical) (19).

The artistic process behind *Was für eine Insel in was für einem Meer* did not advance an agenda of cur-ing or normalizing cognitive disability through medicine or education. Neither the text nor the pictures present the residents' lives as problems to be solved or as case studies of deficiencies to expose and correct. Rather, Fühmann's writing and Riemann's photography focus on achieving more fully drawn portraits that present the residents as fellow human beings with gifts, vulnerabilities, and challenges, valued and acceptable as they are. The humility and self-reflection of the artists were key. Riemann's 1987 interview with Radio DDR 2 describes his growth in understanding of ability and disability:

> Peter Liebert: Für mein Verständnis spitzt Franz Fühmann zu, wenn er sagt, dass man als Normalsinniger von den Behinderten durchaus viel lernen kann. Wie sehen Sie das?Dietmar Riemann: O, ja, ich habe von Behinderten gelernt. Sie sind unkompliziert, und man kann lernen, Freude zu empfinden und auszuleben . . .

> Peter Liebert: To my understanding, Fühmann accentuates that a person with normal intelligence can really learn a lot from disabled people. How do you see that?Dietmar Riemann: Oh, yes, I learned from disabled people. They are uncomplicated, and a person can learn to feel and live out joy . . .

Nearly thirty years later, Riemann reiterated this insight in conversation: "Die Bewohner der Anstalten waren zufrieden mit sich selbst und mit ihrer Welt; das war für mich die größte Überraschung" (The res-idents of the institution were content with themselves and with their world; that was for me the biggest surprise).[31]

Like Fühmann's essay, Riemann's photographs are the result of a substantial investment of time and relationship. They are intimate and respectful pictures of people who in most cultures, even today, remain hidden from public view. They draw heavily from the traditions of portraiture, an art form typically reserved for prominent and powerful people, used here to witness and take seriously the lives of people who are largely kept out of public visibility. The residents are portrayed with dignity, their facial expressions and body language reflecting a trusting relationship with the photographer. These are kind images, notably not designed to enhance sentimentality or pity. Poore notes that Riemann "did not shy away from showing the failings of the GDR institution, such as overcrowding, the use of restraints, inadequate equipment, general shabbiness, and so forth."[32]

Fühmann's essay probes the form and style of Riemann's photographs, earning Riemann's ire yet benefiting the readers. Fühmann is still coming to grips with photography as an art form and surmises that perhaps his readers are too. Of particular interest to him are the processes behind the product. How does the photographer bring about the revelatory image, the telling scene? Fühmann considers the working process of Diane Arbus to describe the power of the camera itself as a license for people to present themselves when they would otherwise not. For him, Arbus's pictures "[fassen] den Alltag in grausamen Bildern . . . , um sein Absurdes sehen zu lehren" (capture the ordinary in cruel pictures in order to teach us to see its absurdity) (15). Convinced of Arbus's artistry, Fühmann leaves open the question of ethics in her process: "ich wage doch kein Urteil, sie ist eine große Künstlerin und hat für ihre Kunst mit dem Leben gezahlt" (I won't wager a judgment, she is a great artist and paid for her art with her life) (15). In Riemann, he observes a fundamentally different method:

> Riemann macht von diesem Freibrief keinen Gebrauch; seine Methode ist die des Gesprächs, er versucht einen Prozeß sich entwickeln zu lassen, in dem sich das Wesen dessen entfaltet, von dem er ein Bild vermitteln will, und er fixiert dann jenen Moment, in dem dieses Entfalten gipfelt: Atom der Ewigkeit, nicht der Zeit. (16)

> Riemann doesn't make use of this license. His method is that of the conversation. He tries to let a process develop on its own, in which the essence of that person unfolds that he would like to impart in image, and he fixes upon the moment in which this unfolding culminates: atom of eternity, not of time.

Riemann confirmed his approach in his 1987 Kulturmagazin radio interview: "ich versuche, Menschen für mich zu gewinnen. Ich laufe keinen Menschen hinterher, ich photographiere nicht heimlich" (I try to win people over. I don't chase people, I don't take pictures secretly). Riemann's process is central to the new insights that the book makes possible, teaching first and foremost Fühmann himself what he can learn about people with cognitive disabilities. Fühmann sees "[h]ier also Ehrfurcht vor der Würde des Menschen, und daraus das Mühen um das Porträt, jene ästhetische Ausdrucksweise, die das Objekt auch als Subjekt braucht, ja sogar vorwiegend als Subjekt" (here, then, awe of human dignity, and from that, the effort to make a portrait, that aesthetic expressive form that needs the object also as a subject, indeed primarily as subject) (15).

"Here, then" are pivotal words. Fühmann has drawn a conclusion about Riemann's medium and method as well as about the revelatory insights these methods produce: dignity, documented; the cognitively disabled, afforded full subject status. "Here, then" is Fühmann's own "aha!" upon engaging with images, insights that he simultaneously presents to the reader. Collaborative learning is again taking place—one recalls the Grieshaber woodcut exhibition—ushered by a writer-interpreter who is himself changed in the course of the viewing.

Riemann's photographs indeed afford an experiential quality of engagement between the viewer and the people portrayed. Nearly thirty years after the book's publication, German author Peter Wawerzinek affirmed the touching impact of the photographs in particular, bringing to bear his personal knowledge of artists' perspectives and proximal understanding of the residents' perspectives. Wawerzinek grew up in an orphanage in the GDR and went on to earn the Bachmann Prize for his 2010 novel, *Rabenliebe*, which incorporates his own experience of living in an institution. Wawerzinek viewed Riemann's photographs with me in 2014, perceiving a richness in them that he attributes to the process of their making. He was deeply moved and offered a powerful appraisal, worth quoting at length:

Was die schwarz-weißen Bilder angeht, so lassen sie kein Grau wie Grauzone oder grauer Alltag entstehen, und sind erstaunlich bunt in der abgelichteten Heiterkeit. Das wird sicher ein Ergebnis einer längeren Zusammenkunft des Fotografen mit seiner Gruppe sein. Die Bilder drücken eine Beziehung zum Fotografen deutlich aus. Der Fotograf darf bis in die intimen Räume seine Arbeit ausführen, was den Eindruck, er ist kein Mann der Schnellschüsse, bestärkt. Das allein ist schon ein Riesengewinn für den Betrachter. Ich mag die Körnigkeit, die den Bildern anhaftet, weil sie auf Arbeit in der Dunkelkammer hinweisen, kaltes Wasser, Handwerk, Persönlichkeit. Für mich ist die Botschaft der Gemeinschaft, des Heimlebens, der Porträts von Leuten, die sonst nicht Beachtung finden, schon die stärkste Botschaft des Buches. Ich danke für den Tipp. Und ich denke, diese Arbeit war in ihrer Zeit eine außergewöhnliche Prozedur. Die insgesamt dann doch eher magere Anerkennung und Aufmerksamkeit für die Bilder steht dazu nicht im Verhältnis. Es sind die richtigen Bilder im falschen Land geschossen, was die Bekanntmachung der Bilder angeht.[33]

As far as the black-and-white pictures are concerned, they don't bring out gray like a gray zone or a gray, daily grind, but are astonishingly colorful, a brightness captured on film. That will surely have come from a longer collaboration between the photographer and his group. The pictures clearly express a relationship to the photographer. The photographer is allowed to do his work even in the more intimate spaces, which only strengthens the perception that he is not a man of quick snapshots. That alone is an enormous benefit for the observer. I love the graininess that appears as imperfections, because they point to the work in the darkroom, cold water, handicraft, personality. For me the messages of community, of life in the home, of portraits of people who otherwise find no recognition, are really the strongest messages of the book. I thank you for pointing me to it. I'm guessing that this work was in its time an extraordinary procedure. Altogether, the rather meager recognition of and attention to the pictures was out of proportion [to the effort to create them]. As far as public circulation is concerned, these were the right pictures in the wrong country.

It is not easy to imagine the "right" country that Wawerzinek envisioned for these photographs; perhaps he surmised that the West Germany of the time of the book's publication would have been more receptive to affirmative pictures of people with cognitive disabilities than the East Germany of 1986. Yet no such volume had appeared in any German context at the time. *Was für eine Insel in was für einem Meer* was unique in presenting such images and narratives and arguing for the need for them. Fühmann expressly connects public images with public consciousness and in turn with public actions, naming what is at stake in examining cultural views of disability.

The awe of human dignity that emerges within the photographs ultimately compels Fühmann's confrontation with its historical antithesis, the murder of disabled people under Nazi rule. Riemann's photographs were, for Fühmann, not only aesthetically beautiful portraits but also the impetus for at last confronting painful facts of the Third Reich: the Nazi campaign to "exterminate life unworthy of living" was first tested on the disabled and met little resistance. Fühmann writes:

Ich will jetzt nicht von Ästhetischem sprechen, dazu ist hier der Ort nicht mehr. Ich nehme das Ja dieser Bilderwelt auf, um in ihrer Aura daran zu erinnern, daß von allen Opfern des nationalsozialistischen Mordens jene am wenigsten Anteilnahme erfuhren, die als erste ins Gas hatten gehen müssen: die psychisch wie physisch Behinderten. Wir sind ihnen so gut wie noch alles schuldig. Ich kenne kein Mahnmal, das an sie erinnert, kein Werk der Kunst hat sie gewürdigt, sie sind aus der Literatur gefallen, keiner ihrer Lebenswege ist aufgezeichnet, als Gruppe Verfolgter sind sie nicht anerkannt, die Namen 'Hadamar' oder 'Grafeneck' oder 'Sonnenstein' oder 'Eglfing-Haar' oder 'Bernburg' oder 'Hartheim' sagen kaum jemand etwas, wiewohl dort die ersten Selektionen geschahen. Der Widerstand in den Anstalten ist wenig erforscht. Einige wenige, sehr verdienstvolle Dokumentationen über die—fälschlich so genannten—Euthanasieverbrechen der Hitlerära bestätigen als Ausnahme die Regel. (22)

I don't want to speak about aesthetics now, this is no longer the place to do that. I am taking in the "yes" of this world of pictures, so that, in its aura, we may remember that of all of the victims of National Socialist murder, those who received the least amount of sympathy were first to have to go into the gas: the mentally and physically disabled. We still owe them as good as everything. I don't know of one monument that memorializes them, no work of art has honored them, they have fallen out of literature, none of their life stories has been chronicled, as a group of persecuted people they have not been recognized, the names "Hadamar" or "Grafeneck" or "Sonnenstein" or "Eglfing-Haar" or "Bernburg" or "Hartheim" hardly mean anything to anyone, although it was in those places that the first selections took place. Resistance within the institutions is little researched. A very few meritorious pieces of documentation about the—wrongly named—crimes of euthanasia in the Hitler era are the exception that prove the rule.

In this concise and sobering passage, Fühmann names the work still needed to correct societal ignorance about those who were killed. The gravity of these words cannot be overestimated, particularly in light of the decades of silence surrounding Nazi killing of disabled people.[34] Fühmann does not exonerate himself even as he takes initial steps toward recovering the neglected history of state-sanctioned medicalized killing. Why this history is neglected has much to do with the dearth of survivors' stories, identified in Fühmann's essay and reiterated in 2015 in Andreas Hechler's research: "Die nicht vorhandenen Berichte von Überlebenden erschweren ein Lernen über, ein Identifizieren mit und ein Erinnern an die als 'lebensunwert' Verfolgten und Ermordeten" (The dearth of reports from survivors impedes learning about, identifying with, and remembering those who were persecuted and murdered for being "unworthy of living").[35] Fühmann attests that eugenic thinking did not begin or end in the Nazi era. He confronts the persistent legitimizing of the question of the "erlösende Spritze" (19), or "merciful injection," to end supposed suffering, but whose? He testifies to pervasive and pernicious doubt about the value of life with disability:

–Die Frage nach der Spritze wird öfter gestellt, als man glaubt, und – versteht sich – immer in einem Timbre, das der Frager für humanistisch hält: Er will ein vermeintliches Unglück enden, Richter über Tod und Leben von andren, und hat doch nur mit der eigenen Not zu tun. (14)

–The question of the injection is posed more often than one might think, and – to be sure – always in a timbre that the questioner holds to be humanistic: he wants to end a presumed unhappiness, judge over death and life of others, and yet is really only concerned with his own need.

With these words and throughout the larger whole of the photo-essay collection, Fühmann and Riemann confront inherited notions, postures, and acts of superiority that dismiss the humanity of people with cognitive disabilities and endanger their lives. By questioning these notions, and through their respectful and self-reflective engagement with the residents of the Samariteranstalten, Fühmann and Riemann testify to their human dignity with new images and new narratives, drawing joy and friendship in the process and documenting lives well worthy of living.

"PHOTOGRAPHIEN VON GEISTIG BEHINDERTEN"

Franz Fühmann

English translation by Elizabeth C. Hamilton

Photographs of intellectually disabled people: How do you approach a challenge like this? –I don't know. –A companion text cannot change photographs, and that is also not my intention.

I will simply tell about my friends, those I made here in Fürstenwalde.

1 As I'm going to the car to get my bags, I encounter Bernd. I want to write the text to this volume at the Samaritans' Institution, that's how the new year should begin, with its frosty air and icicles hanging from the roofs, the linden trees and alders in intermittent hoarfrost, under the thin blue of the sky, freezing away. –My weather, my world. –Bernd, slight, twenty years old, tromping around in clunky brown lace-up shoes, wears a cotton jacket and a stocking cap, blue and white rings of a sturdy wool, the thick pompon dangles on his forehead. When he sees me, he freezes in surprise, sticks his neck out with a thrust of his upper body, and at last recognizing me for sure, jumps in the air, his outstretched arms fluttering behind him with upturned palms and spread fingers, a laughing, oddly flightless bird whom joy makes eager to fly. Three times he jumps up this way, his mouth stretching into a widening laugh, as he's jumping he see-saws his trunk into his hips, a jump within a jump, three- and fourfold: leaping, he lifts his head, which he otherwise lets fall to his chest, and as he's lifting his head, he opens his eyes, and from his knuckles to his eyes he laughs at me. –Oh, that we humans have to be so grave! –Bernd belongs to the Falcons, a group of fourteen young men who spend the time that is given to them in this life at a station of the Samaritans' Institution; most of them sent here at a preschool age with organic brain damage since infancy; impaired intelligence of every degree: spastics and epileptics with cognitive defects; those suffering from Langdon Down syndrome—formerly called "Mongolism"—and also those who are so mysteriously frustrated at a young age, whom we are wont to call "Autists."

Bernd's intellectual capacity—the inadequacy of such a comparison notwithstanding—is about that of a four-year-old child; from the beginning he matured too slowly and has already long since ended his intellectual development: for a few minutes at his birth, his brain received too little oxygen. He was not able to learn to read or to write. His rich feelings, animated by his mirth, often rub up against his poor vocabulary, and so his body says what his tongue remains incapable of; you can see them, if you will, in those attempts at flight. –The group calls his hopping "birding"; the word emerged out of the daily routine of the institution; even those who are linguistically impoverished do their part to build our language.

Early quitting time; Bernd comes out of the leather workshop, he has been sewing pouches and is now going home, which is the upper bunk of the front bunk bed by the window in the sleeping quarters of the Falcons; the Sparrow Hawks live below them, above them the Eagles; every group home area has a dining room and activity room with television and radio and a wall unit for personal belongings; there are toilets and a washroom for all of the groups. The Falcons live in the tightest quarters, altogether four square meters for each of the young men; the minimum amount of space deemed reasonable by law is eight square meters. Even so, the living situations have improved considerably; even as recently as ten years ago there were no lounges or common rooms, only two large dormitory-style sleeping halls for each of the twenty-five, and within them not even lockers; belongings were stashed under the mattresses. –In front of the window, outside on the lawn, four flea market swings, the interlocking seats on very long posts; they are also used in winter: flights to the clouds, from which the snow flows, or to the rambling stars. –Bernd swings often. –He grew up in the institution, although he has no memory of the passage of the years; his life is pure present, sometimes at the margins a shimmer of a near future that promises only happiness; a visit soon or a trip home. Not everyone has such a prospect: Bernd belongs to that minority who are not disowned by their parents.

Altogether, counting the branch locations, four hundred and fifty people with intellectual disabilities live on these ninety-year-old grounds, flanked by ivy, bisected by a public street—from infancy to old age. What kind of island in what kind of sea? "Heh, idiots, wha . . . ?" roars a herd of normal teenagers, liquor bottles in their pants pockets, bellowing all the way down the street to the bus stop; my fury unbolts like a switchblade, yet there is Bernd, running toward me, his arms still fluttering behind him, and in one forward bounce he throws himself around my neck; he says, "Jaaaa," only this, through pitches full of vibrato as he waves his arms, and here comes Peter, the Bear, barreling down toward me in a stream from the workshops, very fast, despite his *pes valgus* limping; he runs, as though he were fox-trotting around his shadow, and behind him Jürgen weighs in, broad shouldered, open chested, sailor's gait, his face full of pimples and pustules, which he's constantly squeezing out with the palm of his hand, and Peter pushed Bernd aside, "Are you coming to visit us again?" and Bernd, hopping, whooping, "Jaaaa!" while Jürgen pushes Peter away so he can hug me, and Klaus shoves his way in between Jürgen and me, and Willi arrives, struggling to find words, and so do Frank, and Heinz, and Thomas, and Andreas, and Peter is the victor over Jürgen, crushing my ribs at a leisurely pace: "Are you back again?"

Yes, I am here.

The first time I held a reading for the fosterlings—it's been three years since then—I told fairy tales and led language games; the event struck a chord, wishes were voiced for doing this again, then partnerships resulted, and now I'm here for the fifth time, but now the joy of return is being broken by an unease that I know all too well, this feeling of anguish that sneaks up whenever someone I respect as a partner becomes someone whom I must degrade to an object. I will have to observe my friends and their companions, stare at them, eavesdrop, take hold of their countenances, mentally take apart their emotional and cognitive processes and fixate upon them, scene by scene, image by image, in order to be able to transform the sequence in the end into a metaphor or to draw an overarching picture: the vexing crux of my profession; enough.

I carry the suitcases to the guest house; along the path, on a frozen sand hill stands a young man, bending over forward, saliva in the corners of his mouth, his head goes slowly back and forth, slowly, very slowly, back and forth, and back and forth, his mouth stands wide open; the dull eyes look nowhere. Now and then, his slow head-bobbing slowing even more, he'll begin, as though he wants to talk, to snap his lips, but he is deaf-mute, and then as though he were afraid of scaring himself, he slowly raises his left hand, almost warped into the shape of a pipe, he looks through it, without seeing it, starts a voiceless talking again; saliva soaks into his coat, and then he lets his hand fall very slowly, turns his head again back and forth, moves in slow motion, pauses and stumbles, picking up speed, down from the hill, four paces, stays at the edge of the path, shakes his head, though only twice now, turns himself around infinitely slowly and climbs, silently gasping from the strain, once again up the hill.

Up from the street the noise of a car, the crack of slamming doors: a young woman, black fur coat with very wide fur trim and a boa-like collar, has locked her Volvo and leads a child, curiously bundled up, to the clinic's evening office hours; the child is also in the same little fur coat as his mother, his face almost completely covered by a black lace scarf. The child looks at the man on the sand hill; the mother pulls him around hastily, as though he could stumble at this sight, and pulls the child up the steps to the clinic. Judging from his size, the child is three or four years old; he could be nine or ten, though, even fourteen or fifteen. He moves haltingly, his head is disproportionately large. –The young man did not perceive anything; he is standing on the hill again and swings his head back and forth, slowly and slobbering. –I know what the mother is afraid of; how she can best serve her child would be—as always—to see "what's the matter."

But that is so easy to say.

An aide comes, ponytail, very young, laughing irresistibly, and the man on the hill turns slowly toward her. He cannot hear her laughing, did he feel it? Laughing, she places an arm around his shoulders and leads him to his station. –The day turns to twilight. –Suddenly, as though this were important, I think that today is Thursday; I haven't yet read a newspaper or heard the news. –Thin sky, freezing away, my weather, and behind a window decorated with stars, on the main floor of the rehabilitation clinic, where the children's groups have their living quarters, sits Heike, still immersed in her work.

II   Thirteen-year-old Heike K., a spastic, lives in the wheelchair; her legs are almost completely paralyzed, her right arm extensively, her left arm significantly hindered from movement; her intellectual capacities are painfully limited. Her active vocabulary of active daily communication comprises little more than a dozen words: "Papa" – "look" – "you" – "they" – "eat" – "my" – "Maget" (Margret, the group's aide) – "pee" – "don' wanna"; her words are more expressions of feeling and perception than carriers of rational information. On request, her vocabulary is richer, she can name quite a number of body parts, can recite the names of the weekdays, if shown a plate, can call it "plate" and cheese "cheese" and spoon "spoon," she performs this moreover with visible pride, but she doesn't do so of her own accord. –She understands a lot. –It's hard for her to articulate; she speaks most forcefully with her glances, or her complete physical being, above all, when she refuses. –She can grip, grab, even hold something, move it, and lift it, though with little strength, and her fingers are always getting in the way. She can also, when she lowers her head, bring a spoonful of broth or a sandwich to her mouth and, if using both hands, even a full cup, and so when her food is placed within her reach, she can eat on her own. –That is a lot; other spastics cannot do that, and all the same it is so bitterly little. Heike will never be able to jump up when she's overcome with joy, she will never hug someone, never be able to pick an apple for herself, she can never use the toilet by herself, never blow her own nose, she cannot swat an annoying fly, she can't even scratch when something itches. She will also never have the ability to ask someone to scratch her itch, and if sadness or pain should overpower her, no god gives her the ability to say what she's suffering.

The mother with the child appears upstairs at the window of the waiting room; she unwraps the scarf from the child. –On the ground floor a light is already turned on. –Heike is the oldest of the Beetles, a group of three girls and seven boys; one of them, Niklas, is an autistic child. He mostly stands back in the darkest corner and plays with a small ball, he throws it vertically to the floor and catches it again and repeats that for hours if no one interrupts him, but should someone interrupt him? –Opinions about that are divided: the majority is probably for allowing him to continue. –Heike is a slim, fully grown girl (I then come to learn that she has been a young woman, physiologically, for a few months now), with a noble, finely sculpted face; her hair, dark, falling in waves across her forehead over her ears to her neck, sits like a cap over beewort brown eyes lying in narrow, drawn-out bays and shadowed by curving eyelashes: living shibboleths of the person. –She has just now straightened herself up, her head remains a little turned to the side, her left lower arm rests on the wheelchair's arm, the right arm she holds bent at a pointed angle and the elbow pulled to the back, so that the hand with the braced thumb seems to hover chest high. –Her feet buckled into the wheelchair's footboard, light brown skirt, dark brown pullover, she sits upright in the wheelchair, almost as on a throne between the massive back wheels, which are as high as her hips. Slender fingers, finely shaped hands, a gothic virgin, not a noble lady, most of all a childlike pietà.

I put down the suitcase; my inaugural visit. –Heike continues her work; she places mosaic blocks next to one another, small pieces of many colors that attach magnetically; she isn't forming a pattern, she can't do that, she's simply trying to put the diamonds in a row, smooth side against smooth side to form a closed band below which another piece can be attached, and so forth, until the honeycomb-shaped game board is filled. –She heard someone open the door and come in, but she cannot move her head far at will, I have to move into her field of vision, and as she sees me, she looks at me. –The last time we met each other was over half a year ago, and even then only a short meeting; I don't believe that she recognizes me. –She draws her gaze deep into my eyes and at the same time opens her mouth a bit, corralled effort of remembering, and then, suddenly, the moment of recognition, a moment that is, to share a word with Kierkegaard, an atom of eternity, not of time. –In everyday life a fleeting episode; in a larger domain, a human feat. –The brown of her eyes begins to light up, as when the sun breaks into a cathedral window, her mouth opens up, she squeals a sound in which the work of remembering unleashes the joy of recognition. The severity that marked her appearance has changed suddenly into exuberance; the transformation starts with her eyes, the brightening spreads across her face, a laughing ripples through her, waves of joy, it makes her shoulders roll a little, she lifts her hands to her temples and pulls her upper lip high, and in doing so, as though she were turning the light toward her inside, she closes her eyes to a crevasse of by now glowing brown. At the same time, an aura has arisen around her that cloaks her with a brightness that lends the ugly, hulking wheelchair a kind of awkward dignity. –An atom of eternity, not of time; a little later this process will become commonplace, and paid no more attention, and hardly even noticed, but in this moment I suddenly recognize the eyes as expressing the essential core of this almost language-less girl, the confluence of all that is unscathed that even the most battered still have at their disposal. –Every one of them possesses such a place; here, it is her eyes. –Even her joyous whoop was broken from the beginning, it comes pressed out of her throat, and the dark tones echo around her mouth; what is voiced is a mixture of whimpering and wheezing, shrill, even screeching, a discordant sound, which, though, beneath these eyes, is unmistakable as a joyous sound. Isolated, played back on a tape recorder, it would certainly not be diagnosed as an expression of joy.

So then, a whoop, and what's more, something else; Heike presses her face to me, but at the same time her shoulder pulls back, and something in her seems to want to flee, girlish shyness, maybe shame, and maybe both already womanly. –Thirteen years old and wrinkles around her mouth and eyes. –But she cannot flee, and the joy is stronger; she gives me permission to hug her gently and to sit down next to her. –Once again, her squeal, by now just a part of everyday life, then she lowers her hands and closes her mouth and abruptly picks up her work again, as though she wanted to show me what she can do. –I write that in the subjunctive; I guard against drawing conclusions too quickly. –The game board is in front of her on the table; she leans her upper body, since she is devoting herself again to her work, almost parallel to the surface of the table, grasps—and that is strenuous enough—a puzzle piece with her left hand, heaves it onto the board, brings it, with its magnet facing downward, to the correct position and steers it to the place where it belongs, making the effort not to disturb the other pieces that are already in place when she puts the new one down. –As though someone with frostbitten fingers wanted to pull a match out of a box. –What for a healthy child would be a playful, casual maneuver poses for Heike a new problem every time, the left hand fights against the right, middle and ring fingers of the left hand won't close, middle and ring fingers of the right hand hardly separate from one another, and if her left hand is busy with the edge of the mosaic, the right elbow pushes everything she has already accomplished to the right.

In a certain sense the work of a spastic resembles my work: enormous effort, tiny successes, very long-lasting pauses of unsatisfying toil toward a recognizable progress, constant doubt about the purpose of this daily work, deep crises verging on despair, and the essence of what is eventually accomplished is hardly noticed by anyone else and all too often not even by oneself. –No, the comparison doesn't hold; subjectively speaking, Heike's achievement is much greater, even though socially and culturally it may appear to be trifling, but I'll come back to that. –Simply that Heike doesn't reflect upon herself; or does she, actually, and we don't know it? She will not be able to tell us. She understands much of our language, we almost nothing of hers, and so she has to reach for blunt means to talk to us, the coarse minded: if they do not keep misjudging the purpose of her actions or, better, can no longer effectively perceive them, she refuses; she falls forward, scrunches her hands, or blows snot onto the table and engages in passive resistance. –I haven't yet experienced her this way; her aide, Margret, reports about it, she tells that one night before her bath, Heike suddenly turned to this passive resistance, without a visible reason; she, who is capable of undressing without help to the point that only her shoes need to be untied and her skirt and underpants pulled over her feet, she sat as though made of stone and didn't move at all, and then Margret attempted to tempt her with the good deed of the bath and pushed the wheelchair toward the tub, Heike launched into the sphere of contemptuous defiance and let it be known that she didn't much care for bathing, although she normally looks forward to it so. –It would be too simple just to call this balking; contempt is a difficult psychic power at a high level of will and value; a great poet, Fantišek Halas, spoke of the "splendor of contempt"—are we not all too ready to judge this negatively?

Yet I don't want to lose myself in this topic; Heike is finishing her work, the third to the last puzzle piece, then the second to last and the last, and the game board would be filled; chance joined black blocks and broken-down yellow bolts of lightning in red, green, white, and blue sprinkles, here comes Maik storming in, that impetuous, joyful Maik, and possessed by the thought of clearing the table thoroughly for dinner, he shoves Heike's work from the table. Heike shrieks and lifts both her hands, she cannot clench her hands to make a fist, she can only raise them in order to scream more shrilly, with freer lungs, and Maik hears Heike's screeching and laughs. She has squeezed her eyes shut, her mouth is wide open, teeth bared, her tongue unusually thick and misshapen, her facial expression tortured, her shaking hands, and all at once I see her as an old woman, heckling and drooling in her wheelchair, in an aura of sullenness and rancor with scrubby hair, warts between her fingers, deteriorating in a circle of deteriorating women—what kind of island in what kind of sea?

III   Photographs of the intellectually disabled: How will they affect the viewer? Whoever approaches this world only out of curiosity, with a tourist's point of view and a tourist's mindset, will only scratch the surface, will only enter into the essence of this world when he makes a sincere effort to share in it, but that presumes understanding, and understanding presumes empathy. But don't photographs in fact satisfy our curiosity? Don't they seduce us into the haughtiness of the Pharisees, who pray, as Luke reports: Lord, I thank you that I am not like these here . . . ?

It would really depend on being able to imagine oneself just like these here.

On another day in work therapy: the wool, textile, leather, and carpentry shop, the rug tying shop and the—somewhat zestfully named—workroom for "industrial manufacturing." –I wanted to see the littlest ones, the Elephants, but Bernd stopped me on the way and simply brought me over here: he had to show me what he was doing—and so I'm now sitting next to him. He is trimming leather pieces, using a stencil, round and longish squares, with rounded-off corners, he marks—again using a stencil—the holes for sewing lengthwise down the sides, and he is punching them out with nippers. The rectangular leather pieces, each of the six, will be glued to one another, the shell of a hexagonal pouch, whose long edges are trimmed in piping made of leather straps that tie two of the rows of holes, and the round leather circle is sewn as the last step as a base. On top a leather lace that closes the bag; a strap out of braided laces, and the little bag takes shape. –The products of the work therapy are sought after: tapestry, carpet runners, fabric and leather bags, Kasper figures and other wooden toys, change purses, baskets, stuffed snakes, and also pieces of pottery: pitchers, dishes, fantastical animals; whatever is made there and sold at carefully calculated prices increases the institution's budget considerably and even at three times the price would sell as much as now: flying out of their hands.

So Bernd shows me what he can do; he is—which is not always the case—completely involved in his work, which to be sure also includes suddenly stopping short and, while seated, attending to stretching his torso, twisting his hands, and fluttering his arms; you could also let him sit and dream; pressuring him is plainly unthinkable; no one is scolded, reprimands are rare. –And yet sometimes tempers flare, above all in the woodshop. –Six-hour day; four working units each of ninety minutes, mornings and afternoons a half, at noon a whole hour break, mornings a snack, afternoons a tea. –Many fosterlings change workshops after the breaks, many work only one unit or their two. –Extra pocket money is paid according to what they produce. –The basic pocket money is 120 Marks; no deductions for food or rent, and since personal needs are minimal—toiletries, treats, or on dance nights, a cola—they save for larger purchases: a watch, a camera, a transistor radio, and it happens time and again that family members take property away from a fosterling when he's at home on a visit: Such an imbecile would only break that; what does he need such expensive things for?! Family ties. The fosterlings could complain, they aren't without rights, but no one encourages them to.

I would like to watch Bernd at work, but it doesn't appear to be in the cards for me. –At the beginning, so as not to be conspicuous, I also took part in the work and punched holes in the leather pieces; but now, as I'm beginning to take notes and am looking at Bernd, he also puts his work down and looks at me and throws his arms like feathers behind him and laughs. –He who has been degraded to an object wants emphatically to be a subject. –I decide to sit down after the break at a table that is somewhat removed, but just at that time Bernd changes to the textile department (where he stitches patterns on leather pouches), and while I think about whether to follow him, I hear a strange shuffling and sloshing, as though a mermaid were traversing the realm of land, and in through the door slides Monika, on her knees, on bulky gauntlets, faster than anyone on healthy feet, laughing as wide-mouthed as a frog, and behind her, rocking a doll, is Peter.

Monika B., epileptic, fosterling of Station 1 in the Bethesda House, a tough, big-boned woman with coarse features, mid-thirties, is paralyzed from her knees to her feet; she moves herself by sliding on knee pads, very thick, green-trimmed rubber cuffs that extend over her toes; as awful as it looks, that is much better than moving in a wheelchair, she can go where she wants, can lift herself onto a chair or a toilet seat and then get back down to the floor again, she possesses the invaluable capacity to get around. –She shuffles around as fast as someone who saunters; later we will dance with each other this way. –Except for the knee cuffs, she is all brown: hair, eyes, complexion, very bulging lips that also play into the brown, added to that a brown jacket, gray pullover, and brown skirt. –She leads me to an insight.

I had never met Monika before, she had never visited my readings (she understands only the simplest sentences, and those only in isolation); now she sets about to work on the leather pouches, next to her Peter with his doll (sometimes he also has a ball with him), and even though I am sitting at a semi-angle across from her at the work table, I can study her at my pleasure, she doesn't take notice of me. She bends forward—occasionally erupting in crimped, peeping falsetto tones that startle you, since you're expecting a bass hum—just like Heike, bends her head deeply over her workpiece, takes up the leather pieces with a clunky hand, pushes the needle with the leather strip through the punched holes, coarsely, yet searching, making the effort to find the right one, licking her lips, pulls the strap tight, and suddenly, as she makes the next stitch, I see of her only her head and her hand, and suddenly I see in the work hall only heads and hands—above all the hands, lunging far back, reaching ahead, smoothing, ordering, piecing together, across the diameter of the room, the hands circling around the workpiece over which heads are bent low— the threefold unity of work: head, hand, and workpiece, the human trinity. –It is a revelation. –I, myself, have for years on end done physical work and again and again searched for the experience of work, on the dock, at the construction site, in the mines; here, I experience work, here, of all places. –Suddenly I understand what I have known for a long time: that the human being enters into the workpiece through the work; he humanizes that piece of dead nature, and what flows into its material is human essence unreduced: in his work, the human being is whole. –The finished purse (apart from its label) will not give any hint that a disabled person made it; it is a human work; its creators are humans, daughters and sons of one genus; in work, all of the fosterlings reveal their wholeness, their defect disappears as immaterial, but doesn't their specialness also disappear, that special quality that isn't only impairment?

In the product, for sure, but not in the work process, which is still entirely undifferentiated from a game and turns every product into an individual piece, a one-of-a-kind product, not only in the sense of artisanal creation. The result of this work is more than the product: it produces not only a use value but also a little bit of humanity.

Insofar as this work is play and thoroughly satisfies its creators, it is at its deepest level human work, commensurate with the human being, worthy of the human being, or, let's say it directly: unalienated work, like—to take its opposite—that kind of work that is a struggle, a struggle with nature, with the elements, as in the work of a miner or a boatman; in the wide middle ground between these spheres, where, according to Hegel, their "sourness" sets in, leads them into the mechanical, in the most extreme consequence into the assembly line, into, still according to Hegel, "the repetition of the same work" as "repetition of a familiar, where there is no longer interest in the thing, no enjoyment, to find oneself in the other . . ." –Such work as a daily occurrence: the terrible price of our civilization. –In the game, the work is new every time even in each repeated hand motion—: finding the right two holes for the needle is for Monika always finding anew an adventure of mind and hand; and finding for each fosterling the work best suited to him becomes the adventure of the therapy: to each is given that work that challenges him to his limits, does not allow mechanical repetition, or, should it, would give him pleasure extending his limits.

To the same extent that enthusiasm grows out of the game, it turns work into a struggle, though it's a struggle that a person fights with himself: the struggle against being disabled. –I know I am talking about an ideal, and that routine, lack of desire, indifference, lack of knowledgeable personnel, or even economic-minded thinking as a primary motivator can make a caricature of occupational therapy, can turn it into its own opposite, into drill, sanding, mechanical work, the very sourness that made Hegel sigh so deeply; only in workshops such as Monika and Peter's does daily life move closer toward the ideal.

Therapy as adventure: the educational path made of work and play can take strange detours. Monika, so I am told, to increase sensitivity in her hand, used to smooth wooden blocks with sandpaper, and at first, she saw the used-up sandpaper as the product she needed to make instead of the smoothed wooden piece, and she proudly scuffled over to her supervisor to show him what she had made: they tell me this anecdote not as an example of intellectual deficiency but as an example of a beginning. At first Monica's eyes grasped this: although the wood remained unchanged in its appearance, the paper changed its color from pale yellow to orange-red, and in the process of recognizing this, Monika saw herself as the agent of change: a great achievement in recognition. After that it was her hand that grasped: the little wooden piece that she sanded became smooth and easy to grip. –Words missing in Monika's vocabulary became her own in the potential of her hand. –At the same time she learned something extraordinary, again, without having a word for it: she learned to differentiate an essential element (smoothing of a workpiece) from an insignificant one (changing color), and this progress in understanding was at the same time the overcoming of that limit set by the purely mechanical; the smoothing of the sandpaper (assuming that that were the task) would in the long run not have been challenging enough; the smoothing of the piece of wood required something new: testing via the hand acquiring feeling. –Now she sews pouches in holy toil, she will complete a pouch, and it will be her pouch. –Peter, next to her, plays with his doll; non-speaking and just a few years ago a will-less and helpless invalid, he rocks it with a monotone mumble, then he puts it to bed in a little box that is always right here for him, and he turns again toward the other little doll, the little leather pouch that he will make here. Work and play in these workshops are as indistinguishable from each other as they are at the stations Play and Work, and out of both into one, pride transforms from achievement into pride in human creativity.

This kind of occupational therapy is not uncontested; in an outpost, in Neuendorf, in a home for mostly older, intellectually disabled women, the emphasis is placed on gardening, work that doesn't culminate in pride in the making and having of a dead object for use but takes the form of midwifery for another living being that needs constant tending and care in order to thrive, repaying in fruit what it incurred for custodial care. Whether the fosterlings identify with their apple tree or their raspberry bush? In any case, they might, and not a coincidence either, that in Neuendorf they nurture every habit of extended family life, such as taking all meals together. –Brotherhood as a basic principle; the notion of work as struggle appears in the garden not as a struggle against raw materials or the raw form of the workpiece but rather the defense against threats; but with that the playful quality of work diminishes; the playful explorer's curiosity that can be taken out on the materials, even to the extent that it destroys the workpiece to investigate its nature and structure (for example: sanding a dent into wood, which shows how sharp the pliable sandpaper bites and how soft the hard wood is)—; this kind of destructive experience is from the outset not allowed in the garden; a living being is no plaything. –All things considered, though: the plaything isn't alive; the teddy bear or the doll are in the end just surrogates. –The difference between both therapies at their core: in the garden, cultivation, in the workshop, subordination; or, if you will: feminine verses masculine engagement with the world; or even: an emphasis on collective nurturing on one side, individual experiences of achievement on the other.

Achievement as a value is certainly often attacked today, and rightfully so, if one is challenging a supremacy of achievement that only traffics in quantitatives, technologically measurable as "more and faster," socially measureable as wholly convertible into money. Achievement as a quantitative entity is based on just that sour repetition of the uncreative; it presupposes alienating work, trades in piecework and assembly line, and the education for it is always training. –In the best case it emerges as sport. –Achievement as a qualitative entity is something else entirely: incommensurable creativity, the singularity of the individual as uniqueness of a person (whether individual or collective), whose value can be immeasurable, even though it might be negligible in monetary terms. This achievement, unalienated, intrinsic, doesn't reside so much in the product as in the process of completion; the process is the creativity, the product is the accomplishment and already part of the past. –The present poses a new challenge. –The product loses importance as something to own; it's not about having but about doing: interestingly, the idea of ownership gives way precisely where you think it to be defining. –The creator will sometimes ask at the beginning whether he may keep what he has made, even though he is little opposed, indeed is even quite happy to learn that his products will be sold, even to someone unknown to him, that someone will treat it as merchandise, even though he may never understand this word: his creation is surely something unique, how could it be common when merchandise is so special!

The item sold is not something divested of the creator; in the pride in the creation it remains his, and as growth in experience too; it has become a piece of his person, the material ownership relationship isn't significant any longer. Yes, even that it was sold makes it even more personally one's own: that which came about as having value for the creator turns out to have use value for another, which is also evident in its character; the exchange value makes no difference. (An aside: since the workshops produce for the market, it makes it extraordinarily difficult to calculate the exact costs; most things are sold below their value.) And those who can be taught to understand, Bernd, maybe, Monika, certainly never, that proceeds from the completed piece will in turn benefit the community, indeed most often very concretely, say, a new leafy plant in the workroom, or even a better weaving loom, they will have been taught via experience what utopia hoped for in vain, the unfolding of unalienating work—; What kind of island in what kind of sea?

IV   Photographs of people with cognitive disabilities—: they all harbor the contradiction that everyone experiences on his first visit to institutions like this: the road toward understanding leads only through experience, through sensual perception, which is also capable of blocking the very path that only it is capable of opening.

   At the beginning of this path, and all too often its swift end, is the shock, or more rarely, the illusion; often a flight or fall from one into the other. –The shock of suddenly meeting people who abruptly, beyond all sympathy, arouse disgust, fear, revulsion, horror, and who, hungry for bodily contact, come close to the repulsed visitor, trying to hug, kiss, or touch; Roswitha, maybe, with the face of a bloody sponge, or Jürgen with his pustules, or the always shadow-boxing Karl. –This shock can drive a person to flight, to flight from the institution or to inner flight, to a fearful internal shutting down, and sometimes to the murderous thought that maybe a "merciful injection" for "these poor, unhappy ones" might be warranted after all. At best, the posture of the Pharisee in the temple. –"Such a shame, such a shame," murmured the lady in the black fur coat, as she brought the mute child from his appointment back to her Volvo. –The question of the injection is posed more often than one might think, and – to be sure – always in a timbre that the questioner holds to be humanistic: he wants to end a presumed unhappiness, judge over death and life of others, and yet is really only concerned with his own need. Outside in public, it comes up more robustly, you even hear the word "gas," all at once, knowing examples will multiply, in the bus, in the stores, even in restaurants.

The other way of obstructing understanding is the illusion of an idyllic world that sees people with cognitive disabilities as some sort of Rousseauean savages, and even the Sermon on the Mount proclaims them blessed and promises them the kingdom of heaven. Sometimes these two combine: shock and illusion; their midpoint an anguished pity, that other kind of selective thinking, or the illusion becomes an escape route and the shock ruptures the idyllic world and destroys any attempt at understanding, its failure already inherent in its construction.

The idyllic world in work therapy: suddenly, as though without a reason, Ingo grabs a hammer and pounds Thomas with it; suddenly, next door in the textile workshop, Viola, howling, reaches under her skirt and begins to masturbate, suddenly Patrick turns into a bundle of rage, and within the dull eyes of Christoph, who lays outside in the hallway in his wheelchair, waiting for the caretaker to pick him up, there pools without warning a dark hate. –And on the hill out of frozen sand, the young man rocks his head slowly back and forth while saliva runs out of his mouth. –"Oh, how cute these little ones are!"—this from the visitor to a children's unit, who exhales in such relief, fleeing from the group to which the cute little ones will soon belong.

I confess that I was not spared this fright—though in a different manner: on my first visit to a psychiatric clinic—not at Fürstenwalde—I stumbled into the lounge for the severely disabled as I was fleeing a downpour. They were passing their time as peacefully as ever in a stark room, filled with school benches and babbling, drooling, coarsely gesticulating people, of whom some came right up to me in order to hug me, to touch me, to say something to me, to show me something; a grunting whirlpool; it sucked me in.

Suddenly thronged by gestures and faces that I took as a threat: clawing fingers, swinging fists, hissing out of bloated mouths; I wasn't prepared for the sight and felt my strength dwindle precipitously, then, near to physical collapse, I saw in front of me Friedrich Hölderlin. A young man, sitting on a school bench, a little bloated; Hölderlin's traits completely, deep lines from his nose across the corners of his mouth, loose curly hair, blond, the very high forehead, Hyperion's sadly rhapsodizing eyes, he stared down at the Peloponnese, and his lips moved inaudibly. He smiled; he wrote with one finger of the right hand onto his left hand, I fixed my gaze upon his smile and on the shoulder of a crocodile-mouthed boy clinging to my sleeve. And upon a scene of brotherliness: an old man, leaning on a windowsill, had to pass water and didn't figure out the problem of how to unbutton his pants, the urine flowed into his shoes; he squealed, and the one near him by the wall came to his aid and unbuttoned the old man's pants. The stream rippled free, both of them laughed and Hölderlin gazed upon them as in a dream. Then my escort came crashing in and saw me, with relief, in company with others and took care of getting a washrag and bucket; then the attendant came, too, and grew surly. –My companion enlightened me about Hölderlin: an upper school student, highly talented, with no apparent conflicts, and suddenly plunging into utter refusal, from one minute to the next, and today without any drive, without goals for his actions, well-nigh lacking all desires, even his language almost completely dismantled. –I saw only that he still dreamed and wrote: my shock became a shiver, and I composed myself enough to understand that what had beset me was their need for words and contact. The crocodile-mouthed boy proudly relayed that he had gone to the movies by himself, he, all by himself, back and forth, without getting lost, back and forth, he found his way there and back all by himself, the whole way, completely alone, to the movies, and he was so obsessed by his achievement that he couldn't hold back the words, they tumbled out of his snapping mouth, which hacked them into chunks, and only the constant repetition and the lively gesticulation revealed their sense. –My companion then went with me along that path; toward the house, down below to the right, and right around the corner across the street; Columbus had only sailed straight ahead. –I suddenly felt the desire to turn back into that room and to embrace the voyager and have him tell me about his trip at length, as long as he felt like talking, and to listen to him without impatience and to meet his companions on the way without fear; I knew suddenly that I could trust them, since they entrusted so much to me; a possibility of life without guile, and out of shock and revulsion grew shame.

On this day I am also shown those who used to be called "raving lunatics" and were paraded in chains or behind bars in front of a gawking public; they lay in bright unlocked halls, under wide, unbarred windows unrestrained in snow-white beds and dozed away, numbed by drugs; a day that was nothing but a twilit night, and a night that dragged the day ahead, and only the rise and fall of breath and small reflexes showed that these bodies were alive. –My attendant was proud. –He spoke admiringly of the power of chemistry, the triumph of human progress that constructed the "soft straitjacket" that rendered the linen version superfluous. –He beamed, speaking of progress. –The eyes of the sick were blank, and their faces seemed suddenly like lard. I was then also shown the dull yellow room in which electroshocks were administered, an examination table covered with oilcloth, flat, with leather straps on the sides, and on one little table a kind of headphone, as stirrup, a clamp adjustable by screws with a black cable cord. –The procedure, said my companion, is not often conducted, but it was therapeutically indispensable; naturally the patient would be informed and his consent sought, to the extent that that was technically possible. –Since then, after certain daily experiences, I see this chamber in my dreams.

Photographs of people with cognitive disabilities—: people have criticized these for showing too little of the misery that besets the caregiver—especially the female caregiver—to the point of despair: aggression, obstinacy, sexual outbursts; people have also, though, criticized these photographs as being crassly superficial, for example in the group shot of children.

I find Dietmar Riemann's way of seeing to be brilliantly suited to opening up the path toward understanding.

His pictures are portraits, or are so in their conception; they take the cognitively disabled as a human being, not only as an object but also as a person, seeing him thus in an aura of dignity, and what guided the camera is veneration and awe. –Such a posture is not a given; ethos is congruent with art, though yes, their relationship is conceivable without intersecting. –It must be extremely tempting for a photographer to try out a way of taking pictures never seen before, a panopticum of the ugly-beautiful, bizarre and grotesque and enthrallingly shocking, in short to play up that shock of a one-way experience into the aesthetic-sensational realm; on the other hand, it would be just as tempting to unfurl the illusion as an idyll and to idealize within a picture an everyday that—we must concede—is not infrequently idealized.

The fascinating-shocking part: Diane Arbus, for instance, took these kinds of pictures, everyday life on the street, on a nude beach, inside the apartment, at the fairground, in Hollywood, a panopticum of the abnormal in a society that is abnormal in other ways; ultimately, in order to find new models, she looked for a psychiatric institute—or to be more precise, an "insane asylum." –Her pictures from there remain untitled: numbers in a horror show. Certainly you can't object to capturing the ordinary in merciless pictures in order to teach us to see its absurdity, the sheer decision to go to a psychiatric institution, and once there, also to a masked ball, or better: a masquerade—; no, I won't wager a judgment, she is a great artist and paid for her art with her life.

Here, then, awe of human dignity and, from that, the effort to make a portrait, that aesthetic expressive form that needs the object also as a subject, indeed primarily as subject. The portraitist has to court partnership; he has to cultivate the cooperation of the person to be photographed, since without that cooperation, no portrait will succeed. In an interview, Diane Arbus described her manner of gaining this cooperation this way: "If I were merely curious, then it would be hard to say to someone, 'I would like to visit you so that you talk with me and can tell me your life story.' People would tell me 'you're crazy!' And they would behave extremely cautiously. But the camera is a kind of license. There are a whole lot of people who desire exactly this kind of attention, and that is an attention within reasonable limits."

Riemann doesn't make use of this license. His method is that of the conversation. He tries to let a process develop on its own, in which the essence of a person unfolds that he would like to impart in image, and he fixes upon the moment in which this unfolding culminates: atom of eternity, not of time. This moment is condensed daily life; although not in a naturalistic sense: such a conversation is after all just as much daily life as another; it concentrates what daily routine diffuses. The old man in the bathtub, for one: if someone filmed the course of a bath and then isolated the stills of this procedure, shot for shot, a person would not land upon the moment that Riemann's photograph shows us—; he extracted that moment out of the everyday that is *also* myth, and whose essence emerges when it is distilled: in walking, standing, playing, dancing, sleeping, waking, dreaming, learning, taking, giving, breathing, singing, being silent, laughing, crying, celebrating, taking, eating, drinking, yes, even while defecating. –I find it worthy of his topic that this volume shows a scene of toileting: humanity is right here. –And so bathing, too, is routine as well as myth: Susanna in the bath, the Pool of Bethesda, of which the Gospel of John speaks, bathing in the sea, bathing in the Ganges, the bath of the Baptist, the bath of Agamemnon, the bath of the newborn, and here, then, a new one: the bath of the aged: near to the gate of death, hunching up into the state in which he was when he first began his existence, and at the same time approaching the final stretch: amniotic fluid of life, amniotic fluid of death, and both opaque: the residue of life. –You wash it off so as to persist in it. –The hands, opened to encompass the world, can only just encircle the body: the toes that an infant sticks in his mouth in order to recognize them as his own, you play with them the way you play with something foreign, and at the same time, you attach yourself to them: the borders of that which is granted to us, something we can cling to. You will be alone this way. Old; naked; poor in spirit; helpless in the tub, and nonetheless, what the arms embrace endures, the person, the self that is facing you: again these eyes that look at you, facing them, you must now live on.

I ask the reader to look at the hands, these hands and these feet, and when he can no longer take it, to look in the eyes that quietly tell him: you'll also be like this.

The old man with his covered genitals, behind the sheer curtain—: I cannot look at this photograph without thinking about Auschwitz: the shower pipe positioned at eye level, black, threateningly open; it is aimed to cross the viewer's eyes. –Whoever has seen this sees it forever. –It is good to find a MEMENTO of AUSCHWITZ in a place, to remember Auschwitz again and again. This conversation from the bathtub, dispensing with any hint of strangeness, is a conversation from an open casket, doubly accentuated by that pipe: as conversation from the tub, and as conversation in the face of death.

That a photograph can bear such a burden makes it great.

Diane Arbus created many pictures of old people, great photographs, such as "A Woman in Her Negligé." She shows her frontally, sitting on the left corner of a pillow-less double bed covered with an antimacassar, to the right, behind an open purse, a hazy little pile of laundry, in between them, indistinct, a brassiere. Her hands are spread out over the edge, on the right her wedding ring is visible, but nothing in the room indicates that a partner uses it with her. The negligé attempts to be seductive: little slippers of a kind of snakeskin, stockings and shirt of whisper-thin nylon, under which black panties show through, but the person who presents herself this way is an old lady, and her underwear, telling a lie of youth, stands in crass contrast to the shriveled face and the withered, varicose-veined, and hairy limbs riddled with dye so that the stately stature appears as a monstrosity, an everyday rendering of the cry, "How vain it all is!" A shock to our being. –The longer one observes this portrait, the more a giant stingray emerges, the curved triangle of the bed wall, and the black triangle of the panties, and diagonally on the edge the black bag, open, empty, a quilted advertising sign, and far in the background, blurry, on a chest of drawers, a black telephone. Behind it a window, morning sun, half-open drape, the night table lamp, and all of that in the mirror of the dresser. The early light breaks into this gloomy room, and it flares up into the eye, not in that of the old woman but the eye of the ray. Only in one, the left one, the other rests. –All of the woman's energy is mustered for the jump, to be there if the miracle would commence, if the telephone would begin to ring, if someone would enter her room in which she waits in a negligé, but the one who did come in was the woman photographer, her camera her free pass, her victim ready to surrender. –How vain it all is. –This portrait, one of perfection, is missing only one thing, a whiff of sadness, and this lack veers into a ridicule that counteracts the shock.

Through this doubled refraction a third ensues: the consciously and emphatically amoral posture, as peculiar as it sounds, puts in play a streak of cheap moralizing. It imposes itself upon the viewer to assure us with this portrait of the waiting woman that we don't have to be this way in old age; the observer joins forces with the photographer in derision. –The old man in the bathtub expresses the "have to" with an unsparing look and calls it into question differently: The imperative to become an old man is inevitable, but will the dignity endure that speaks from his eyes? And when this old man is shaved, he, by raising his pullover elevates a trivial daily occurrence to a festive act, to a great event in his life that conveys its magnitude to the viewer, and, gingerly touching upon the comical, even though it shocks with its dignity. In the dignity of this gesture, in the pose of enthronement in the dreary washroom, there is a draft of senility, but he inhabits the dignity of age and makes a myth visible: the old man being shaved is a King Lear. In the act of civilizing, he is made lower, and his being a king is diminished if not entirely annulled; as he spoke from the bathtub, he was stubbly, and that was certainly not a stroke of fate: whiskers are the most resilient life form; it is they that still grow in a coffin.

Like every real work of art, photographs can be understood as conveyers of a myth; they hold fast that place and that moment where the everyday is transcended, or to say it once more, where an atom of time becomes an atom of eternity. –The boy, confined behind bars, "restrained," in the words of the experts, since, largely impervious to pain, he would otherwise begin to rage against himself, maybe tearing his hair out in clumps or mauling his own cheeks and brow. It is the age-old form of the most painful lamentation, ritualized form of reaction to a loss that has suddenly broken into being, which then, as the healing of the self, only mourning can overcome. –Over whom does the boy grieve? Whom or what has he lost? Or what other kind of enemy than the grim reaper has broken into his being and his soul, against whom, sitting within, the young boy beats as though against himself? —Among the ancients, every mania, every intrusion of madness, like every drive, was caused by a god, in that god's specific sphere of being, with Ares, say, it would be different from how it would be with Hera or Apollo, and as the warriors of the illustrious Ajax saw their commander on Troy's coast, raging in madness with his sword on a pile of slaughtered cattle, believing them to be the enemies who betrayed him out of the victor's prize, the armor of Achilles—seeing their field commander defeated this way, his warriors, Sophocles tells us, began by asking which deity sent this mania, so that according to the uniqueness of the deity, they could recognize the uniqueness of the madness. It was Athena, and from the seer's adage we learn that Ajax could be healed if someone would protect him from himself for one day, guard him for one day, not let him out of his tent, if necessary, bind him to a post, then the anger of the goddess would be over. This day is wasted, and Ajax heals himself in his own way, in hubris, without divine help, by casting away the source of the madness, throwing himself onto his own sword.

Ajax as a boy, struck with madness, bound—I cannot see this photograph any differently, and the aloneness of this boy shocks me; maybe it is precisely his mania that he cannot suffer being alone. The use of restraints—in this institution, naturally—is not regarded as therapy; it is a manifestation of the lack of suitable personnel, friends tell us, who can stay by the ill during the day and then also during the night until the blessing of sleep is granted him. The elders in olden days knew a lot: I take from a little pamphlet "Mental Illness in Classical Antiquity" by Prof. J.L. Heiberg (Berlin and Leipzig: Walter de Gruyter & Co., 1927) this rendition of therapeutic recommendations of the Syrian doctor Archigenes, in the first century B.C. "It is important to keep the patient in a good mood, for that reason his best friends should visit and encourage him through stories and chaste conversations. Sickness is often accompanied by sleeplessness . . . In such cases one must use powerful sleeping pills, head baths, rubbing on the soles of the feet, massaging at the temples or behind the ears (like with animals). Often it can also help to create for the patient the conditions under which he is used to sleeping; the sailor can be placed in a boat, rocked by the waves, noticing the smell of the sea and ship, let him hear the surf and the rush of the wind; the musician should be ushered to sleep by playing of music and singing, the teacher through the chattering of children." Imagine what is lost. –One question that this photograph provokes even beyond the institution runs in two directions, as does every limitation of freedom: one can strive to perfect the restraint or look for means to make it superfluous.

This boy would have to have someone who takes care of him exclusively; he doesn't have anyone; does he long for someone? I wasn't able to get to know him; so I focus on the photography: what a technical display against someone dissected by these bars. Where do the shadows come from that circle around his head, strange meridians of delusion, and sections of the body lie in the darkness with the left arm, also the left leg. –The restraint protects him from damage; what kind of damages does it cause? Who would take stock? –I don't want to stir up hard feelings toward the institution, nor does Riemann's photograph; the people in Fürstenwalde are aware of their own deficiencies, of the never- (or hardly ever-?) ending dearth of caregiving personnel—though the Samaritans' Institution, supported by the Church, has a far greater reservoir of selfless young people who are willing to help than every state-run institution, and it still enjoys the advantage of being able to commit highly aggressive people to closed institutions. Nevertheless; and I find it good that we don't push borderline situations out of our consciousness.

The same holds true for another photograph that—facing an agonizing choice—I would regard as the most distressing of this series: the group portrait of children in the dormitory that opens the photo portion of this volume. It also speaks of a myth, that of the onset of sexuality in adolescent life, the myth of Kore, the daughter of Demeter, whom Hades lured into his underworld kingdom; he lives on in fairy tales: Do you remember the futile efforts to protect Sleeping Beauty from the spindle that makes her bleed unrelentingly?

Five children, around ten years old, two girls, three boys, in underwear, T-shirts and underpants, one of them chewing on his key lanyard, three in a group in the left wing, one with a hand on his genitals; one with his head in his hand. –The worrying child. –The girl in the background laughs, the boy in front smiles, but even in their laughter and smiles there is little cheer; there is a defiance in the facial expression of the smiling boy, in the laughter of the girl a fatuity. –The girl with the key casts a scrutinizing look; the boy on the outer left knows a lot. –All around them, beds; they surround the children; the wall behind them windowless, a wall of cabinets, lacquered, reflecting the beds, and through the single, slightly cracked door, in front of which the worrying boy is sitting, darkness and within it two slits; eyes of a demonic being; they are door handles that glow from a light whose origin no one here recognizes; even the function of this door during the day is not clear, in the photo the future peers in through it.

Sex is a heavy burden in the world of the intellectually disabled as in the surrounding world, only that those here are denied what is called "normal fulfillment." Marriages are legally possible, the disabled are not deprived of their rights; up until now no wish for that has been articulated; one doesn't know how one would decide, were it to be spoken aloud. –No opportunity is provided for more intimate attachments between the sexes; the outermost form of a partnership shows up in the weekly dance party as modest cuddling: holding hands, sitting arm-in-arm, stroking each other's hair, a hug that passes for playful, just nothing near an erotic kiss. What remains are homosexual encounters, which they tolerate at night in the sleeping areas without making a big fuss about it, and masturbation, which they view as natural, they'll even allow in certain cases during the day; they'll send the fosterling to the bathroom and then just leave him undisturbed as long as he needs. –Measures that dampen human drive are frowned upon; they use medications sparingly, only sedate in urgent cases (this, too, is a legacy of antiquity), don't have an electro-shock device and staunchly reject the "white straitjacket," the stifling of aggressions with narcotizing drugs.

So far, so good; not everywhere is there such insight, above all regarding homosexual sex (about which practices, since one doesn't observe, one doesn't really know and doesn't want to know); but yet again: behind the door that is ajar the darkness with the two slits of eyes. –Who sees the whole of its form? –We should be free to look it directly in the eye, be called upon to reflect further whether all possible allowances have been exhausted. From another institution, for instance, I know the example of a kind of marriage in which at least one partner has been sterilized; or for a heterosexual couple the opportunity of mutual masturbation. –Only the institution's problems? –Even in the world outside, sexual fulfillment eludes all too many who long for it; here, though, the need stares us in the face. From the outset, nonconformity is without exception the norm. On the outside there is always hope, and from that, a striving for instinctually appropriate satisfaction; the possibility for it exists outside, here inside severity reigns, and people say you have to resign yourself to that just like you do with your disability. But the disability is located in the mind, the drive in the flesh, and where the defect is physical, as in the case of many spastics, then the flesh cannot help its own flesh, preventing even masturbation. Should all help be denied? Assuaging words fall quickly from our mouths that "they" didn't feel it that way and that outside there are also similarly urgent cases. The latter is true, and it is certainly also right not to make human sexuality the main point when and where it doesn't play that role.

Nonetheless.

Consider Riemann's photographs.

V   The question of the "merciful injection," if we want to take it objectively, is the question of meaning in psychiatry. It could be posed three ways: as a question of the meaning of impaired existence, essentially its social aspect; in metaphysical terms, the question of the meaning of impairment itself (let's retain—for the moment—the simplified pairing of sickness and disability, which after all do not have to be identical); and, finally, as a question of the meaning of medical and caregiving work, its scientific form. The answers to these clusters of questions may in turn be further sorted into those that people with impairments might give if they could and which one could surprisingly often interpret as "happiness"; answers from those who take care of them; and, finally, answers from the society in which both live. All of these questions are knotted up, unraveled only with painstaking effort, their contours interlocking without ever being exactly identical, and in their historical progression, the answers acquire multiple forms, above all, viewed through a social lens: they range from the "holy fool" as the mouthpiece of divine revelation to the object of ridicule to be stared at, when people with bodily or intellectual impairments or other different kinds of living beings were paraded like animals in front of an audience that reveled in it, enjoying the delights of their own normalcy. After that, this normalcy saw the "aberrant" as objects that have to be tamed in order to be managed; ultimately, National Socialism decisively negated the value of such an existence, and the chimneys of the crematoria billowed smoke.

All of these configurations persist: at night in our dreams, and not only there.

In order to distill these questions and fully comprehend their essential nature, let us pose an extreme case, one in which the district medical leader under Nazi rule would not have hesitated to decide: "to the gas!" So: What meaning would there be in a human existence as a being whom one cannot even ask indirectly about the meaning of his life, since he wastes away without a will, lethargic, hardly even grunting or babbling, unable to hold feces and urine, unable, too, to lift himself, whom someone has to feed and toilet and clean without even gleaning a hint of a smile as a reward for such painstaking care? Now precisely this was Peter's case three years ago, an absolute full-care case, Langdon Down syndrome with cognitive disability of the third degree, the kind of extreme, severe degree that one used to call "idiocy," and this Peter has become that boy who shows up in the workshop with a ball or a doll, in order to sew a pouch when he feels like it, and on a walk he drives the spastic Ulli in his wheelchair, outside, of course under close supervision: Peter thinks that cars are friendly creatures and when he sees one, steers his friend Ulli in the wheelchair right toward it.

Even this Peter of today, whose development is now probably complete—it is necessary to safeguard his accomplishments instead of placing further demands on him, which he will either fail or meet only after drilling, that is, which would diminish him in his personality—: even this Peter of today whom the Nazi district medical leader would have casually waved into the gas; and the driver who steered toward Peter will probably angrily curse the scandal of allowing "people like that" to move freely on the street. Yet for someone who knows Peter's development, the value of therapeutic effort shines forth even where success is thwarted: its potential still remains, and being out and about is a way to realize this potential. –The person who played an essential role in this quiet miracle of human development, Gabriele D., the caregiver on the outing, is also captured with Peter in the picture, cheerfully giving him a goodnight kiss. She gave him this kiss before, too, every evening, even when Peter seemed like a hopeless case, and it is the devotion of love and warmth, of hope and of meaning, that awakened Peter's human dignity: the meaning of the human being is the human being.

The metaphysical meaning, which falls completely outside of science, is answered for the religiously devoted person beyond a shadow of a doubt in the Gospel of John, chapter 9, verses 1–3: "And passing by he saw a person who was blind since birth. And his disciples asked him, 'Rabbi, who sinned, this man or his parents, that he was born blind?' Jesus answered: 'Neither he nor his parents sinned. How much more should the workings of God be revealed through him.'"

For a Christian this saying is probably the meaning of revelation, it's just that for many outside the faith the question persists and they have to think through whether and how the saying might also have relevance for them.

Viewing sickness as divine punishment or a warning for others to avoid evil or as an impetus for penance is old; the disciples' question stems from it, and Ajax's mania was seen by his contemporaries as a punishment for his hubris in spurning Athena's aid to prevail in battle, alone, without the deity.

Here is what we read in Sophocles:

When the goddess Athena once drove him to battle,

so that he dipped his hand in enemy blood,

He called out to her in brazen swagger:

Go help the other Greeks, madam, stand by them with your protection,

But here, where I stand, no enemy breaks through.

Through such brash talk he drew upon himself the rage

of the goddess, who bids defiance to this haughtiness

But if he lives through this current day,

so could you rescue him with the help of God.

Except Ajax, consistent to the end, rejects this type of help; he'd rather be cured by giving up, and so he falls at his own hand. –A mercilessly hard, logical chain. –Even Jesus' disciples still think completely in the tradition of a causal relationship in which sin is the cause and punishing illness the effect, trembling before the rage of a God who punishes to the seventh generation: "Because I, Yahweh, your God, am a jealous God, punishing the children for the sin of the parents to the third and fourth generation of those who hate me," as it is proclaimed in the Decalogue, in the Book of Exodus. Rabbi Jesus breaks this chain: neither the blind man nor his parents had sinned, the meaning of the illness lay all the more in that God revealed His power through it. –Through what? –In the power to destroy human capacity? Antiquity saw it this way. "I can strike the seeing with blindness," Athena declares about herself in Sophocles' *Ajax*, and Odysseus hurries to agree with her: "The power of the gods can do everything it wills."

The revelation of divine power through the destruction of human power would hardly have been the way to understand that passage; its consequence, the healing, points to the other possibility: the unfolding of impaired humanity. Jesus "spat . . . on the ground, made some mud from the saliva, put it on his eyes (the blind man's) and said to him: 'Go, wash in the pool of Siloam' . . . So he went and washed and came back seeing."

This was a doctor's work, it happened on the Sabbath, and it was undertaken under penalty of death. –Nevertheless. –Every commentator on this passage, Saint Augustine, for example, sees the revelation of divine power in the healing of the blind and in the healing of a blind person the revelation of divine power. Yet not even the believing Christian would be able to see blasphemy in the secularization of this thought, that in healing in its various degrees, the power of being human unfolds, both within those being healed and in those doing the healing.

The meaning of an impairment would reside, then—presuming we accept the question—in that the power of humanness unfolds both within impairment and by virtue of it, for the impaired as well as for his caregiver, both of whom belong to the species human, whether one sees them as creature and divine helper or simply as people left to their own devices. Of course, meaning has to be assigned, it isn't in the impairment itself, it is projected onto it, and even when science dismisses the question—the question of what, say, epilepsy might mean is nonsense from a scientific perspective—meaning confronts science as a value to take up, if not by the field per se then by its practitioners, for whom the impaired person is a human being and not merely an object of expertise.

To accept another person as a human being means first to recognize him as a human being like yourself; heads will nod very quickly at that notion, but if the question is posed so that you look at yourself as being just like the other and, in doing so, become aware of the impairment allotted to each of us, you imagine yourself in the position of the one who needs care, then nodding turns into head shaking. But meaning would rest or fall on exactly that: that you're ready not only to give to the impaired but also to take something from them.

We who distract ourselves in work as well as in leisure, who have such a hard time concentrating, who jump so quickly from one thing to another, we could learn from Heike and Monika what devotion to work means, and we who are pulled in different directions in our work as in our free time, overwhelmed, in career and hobby alike, slaves to and not masters over our actions, we could learn from Bernd and Peter to be easier on ourselves. Laid back isn't scattered, and focused isn't dogged. –The driver who criticizes Peter should certainly not pick up Peter's habit of steering toward another car, but meeting one another as friend rather than enemy wouldn't be the worst lesson. Who among us is allowed to be as happy as Willi or Jürgen, to make no secret of his feelings, to show his true face without guile? Please, let's not say that this is only the simplicity of the poor in spirit, let us rather ask whether a spirit isn't itself limited when humanity requires so much constraint, like that spirit that demands we "keep smiling," that all of our faces show the same uniform expression; sugary optimism snuffs out the variety of our emotions right along with every manifestation of trust. –Every society has its own experience of that, and apparently no one learns from it. –"Whoever wants to accomplish something has to be happy!" I shudder at this imperative. I see his picture; that's how one looks at people: bustling and turning himself inside out with laughter when the boss tells a joke. There isn't much laughter in the Fürstenwalde workshops, the prevailing mood is concentrated effort, and from that emerges, without imposition, the quiet joy of meaning gained.

What would there have been to learn from Peter when he lay limply on his bed? Nothing yet from the figure embodied at that time, yet everything from all that happened to him since: becoming. In becoming, meaning unfolds, and it does so in a reciprocal manner: in the situation into which he is brought as well as within that person who brought him in.

If the purpose of the care given by Gabriele and the other aides has been that Peter's humanity develops, then Peter's development has also had an effect on his caregivers: they are not only affirmed through him, they, too, are boosted by his meaningful existence. And today that includes that he decides whether he sews or plays ball, that he considers the cars to be his friends, that he constantly cuddles a doll, that he only paints black dogs with outsized heads and mostly two or three horizontally splayed legs, with plate-like paws that look like the discs that weightlifters use. He has a right to his personality, and no one thinks of training him only to sew purses all day or to paint a "real" dog instead of the creation of his mythology. It might be achievable, this sort of training, but it would not develop anything more, it would diminish Peter's personality from a social standpoint, and would therefore not only be bad for Peter but also bad for us too: training also trains the trainer.

Being a disciplinarian is not a good occupation.

To accept the disabled person as a human being means to accept his personhood so as to recognize him as a partner. The valid answer to the question of the "merciful injection" is not found in a warm-hearted appeal to humane behavior toward "them too" or, worse yet, "even them," imputing a useless existence that in another place was called "life unworthy of living"; this answer, it can only be an avowal of all people with cognitive disabilities as bearers of benefit to the whole, bearers of meaningful lives.

That's the reason why it is so meaningful that Heike fills her board with blocks, she's building a piece of culture that is more valuable than so many products in store windows or galleries, whose only approximation of personal achievement is one of reproduction. What Heike brings forth is creativity, and it shows itself as such in that it can radiate out toward others: not only Heike grows with them, they themselves also grow through Heike's activity. And the doctor, who after a long day's work still spends each evening with an autistic child, encouraging him to put a tapered block into a board with holes, only this, nothing but this: "Put it in!" and a caress, when the difficult work is successful, and—glossing without fuss over a failure, the challenge to try again: "Put it in!"; every evening, a whole hour, and the success of six weeks would be that this work is accomplished four times in a row without error—; this doctor, giving of herself, doesn't only give, she also receives something, and the child, in the deepest region of the soul, feels himself as well to be a giver and can also build up a partnership, the saving grace in his senses that see the external as a singular adversary.

VI   Photographs of people with cognitive disabilities—; they pull me under their spell through something that is well nigh suspect: through their affirmation. These pictures say yes, yes to the disabled and to their caregivers, and they say their "yes" out of a double necessity: Riemann's principle of placing the object of his camera in a partner relationship meets a world whose principle for existence is in fact partnership.

This "yes" does not glorify its subject, it even includes painful criticism and sharpens pressing hard questions: a "yes," how and where it is appropriate. I try to imagine a "yes" to an institution with pharmaceutical straitjackets, with attendants who beat and with doctors who imagine themselves to be like gods, with electroshocks, with humiliated souls in managed bodies; a "yes" to that question would be cynicism or lie, whereby cynicism as a foundation for art is at least conceivable.

I don't want to speak about aesthetics now, this is no longer the place to do that. I am taking in the "yes" of this world of pictures, so that, in its aura, we may remember that of all of the victims of National Socialist murder, those who received the least amount of sympathy were first to have to go into the gas chambers:

the mentally and physically disabled. We still owe them as good as everything. I don't know of one monument that memorializes them, no work of art has honored them, they have fallen out of literature, none of their life stories has been chronicled, as a group of people persecuted they have not been recognized, the names "Hadamar" or "Grafeneck" or "Sonnenstein" or "Eglfing-Haar" or "Bernburg" or "Hartheim" hardly mean anything to anyone, although it was in those places that the first selections took place. Resistance within the institutions is little researched. A very few meritorious pieces of documentation about the—wrongly named—crimes of euthanasia in the Hitler era are the exception that prove the rule.

The moral rehabilitation, like the grappling with theories about the "merciful injection," is basically stuck in half measures, with a "they too" and "even they," with cost-benefit analyses of the value of caregiving, with recourse to the fifth commandment. Even today we still see in theoretical discourses the completely differently situated problem of assisted suicide drawn into that of the murder of intellectually or physically disabled people: it is precisely these people whose lives evince the famous Marxist axiom that the free development of each is the condition for the free development of all.

So that no one misunderstands me: I don't want to turn a scourge into an act of charity. Every impairment is a malady, every step toward its prevention an act of goodness, and every rehabilitation a blessing. The purpose of a sickness should be its healing and the redemption that comes from it. Humans have succeeded in ridding the world of epidemics: plague, cholera, tuberculosis; manifold disabilities are never going to be eradicated. As long as disabilities are among us, though, those who bear them are of our kind, and we are of their kind. What happens to them happens to us too.

The development of the one as a condition for the development of all. Fürstenwalde is an example of that. These photographs make it visible. I have hung one from this volume, framed, on the wall of the room in which I work, eat, and sleep.

It is a portrait of Monika.

I'm learning from her to go on my knees too.

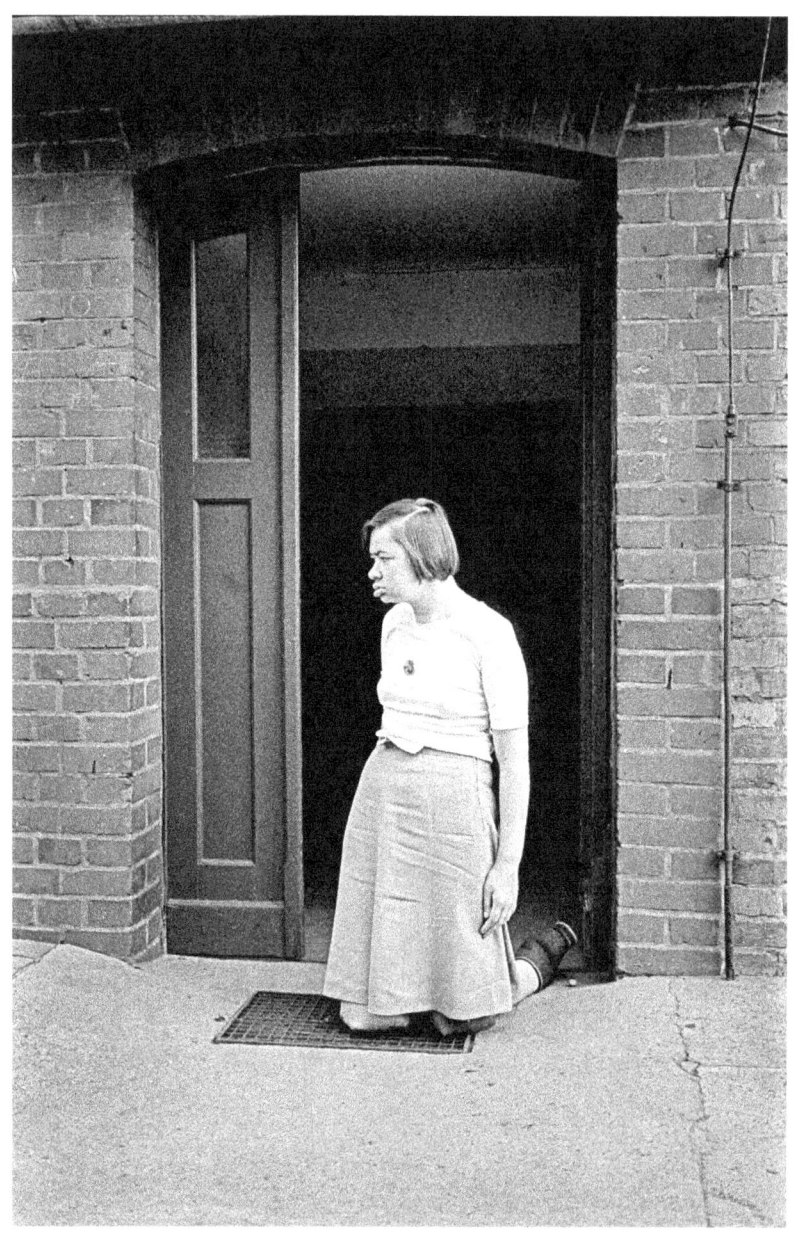

Photographien von geistig Behinderten: Wie wird man eine solche Herausforderung aufnehmen? –Ich weiß es nicht. –Ein Begleittext kann Photographien nicht verändern, und das ist auch nicht meine Absicht.

Ich werde einfach von meinen Freunden erzählen, die ich hier in Fürstenwalde gewann.

1   Da ich zum Auto gehe, mein Gepäck zu holen, begegnet mir Bernd. Ich will den Text zu diesem Band in der Samariteranstalt schreiben, das neue Jahr soll damit beginnen, mit seiner Frostluft und den Eiszapfen von den Dächern, die Linden und Erlen in wechselndem Rauhreif unterm dünnen, wegfrierenden Himmelsblau. –Mein Wetter, meine Welt. –Bernd, schmal, zwanzigjährig, in klobigen braunen Schnürschuhen stapfend, trägt Wattejoppe und Zipfelmütze, blauweiße Ringe kräftiger Wolle, die dicke Troddel baumelt vorn in die Stirn. Da er mich erblickt, bleibt er überrascht stehen, schiebt mit einer Bewegung des Oberkörpers Hals und Kopf vor, und mich endgültig erkennend, springt er in die Höhe, die gestreckten Arme rückwärts hochfedernd, Handflächen nach oben, Finger gespreizt, ein lachender, seltsam unflügger Vogel, den Freunde das Fliegen verlangen macht. Dreimal hüpft er noch solcherart auf, den Mund immer breiter ins Lachen ziehend, und er wippt während dieses Hüpfens auch noch den Rumpf in den Hüften, ein Sprung im Sprung, und verdrei-, ja vervierfacht: Aufschnellend hebt er den Kopf, den er sonst zur Brust senkt, und da er den Kopf hebt, schlägt er die Augen auf, und vom Knöchel bis zum Auge lacht er mich an. –Ach, daß wir Menschen so erdschwer sein müssen!—Bernd gehört zu den Falken, einer Gruppe von vierzehn jungen Männern, die auf einer Station der Samariteranstalt die Zeit verbringen, die ihnen auf Erden gegeben ist; die meisten schon im Vorschulalter mit frühkindlichen organischen Hirnschäden hier eingewiesen: Intelligenzgeminderte aller Grade; Spastiker und Epileptiker mit geistigen Defekten; am— früher—"Mogolismus" genannten—Langdon-Down-Syndrom Leidende, und auch jene so rätselhaft früh Enttäuschten, die man "Autisten" zu nennen pflegt.

Bernds Intelligenzleistungen—die Unzulänglichkeit solchen Vergleiches einmal außer acht gelassen— entsprechen etwa denen eines vierjährigen Kindes; er reifte von Anfang an zu langsam und hat längst seine geistige Entwicklung geendet: Als er in die Welt geboren wurde, erhielt, für einige Minuten, sein Gehirn zuwenig Sauerstoff. Er konnte weder Lesen noch Schreiben erlernen; sein reiches, von Frohsinn bewegtes Gefühl stößt oft an die Grenze eines dürftigen Wortschatzes, und so sagt der Leib, was der Zunge verwehrt bleibt, gern in jenen Ansätzen zum Flug. –Die Gruppe nennt sein Hüpfen "vogeln"; das Wort ist im Anstaltsalltag entstanden; auch die Spracharmen baun an der Sprache mit.

Früher Feierabend; Bernd kommt aus der Lederwerkstatt, hat Taschen genäht und geht nun nach Hause, das ist das obere Lager des vorderen Doppelbettes am Fenster im Schlafsaal der Falken; unter ihnen wohnen die Sperber, über ihnen die Adler; zu jedem Gruppen-Zuhause gehören auch ein Eß- und ein Aufenthaltsraum mit Fernseher und Radio und einer Schrankwand für die persönliche Habe; für alle Gruppen gemeinsam sind Toilette und Waschraum. Die Falken wohnen am beengtesten, insgesamt vier Quadratmeter für jeden der jungen Männer; als zumutbar unterstes Wohnraumlimit schreibt das Gesetz acht Quadratmeter vor. Dabei haben sich die Wohnverhältnisse erheblich verbessert; noch vor zehn Jahren gab es keine Aufenthaltsräume, nur zwei Schlafsäle für je ihrer fünfundzwanzig, und darin noch nicht einmal Spinde; die Habseligkeiten lagen unter den Matratzen versteckt. –Vorm Fenster, im Grün, vier Jahrmarktsschaukeln, die verkettbaren Sitze an sehr langen Stangen; sie werden auch im Winter benutzt: Flüge zu den Wolken, aus denen der Schnee rinnt, oder zu den schweifenden Sternen. –Bernd schaukelt oft. –Er ist in der Anstalt aufgewachsen, doch er hat keine Erinnerung an den Ablauf der Jahre; sein Leben ist pure Gegenwart, am Saum manchmal ein Schimmer naher, ausschließlich Freude verheißender Zukunft: bald ein Besuch oder eine Nachhausefahrt. Nicht jeder hat so eine Perspektive; Bernd zählt zu jener Minderheit, die von den Eltern nicht verleugnet wird.

Insgesamt, die Außenstellen mitgerechnet, leben auf diesem durch nunmehr neunzig Jahre gewachsenen, efeuflankierten, von einer öffentlichen Straße durchschnittenen Gelände vierhundertfünfzig geistig Behinderte vom Kleinkind bis zur Greisin. Was für eine Insel in was für einem Meer? "Eh, blöde, wa?" brüllt die Gruppe normaler Jugendlicher, die Schnapsflaschen in den Hosentaschen, die Straße hinab zur Bushaltestelle grölt; meine Wut spring wie ein Schnappmesser auf, allein da läuft mir Bernd schon entgegen, immer noch die Arme nach hinten hochwippend, und im Vorwärtsschwung fällt er mir um den Hals; er sagt: "Jaaaa", nur dies, durch Tonhöhen so schwingend, wie er seine Arme wirft, und nun kommt im Strom aus den Werkstätten auch Peter, der Bär, herangestürmt, sehr schnell, trotz seines Knickfuß-Hinkens; er läuft, als umtänzle er seinen Schatten, und hinter ihm wiegt sich Jürgen einher, breitschultrig, brustoffen, Seemannsgang, das Gesicht voller Pickel und Eiterflatschen, die er ständig mit seiner Handfläche ausquetscht, und Peter hat Bernd zur Seite geschoben: "Hommsu wiede bei uns?" und Bernd, hüpfend, jauchzt: "Jaaaa!", dieweil Jürgen, mich zu umarmen, Peter wegstößt, und Klaus schiebt sich zwischen Jürgen und mich, und Willi kommt, um Worte sich mühend, und Frank, und Heinz, und Thomas, und Andreas, und Peter hat über Jürgen gesiegt und zerdrückt mir gemächlich die Rippen: "Bissu wiede da?"

Ja, ich bin da.

Beim ersten Mal, drei Jahre sind's her, hatte ich vor den Pfleglingen gelesen, Märchen erzählt und Sprachspiele getrieben, die Veranstaltung hatte Anklang gefunden, Wünsche nach Wiederholung wurden geäußert, dann hatten sich Partnerschaften ergeben, und nun bin ich das fünfte Mal hier, doch jetzt wird die Freude des Wiederkommens durch ein Unbehagen gebrochen, das mir nur zu gut bekannt ist, jenes Peingefühl, das sich immer heranschleicht, wenn ich jemand, den ich als Partner schätze, zum Objekt degradieren muß. Ich werde meine Freunde und ihre Gefährten beobachten müssen, anstarren, belauern, ihre Mienen festhalten, ihre Gefühls- und Begreifensprozesse gedanklich zerstücken und Bild für Bild davon fixieren, um die Sequenz schließlich in eine Metapher umsetzen oder als Summe ziehen zu können: die leidige crux meines Berufs; genug.

Ich trage die Koffer zum Gästehaus; am Weg, auf einem gefrorenen Sandhügel, steht ein junger Mann, vornübergebeugt, im Mundwinkel Speichel, sein Kopf geht langsam hin und her, langsam, sehr langsam, hin, und her, und hin, und her, sein Mund steht weit offen; die glanzlosen Augen schauen nirgendwohin. Mitunter, sein langsames Kopfschwenken noch mehr verzögernd, setzt er an, als ob er reden wolle, seine Lippen schnappen, doch er ist taubstumm, und dann hebt er, als fürchte er, sich selbst zu erschrecken, langsam seine linke, fast zum Rohr gekrümmte Hand vor die Augen, schaut durch sie hindurch, ohne sie anzusehen, setzt wieder zur lautlosen Rede an; der Speichel sickert ihm auf den Mantel, und dann läßt er die Hand ganz langsam sinken, dreht wieder seinen Kopf hin und her, wird zeitlupenhaft, hält schließlich inne und stolpert, beschleunigt, vom Hügel herunter, vier Schritt, bleibt am Rand des Weges stehen, schüttelt, doch jetzt nur zweimal, den Kopf, dreht sich unendlich langsam um und klimmt, vor Anstrengung unhörbar keuchend, abermals den Hügel hinauf.

    Von der Straße her Autolärm, Knallen zugeschlagener Türen: Eine junge Frau, schwarzer Fellmantel mit sehr breitem weißem Fellsaum und boaartigem Kragen, hat ihren Volvo abgeschlossen und führt ein merkwürdig vermummtes Kind zur Klinik, in die Spätsprechstunde; auch das Kind im gleichen Pelzmäntelchen wie seine Mutter, das Gesicht von einem schwarzen Spitzenschal fast verdeckt. Das Kind schaut den Mann auf dem Sandhügel an; die Mutter reißt es hastig herum, als könne es sich an diesem Anblick versehen, und zieht es die Stufen zur Klinik hinauf. Seinem Wuchs nach ist das Kind drei, vier Jahre alt, es könnte aber auch neun, oder zehn, ja vielleicht vierzehn oder fünfzehn Jahre zählen. Es geht stolpernd, sein Kopf ist unproportioniert groß. –Der junge Mann hat nichts wahrgenommen; er steht nun wieder auf dem Hügel und schwenkt, langsam und sabbernd, den Kopf hin und her. –Ich weiß, wovor die Mutter zittert; womit sie ihrem Kind am besten diente, wäre—wie immer—sehen "was ist".

Aber das ist so leicht gesagt.

Eine Betreuerin kommt, Pferdeschwanz, blutjung, unwiderstehlich lachend, und der Mann auf dem Hügel dreht sich ihr langsam entgegen. Er kann ihr Lachen nicht hören, hat er es gefühlt? Sie legt ihm, lachend, den Arm um die Schultern und führt ihn auf seine Station. –Der Tag geht ins Dämmern. –Plötzlich, als wäre dies von Bedeutung, denke ich, daß heute Donnerstag ist; ich habe noch keine Zeitung gelesen oder Nachrichten gehört. –Dünner, wegfrierender Himmel, mein Wetter, und hinter einem sternengeschmückten Fenster im Erdgeschoß der Rehabilitationsklinik, wo die Kindergruppen ihre Heimstätten haben, sitzt Heike, noch in ihre Arbeit vertieft.

II   Die dreizehnjährige Heike K., eine Spastistikerin, lebt im Rollstuhl; ihre Beine sind fast vollständig gelähmt, der rechte Arm ist weitgehend, der linke erheblich bewegungsbehindert; die intellektuellen Fähigkeiten sind schmerzlich beschränkt. Ihr aktiver Wortschatz aktiver Alltagskommunikation umfaßt wenig mehr als ein Duzend Wörter: "Papa" – "guck" – "du" – "die" – "eß" – "mein" – "Maget" (Margret: die Gruppenbetreuerin)—"pullan"—"winnich" (will nicht); es sind mehr Ausdrücke von Gefühl und Empfindung als Träger rationaler Information. Auf Abruf ist ihr Wortschatz reicher, sie kann etliche Körperteile benennen, weiß die Wochentage herzusagen, nennt, wird er gezeigt, den Teller "Teller" und den Käse "Käse" und den Löffel "Löffel", sie leistet dies auch mit sichtlichem Stolz, jedoch nie aus eigenem Antrieb. –Verstehn kann sie viel. –Es fällt ihr schwer, zu artikulieren; am eindringlichsten spricht sie mit ihren Blicken, oder ihrem gesamten leiblichen Sein, vor allem, wenn sie sich verweigert. –Sie kann greifen, zupacken, auch etwas halten und bewegen und heben, allerdings mit geringen Kräften, und ihre Finger stehen einander im Weg. Sie kann auch, wenn sie den Kopf tief senkt, einen Löffel Brei oder ein Butterbrot, beidhändig sogar eine gefüllte Tasse zum Mund führen und also, wenn ihr Speisen in Griffnähe gestellt werden, selbständig essen. –Das ist viel; andre Spastiker können das nicht, und dennoch ist es so bitter wenig. Heike wird niemals aufspringen können, wenn sie Freude überwältigt, sie wird niemals jemand umarmen, sich niemals einen Apfel abflücken können, sie kann niemals allein die Toilette benutzen, sich nicht allein die Nase schnauben, sie kann keine lästige Fliege erschlagen, ja sich nicht einmal kratzen, wenn es sie juckt. Sie wird es auch nicht zu fordern vermögen, und wenn sie Trauer oder Schmerz übermannt, gibt ihr kein Gott, zu sagen, was sie leidet.

Die Mutter mit ihrem Kind erscheint oben am Fenster des Wartezimmers; sie wickelt dem Kleinen den Spitzenschal ab. –Im Erdgeschoß wird schon Licht angedreht. –Heike ist die Älteste der Käfer, einer Gruppe dreier Mädchen und sieben Jungen; einer von ihnen, Niklas, ist ein autistisches Kind. Er steht meist hinten im dunkelsten Winkel und spielt mit einem kleinen Ball, er wirft ihn senkrecht zu Boden und fängt ihn wieder, und wiederholt das stundenlang, falls man ihn nicht unterbricht, aber soll man ihn unterbrechen? –Die Meinungen darüber sind geteilt: die Mehrheit geht wohl dahin, ihn gewähren zu lassen. –Heike ist ein schmales, hochgewachsenes Mädchen (ich erfahre dann, daß sie seit einigen Monaten physisch eine junge Frau ist), mit edlem, strenggeschnittnem Gesicht; ihr dunkel in Bogen von der Stirn über die Ohren zum Nacken niederfallendes Haar sitzt wie eine Kappe über kalmusbraunen, von sehr weit geschwungenen Wimpern überschatteten Augen, die in schmalen, langgezogenen Buchten liegen: lebendige Schibboleths der Person. –Soeben hat sie sich aufgerichtet, ihr Kopf bleibt ein wenig zur Seite gedreht, ihr linker Unterarm ruht auf der Rollstuhllehne, den rechten Arm hält sie spitzwinklig geknickt und im Ellbogen nach hinten gezogen, so daß die Hand mit dem abgespreizten Daumen in Brusthöhe zu schweben scheint. –Die Füße ans Rollstuhltrittbrett geschnallt, hellbrauner Rock, dunkelbrauner Pullover, sie sitzt aufrecht im Rollstuhl, beinah thronend zwischen den massigen Hinterrädern, die ihr bis an die Hüften reichen. Schmale Finger, feingegliederte Hände, eine gotische Jungfrau, kein Edelfräulein, am ehesten eine kindhafte Pietà.

Ich lasse die Koffer stehen; mein Antrittsbesuch. –Heike setzt ihre Arbeit fort; sie legt Mosaiksteine aneinander, kleine, magnetisch haftende Plättchen verschiedener Farben; sie baut keine Muster, das schaffte sie nicht, sie ist nur bemüht, die Rhomben richtig zu reihen, gleiche Seite an gleiche Seite, so daß ein geschlossenes Band entsteht, dem sich ein tieferliegendes anfügt, und so fort, bis das wabenförmige Spielbrett gefüllt ist. –Sie hat jemand die Tür öffnen und hereinkommen gehört, aber sie kann den Kopf nicht beliebig weit drehen, ich muß mich in ihr Sichtfeld begeben, und da sie mich sieht, schaut sie mich an. –Das letzte Mal sind wir einander vor mehr als einem halben Jahr begegnet, und auch da nur ein kurzes Zusammentreffen; ich glaube nicht, daß sie mich erkennt. –Sie zieht den Blick tief in die Augen und öffnet dabei ein wenig den Mund, versammelte Arbeit des Erinnerns, und dann, jäh, der Moment des Erkennens, und der ist, um mit Kierkegaard zu sprechen, ein Atom der Ewigkeit, nicht der Zeit. –Im Alltag eine flüchtige Episode; vor einer andern Instanz ein Akt der Person. –Das Braun ihrer Augen beginnt zu leuchten, wie wenn Sonne in ein Domfenster bricht, ihr Mund tut sich auf, sie jauchzt einen Laut, in dem die Arbeit des Erinnerns sich in der Freude des Wiedererkennens befreit. Die Strenge, die ihre Erscheinung bestimmt hat, ist beinahe in Überschwang umgeschlagen; die Veränderung geht von den Augen aus, das Leuchten teilt sich dem Gesicht mit, ein Lachen durchwellt sie, Wellen der Freude, es macht ihre Schultern ein wenig rollen, sie hebt die Hände bis über die Schläfen und zieht die Oberlippe sehr hoch, und dabei, als wende sie das Leuchten nach innen, schließt sie die Augen zu einem Spalt nunmehr glühend gewordenen Brauns.

Gleichzeitig ist um sie eine Aura entstanden, die sie wie ein Mantel aus Helle einhüllt und die selbst dem häßlichen, plumpen Rollstuhl eine Art ungelenker Würde verleiht. –Ein Atom der Ewigkeit, nicht der Zeit; wenig später schon wird dieser Vorgang alltäglich werden, und nicht mehr beachtet, und kaum noch bemerkt, doch jetzt erkenne ich plötzlich die Augen als Ausdruck des Wesenskerns dieses fast sprachlosen Mädchens, des Sammelpunkts aller Unversehrtheit, über die der Geschlagenste noch verfügt. –Jeder von ihnen besitzt solch einen Ort; hier sind es die Augen. –Schon das Freudenjauchzen war von Beginn an gebrochen, es kommt gequetscht aus ihrer Kehle, und die dunklen Töne verhallen im Mundraum; was laut wird, ist ein Gemisch aus Winseln und Röcheln, schrill, sogar kreischend, ein mißtönender Laut, der jedoch unter diesen Augen unverloren als Jauchzen erklingt. Isoliert, vom Tonband abgespielt, wäre er als Freudenäußerung gewiß nicht zu diagnostizieren gewesen.

So also ein Jauchzen, und übersteigernd noch eines; Heike drängt mir ihr Gesicht entgegen, doch zugleich schiebt sich ihre Schulter zurück, und etwas in ihr scheint fliehen zu wollen, mädchenhafte Scheu, vielleicht auch Scham, und vielleicht beides schon frauenhaft. –Dreizehn Jahre, und Falten um Mund und Augen. –Doch sie kann nicht fliehen, und die Freude ist stärker; sie gibt mir das Recht, sie sacht zu umarmen und mich neben sie zu setzen. –Noch einmal ihr Jauchzen, nun schon ganz ein Stück Alltag, dann senkt sie die Hände und schließt den Mund und arbeitet unvermittelt weiter, als wolle sie mir zeigen, was sie kann. –Ich schreibe das im Konjunktiv; ich hüte mich vor übereilten Schlüssen. –Das Spielbrett steht vor ihr auf dem Tisch; sie neigt, da sie sich wieder der Arbeit hingibt, den Oberkörper fast parallel zur Tischplatte, greift—und schon das ist mühvoll genug—mit der Linken ein Plättchen, hievt es aufs Brett, bringt es, Magnetsteinchen nach unten, in die richtige Lage und steuert es an den ihm zukommenden Platz, bemüht, die schon geordneten Plättchen durch das neue nicht wieder auseinanderzudrücken. –Als wollte einer mit froststarren Fingern ein Streichholz aus der Schachtel ziehn. –Was für ein gesundes Kind ein Handgriff ist, den es spielerisch-lässig ausführt, stellt für Heike ein immer neues Problem dar, die linke Hand streitet wider die rechte, Mittel- und Ringfinger der Linken lassen sich nicht schließen, Mittel- und Ringfinger der Rechten kaum voneinander trennen, und ist ihre linke Hand am linken Mosaikrand tätig, verschiebt der rechte Ellenbogen das Geleistete nach rechts.

In gewisser Hinsicht ähnelt die Arbeit des Spastikers der meinen: enorme Anstrengung, kleine Erfolge, sehr lang dauernde Phasen unbefriedigenden Mühens bis zu einem erkennbaren Fortschritt, steter Zweifel am Sinn des Tagwerks, tiefe Krisen bis zur Verzweifulung, und das Wesentliche des Geleisteten wird von andern, ja von einem selbst allzuoft nicht bemerkt. –Nein, der Vergleich ist unzulässig; subjektiv ist Heikes Leistung weit größer, mag sie sozial und kulturell auch als nichtig erscheinen, doch darüber wird noch zu sprechen sein. –Schon daß Heike sich selbst nicht reflektiert; oder tut sie es doch, und wir wissen es nicht? Sie wird es uns nicht sagen können. Sie versteht viel von unserer Sprache, wir fast nichts von der ihren, und so muß sie zu groben Mitteln greifen, um zu uns Grobsinnigen zu reden: Wenn sie den Sinn ihres Tuns nicht mehr verkennen, oder vielleicht besser: nicht mehr erfühlen kann, verweigert sie sich; sie fällt dann vornüber, verkrampft die Hände, oder rotzt auf den Tisch, und leistet passiven Widerstand. –Ich habe sie so noch nicht erlebt; ihre Betreuerin, Margret, berichtet davon, sie erzählt, daß eines Abends, vorm Baden, Heike plötzlich ohne ersehbaren Grund zu diesem passiven Widerstand überging; sie, die fähig ist, sich ohne Hilfe so weit auszuziehen, daß nur mehr die Schuhe aufgeschnürt und Rock und Schlüpfer über die Füße gestreift werden müssen, sie saß wie versteint und regte sich nicht, und als dann Margret mit den Wohltaten des Bades zu locken versuchte und den Rollstuhl an die Wanne schob, begab sich Heike in die Sphäre verachtenden Trotzes und ließ erkennen, daß sie sich aus dem Baden nichts mache, wiewohl sie sich sonst darauf freut. –Es wäre zu einfach, hier nur von "bocken" zu reden; Verachtung ist eine schwierige psychische Leistung auf einem hohen Willens- und Wertensniveau; ein großer Dichter, František Halas, hat von der "Herrlichkeit der Verachtung" gesprochen—sind wir nicht allzu vorschnell bereit, diese Leistung nur negativ einzustufen?

Allein ich will mich nicht hierin verlieren; Heike bringt ihre Arbeit zu Ende, das drittletzte Steinchen, dann nur noch ein vorletztes und letztes, und das Spielbrett wäre gefüllt; der Zufall hat schwarze Blöcke gefügt und zerfallende gelbe Blitze in roten, grünen, weißen und blauen Sprenkeln, da kommt Maik herangestürmt, der ungestüme, fröhliche Maik, und besessen vom Gedanken, gründlich fürs Abendbrot aufzuräumen, stößt er Heikes Werk vom Tisch. Heike kreischt auf und hebt beide Hände, sie kann sie nicht zu Fäusten ballen, sie kann mit ihnen nicht einmal drohen, sie kann sie hur heben, um schriller, mit freierer Lunge zu schreien, und Maik hört Heike kreischen und lacht. Sie hat ihre Augen zugekniffen, der Mund steht weit offen, gebleckte Zähne, ungewöhnlich dick und mißförmig die Zunge, zerrißnes Gesicht, die bebenden Hände, und da sehe ich sie jählings als alte Frau, hechelnd und sabbernd in ihrem Rollstuhl, in einer Aura aus Mißmut und Hader, mit struppigem Haar, Warzen zwischen den Fingern, verfallen im Kreis verfallender Frauen—was für eine Insel in was für einem Meer?

III   Photographien von geistig Behinderten: Wie werden sie auf den Betrachter wirken? Wer sich dieser Welt nur aus Schaulust naht, mit Touristenblick und Touristenbewußtsein, der erreicht nur ihre Oberfläche, in ihren Wesensbereich wird er erst dringen, wenn er ernsthaft Anteil zu nehmen versucht, aber das setzt Verstehen voraus, und das wieder Einfühlungskraft. Aber befriedigen Photographien nicht gerade die Schaulust? Verführen sie nicht zu der Hoffart des Pharisäers, wie sie Lukas berichtet: Herr, ich danke dir, daß ich nicht bin wie diese da?

Es käme aber, fürs erste, alles drauf an, sich vorstellen zu können, wie diese zu sein.

Anderntags in der Arbeitstherapie: die Woll-, Stoff-, Leder- und Holzwerkstatt, die Teppichknüpferei und der—ein bißchen sehr schwungvoll so genannte—Arbeitsraum der "industriellen Fertigung". –Ich wollte zu den Kleinsten, den Elefanten, gehen, aber Bernd hat mich unterwegs angehalten und einfach hierher mitgenommen: er müsse mir zeigen, was er schaffe—und so sitze ich nun neben ihm. Er schneidet, nach einer Schablone, Lederstücke zurecht, runde und länglich-rechteckige, mit abgerundeten Ecken, markiert—wieder mittels einer Schablone—längs der Seiten Löcher fürs Nähen und stanzt sie mit einer Zange aus. Die rechteckigen Lederstücke werden, jeweils ihrer sechs, aneinandergeklebt, Mantel eines hexagonalen Beutels, dessen Längskanten durch Lederriemchen herausgestreift werden, die zwei der Löcherreihen verschnüren, und die runde Lederscheibe wird schließlich als Boden angenäht. Oben eine Lederschnur, den Beutel zu schließen; ein Henkel aus geflochtenen Riemen, und das Täschlein kann sich sehen lassen. –Die Produkte der Arbeitstherapie sind beghert: Wandteppiche, Läufer, Stoff- und Ledertaschen, Kasperlefiguren und andres Holzspielzeug, Geldbeutel, Körbe, Kuschelschlangen, dazu die Stücke der Töpferei: Krüge, Geschirr, die phantastichten Tiere; was da geschaffen und zu sorgfältig kalkulierten Preisen verkauft wird, stärkt das Anstaltsbudget erheblich und ginge zum dreifachen Preis noch so weg wie jetzt: aus den Händen gerissen.

Bernd also zeigt mir, was er kann; er ist—was durchaus nicht immer der Fall—voll Hingabe bei seiner Arbeit, wozu allerdings auch gehört, plötzlich innezuhalten und nun im Sitzen das Rumpfstrecken, Händeverdrehen und Armfedern nach hinten zu absolvieren; man ließe ihn auch sitzen und träumen; Antreiberei ist schlechthin undenkbar; gescholten wird nicht, Ermahnungen sind rar. –Dennoch bricht manchmal Angriffswut durch, vor allem in der Holzwerkstatt. –Sechsstundentag; vier Arbeitseinheiten von je neunzig Minuten, vor- und nachmittags eine halbe, mittags eine volle Stunde Pause, vormittags ein Imbiß, nachmittages ein Tee. –Viele Pfleglinge wechseln nach den Pausen die Arbeitsstätten, manche arbeiten nur eine Einheit oder ihrer zwei. –Je nach Leistung wird Zusatztaschengeld gezahlt. –Das Grundtaschengeld beträgt 120 Mark; kein Abzüge für Essen oder Wohnung, und da der persönliche Bedarf gering ist—Toilettenartikel, ein paar Näschereien, oder zum Tanzabend eine Cola—wird viel und für größere Anschaffungen gespart: eine Armbanduhr, eine Kamera, ein Transistorradio, und es kommt immer wieder vor, daß Familienangehörige einem Pflegling, wenn er zu Besuch daheim ist, dies Besitztum dann abnehmen: So ein Blöder

mache das doch nur kaputt; wozu brauche denn der solch kostbare Sachen!—Familienbande. –Die Pfleglinge könnten klagen, sie sind nicht entmündigt, doch man ermutigt sie nicht dazu.

Ich möchte Bernd bei der Arbeit zusehn, aber es soll mir nicht gelingen. –Anfangs habe ich, um nicht
aufzufallen, mich ebenfalls an der Arbeit beteiligt und Löcher in die Lederstücke gestanzt; doch da ich
beginne, Notizen zu machen, und Bernd anschaue, legt auch er die Arbeit hin und schaut nun mich an
und wirft federnd die Arme nach hinten und lacht. –Der zum Objekt Degradierte will durchaus Subjekt
sein. –Ich beschließe, mich nach der Pause an einen abgelegenen Tisch zu setzen, doch da wechselt Bernd
zur Stoffabteilung (wo er Muster auf Leinentaschen stickt), und während ich überlege, ob ich ihm folge,
höre ich ein merkwürdiges Schlurfen und Platschen, als ob eine Melusine das Landreich durchquere, und
durch die Tür, auf den Knien, auf unförmigen Stulpen, rutscht, schneller als wer auf gesunden Füßen,
froschmäulig lachend, Monika, und hinter ihr, ein Püppchen wiegend, kommt Peter.

Monika B., Epileptikerin, Pflegling der Station 1 im Hause Bethesda, eine derbe, grobknochige, von groben Zügen geprägte Frau Mitte der Dreißig, ist von den Knien bis zu den Füßen gelähmt; sie bewegt sich
auf den Knieschützern schlurfend, sehr dicken grünumrandeten Gummistulpen, die bis über die Zehen
reichen; das ist, wiewohl es grausam aussieht, viel besser, als im Rollstuhl zu fahren, sie kann solcherart
gehen, wohin sie will, kann sich allein auf einen Stuhl oder den Toilettensitz hebeln und von dort wieder
zu Boden kommen, verfügt also über ein unschätzbares Bewegungspotential. –Sie schlurft so schnell daher
wie jemand, der schlendert; später werden wir derart miteinander tanzen. –Bis auf die Kniestulpen ist sie
braun: Haar, Augen, Teint, sehr wulstige Lippen, die ebenfalls ins Braune spielen, dazu braune Jacke, grauer
Pullover und brauner Rock. –An ihr erfahre ich eine Erkenntnis.

Ich war Monika vorher nicht begegnet, meine Lesungen hatte sie nie besucht (sie versteht nur die
einfachsten Sätze, und auch die nur isoliert); nun setzt sie sich an die Ledertaschen, neben ihr Peter mit
seinem Püppchen (manchmal hat er auch einen Ball dabei), und wiewohl ich am Arbeitstisch ihr halbschräg
gegenübersitze, kann ich sie nach Belieben studieren, sie beachtet mich nicht. Sie beugt – mitunter in
gequetschte, piepsende Fisteltöne ausbrechend, die überraschen, da man Baßgebrumm erwartet – ähnlich
wie Heike den Kopf tief übers Werkstück, nimmt die Lederteile mit klobiger Hand auf, stößt die Nadel mit
dem Lederriemchen durch die gestanzten Löcher, derb und doch suchend bemüht, die rechten zu treffen,
zieht, die Lippen leckend, das Riemchen nach, und plötzlich, da sie den nächsten Stich tut, sehe ich von
ihr nur den Kopf und die Hand, und plötzlich sehe ich im Werksaal nur Köpfe und Hände – vor allem die
Hände, weitausholend, zugreifend, glättend, ordnend, fügend, den Raum durchmessend, die Hände, die
um das Werkstück kreisen, darüber die Köpfe tief gebeugt sind—, die Dreiheit der Arbeit: Kopf, Hand

und Werkstück, die menschliche Dreifaltigkeit. –Es ist eine Offenbarung. –Ich habe selbst Jahre hindurch physisch gearbeitet und immer wieder das Arbeitserlebnis gesucht, auf der Werft, auf der Großbaustelle, im Bergwerk; hier erfahre ich Arbeit, eben hier. –Plötzlich begreife ich, was ich schon lange wußte: Daß der Mensch durch die Arbeit in das Werkstück eingeht; er vermenschlicht das Stück toter Natur, und was in dessen Materie einfließt, ist menschliches Wesen ohne Abstrich: In seiner Arbeit ist der Mensch heil. –Die fertige Tasche wird (außer durch ihre Etikettierung) in nichts darauf hinweisen, daß ein Behinderter sie geschaffen; sie ist Menschenwerk; ihre Schöpfer sind Menschen, Töchter und Söhne einer Gattung; in der Arbeit offenbaren alle Pfleglinge ihr Heiles, ihr Defekt verschwindet als das Unwesentliche, aber verschwindet damit nicht auch ihr Besonderes, das ja nicht nur Minderung bedeutet?

Im Produkt wohl, doch nicht im Arbeitsprozeß, der noch ganz ungeschieden vom Spiel ist und jedes Erzeugnis zum Einzelstück macht, nicht nur im Sinn handwerklichen Schaffens. Das Ergebnis dieser Arbeit ist mehr als ihr Produkt: Sie produziert nicht nur einen Gebrauchswert, sondern auch ein Stückchen Menschentum.

Dadurch, daß diese Arbeit auch Spiel ist und ihre Vollbringer unmittelbar befriedigt, ist sie zutiefst menschliche Arbeit, dem Menschen gemäße, seiner würdige, oder sagen wir's direkt: unentfremdete Arbeit, wie—auf gegenpolige Weise—da, wo sie Kampf ist, Kampf mit der Natur, mit den Elementen, etwa in der Arbeit des Bergmanns oder des Schiffers; im weiten Mittelbereich zwischen diesen Sphären, wo, nach Hegel, ihr "Saures" einsetzt, gleitet sie ins Mechanische ab, in der äußersten Konsequenz ins Fließband, in das, immer noch Hegel, "Wiederholen derselben Arbeit" als "Wiederholen eines Bekannten, wo kein Interesse mehr an der Sache ist, kein Genuß, sich im Andern zu finden . . ." –Solche Arbeit als Alltagserscheinung: der entsetzliche Preis unserer Zivilisation. –Im Spiel ist die Arbeit jedesmal neu, selbst in jedem wiederholten Handgriff–: Die richtigen zwei Löcher für die Nadel zu finden ist für Monika immer aufs neue ein Abenteuer des Kopfs und der Hand; und für jeden Pflegling die ihm gemäße Arbeit zu finden wird das Abenteuer der Therapie: jedem werde die Arbeit zuteil, die, ihn bis an seine Grenze fordernd, kein mechanisches Wiederholen erlaubt oder, rückte dies in die Nähe, ihm Lust machte, seine Grenze überschreiten.

Im gleichen Maß, wie die Lust aus dem Spiel wächst, führt sie die Arbeit zum Kampf hinüber, allerdings zu einem, den man gegen sich selbst ficht: den Kampf gegen sein Behindertsein. –Ich weiß, daß ich vom Ideal rede, und daß Routine, Unlust, Gleichgültigkeit, Mangel an kundigem Personal oder gar ökonomisches Denken als Leitwert die Arbeitstherapie karikieren können, ins Gegenteil ihrer selbst verwandeln, in Drill, Schliff, Mechanik, ebendas Saure, dem Hegels tiefer Seufzer galt; allein in Werksälen wie denen Monikas und Peters rückt der Alltag nach ans Ideal.

Therapie als Abenteuer: der Bildungsgang aus Arbeit und Spiel kann höchst seltsame Umwege einschlagen. Monika, so wird mir erzählt, hat früher, daß ihre Hand fühlender werde, Holzklötzchen mit Sandpapier abgeschmirgelt, und sie hat zuerst statt des geglätteten Holzstücks das abgenutzte Papier als gefordertes Produkt angesehen und war damit stolz zum Betreuer geschlurft, ihm zu zeigen, was sie geschafen: man erzählt mir diese Anekdote nicht als Beleg intellektueller Minderbemittlung, sondern als Beispiel für einen Anfang. Zuerst hatte Monikas Auge begriffen: Dieweil das Holz unverändert erschien, veränderte das Papier seine Farbe vom Fahlbelb zum Orange-rot, und im Prozeß dieses Begreifens hatte Monika sich als Bewirkerin der Veränderung begriffen: eine große, erkennende Leistung. Danach war es ihre Hand, die begriff: Das Holzstückchen, das sie da schmirgelte, wurde glatt und zugleich griffig. –Wörter, Monikas Sprachschatz fehlend, doch ihr eigen geworden im Potential ihrer Hand. –Zugleich lernte sie, wieder ohne Namen dafür zu haben, etwas Außerordentliches: Sie lernte ein Wesentliches (Glätten des Werkstücks) von einem Unwesentlichen (Farbveränderung) zu trennen, und dieser Fortschritt im Begreifen war zugleich die Überwindung jener Grenze, da das Nur-Mechanische einsetzt; das Abschmirgeln des Sandpapiers (gesetzt, es wäre der Auftrag gewesen) hätte sie auf die Dauer unterfordert; das Glätten des Holzstücks verlangte ein Neues: Prüfung durch die fühlend werdende Hand. –Nun näht sie Taschen, in heiligem Mühen, sie wird eine Tasche fertigstellen, und es wird ihre Tasche sein. –Peter, neben ihr, spielt mit seinem Püppchen; er, sprachlos, und noch vor wenigen Jahren gänzlich willen- und hilfloser Pflegefall, wiegt es mit monotonem Gemurmel, dann bettet er es in ein Kästchen, das hier immer für ihn bereitsteht, und wendet sich wieder dem anderen Püppchen, dem Ledertäschlein, das er erschaffen wird, zu. Arbeit und Spiel sind in diesen Werkstätten sowenig voneinander zu trennen wie auf den Stationen Spiel und Arbeit, und aus Beidem in Einem wächst der Stolz auf die Leistung als Stolz auf des Menschen Schöpfertum.

Diese Art Arbeitstherapie ist nicht unangefochten; in einer Außenstelle, in Neuendorf, einem Heim für geistig behinderte, zumeist ältere Frauen, wird das Schwergewicht auf die Gärtnerei gelegt, eine Arbeit, die nicht im Stolz aufs Erschaffen-Haben eines toten Gebrauchsgegenstandes gipfelt, sondern sich als Geburtshelfertum für ein anderes lebendes Wesen darstellt, das, um fortgedeihen zu können, ständige Pflege und Obhut verlangt, jedoch als Frucht zurückerstattet, was ihm als Sorge angediehn ward. Ob die Pfleglinge sich mit ihrem Apfelbaum oder ihrem Himmbeerstrauch identifizieren? Jedenfalls könnten sie es, und kein Zufall wohl auch, daß in Neuendorf alle Tendenzen gefördert werden, die zur Großfamilie drängen, gemeinsames Einnehmen der Mahlzeiten etwa. –Brüderlichkeit als Grundprinzip; der Kampfcharakter der Arbeit erscheint im Garten nicht als Kampf gegen das Rohmaterial oder die Rohform des Werkstücks, sondern als Abwehr von Bedrohern; doch damit ist auch der Spielcharakter der Arbeit gemindert: Das, was spielhafte Foscherlust sich in der Werkstatt gegen das Material herausnehmen darf, letztlich sogar die Zerstörung des Werkstücks als Erprobung seiner Art und Struktur (zum Beispiel: ins Holz eine Rille schmirgeln, die erkennen macht, wie scharf das biegsame Sandpapier beißt und wie weich das harte Holz ist)—; diese Art von zerstörender Erfahrung ist im Garten von vornherein unzulässig; ein Lebendiges ist kein Spielzeug. –Allerdings dann auch: Das Spielzeug lebt nicht; der Teddy oder das Püppchen sind letztlich doch Surrogat. –Der Unterschied beider Therapien auf eine gröbste Formel gebracht: im Garten Kultivierung, in der Werkstatt Unterwerfung; oder, wenn man will: weibliches gegen männliches Welt-Aneignen; oder auch: dort Schwergewicht auf kollektive Hege-, hier auf individuelle Leistungserlebnisse.

Die Leistung als Wert wird ja heute oft attackiert, und zu Recht, wenn man eine Leistungssuprematie angreift, die sich nur im Quantitativen bewegt, technologisch meßbar als "mehr und schneller", sozial als restlos überführbar in Geld. Die Leistung, als quantitative Größe basiert auf ebenjener sauren Wiederholung des unschöpferisch Gewordenen; sie setzt entfremdete Arbeit voraus, hat mit Akkord und Fließband zu tun, und die Erziehung zu ihr ist immer Dressur. –Im günstigsten Fall erscheint sie als Sport. –Die Leistung als qualitative Größe ist etwas ganz Andres: das inkommensurabel Schöpferische, das Einzelne eines Einzelnen als Einzigartiges einer Person (ob Individuum oder Kollektiv), dessen Wert auch dann unermeßlich sein kann, wenn er in Geld gefaßt nichtig wäre. Diese Leistung als unentfremdet Eigenes liegt nicht so sehr im Produkt als im Prozeß des Vollbringens; der Prozeß ist das Schöpferische, das Produkt das Vollbrachte, und damit schon Vergangenheit. –Die Gegenwart fordert aufs neue heraus. –Das Erzeugte wird als Besitz unwichtig; es kommt nicht aufs Haben an, sondern aufs Tun: Merkwürdig, daß der Eigentumsbegriff ebenda zurücktritt, wo man ihn als bestimmend glaubt. –Der Schöpfer fragt zwar anfangs manchmal, ob er behalten dürfe, was er geschaffen, allein er hat merkwürdig wenig dagegen, ja freut sich noch, wenn er erfährt, daß seine Produkte veräußert werden, auch an einen ihm noch Unbekannten, daß man sie also als Ware behandelt, wiewohl er dies Wort nie begriffe: Sein Erzeugnis ist doch ein Einziges, wie wäre es da ein Allgemeines, das eine Ware doch vornehmlich ist!

Das Veräußerte ist nicht das dem Schöpfer Entäußerte; im Stolz aufs Vollbrachte bleibt es seines, und als Zuwachs von Erfahrung auch; es ist ein Stück seiner Person geworden, das materielle Eigentumsverhältnis interessiert nicht mehr. Ja sogar daß es veräußert wird, macht es noch inniger zu einem Eignen: Das, was als Gebrauchswert für den Schöpfer entstand, erweist sich als Gebrauchswert auch für einen andern, wird also in seinem Charakter bestätigt: der Tauschwert hat keine Rolle gespielt. (Nebenbei: Da die Werkstätten trozt alledem für den Markt produzieren, macht die exakte Kostenberechnung außerordentliche Schwierigkeiten; es wird wohl meist unterm Wert verkauft.) Und wem man begreiflich machen kann, Bernd etwa, Monika gewiß nie, daß der Erlös aus dem veräußerten Werkstück der Gemeinschaft wieder zugute kommt, und zwar meist in konkreter Gestalt, etwa einer neuen Blattpflanze im Werkraum, oder auch eines verbesserten Webstuhls, dem hat man als Erfahrung vermittelt, was Utopie vergebens erhofft hat, die Entfaltung unentfremdeter Arbeit—; Was für eine Insel in was für einem Meer?

IV   Photographien geistig Behinderter—: Sie alle bergen den Widerspruch in sich, den jeder bei seinem ersten Besuch in solchen Anstalten erfährt: Der Weg zum Verstehen führt nur übers Erfahren, über die sinnliche Rezeption, und die hat es an sich, ebenden Weg zu versperren, den nur sie zu öffnen vermag.

Am Anfang dieses Wegs, und allzuoft gleich als sein Ende, steht der Schock oder, seltner, die Illusion; oft Flucht oder Sturz von Einem ins Andre. –Der Schock, plötzlich Menschen zu begegnen, die jäh über jedes Mitleid hinaus Abscheu, Furcht, Ekel, Entsetzen erregen und die sich, nach Körperkontakten gierend, dem Angewiderten auch noch nähern, ihn zu umarmen, zu küssen, zu berühren versuchen, Roswitha vielleicht, mit dem Gesicht aus Blutschwamm, oder Jürgen mit seinen Eiterbatzen, oder der ständig schattenboxende Karl. –Dieser Schock kann bis zu Fluchten treiben, zu der Flucht aus der Anstalt oder der Flucht nach innen, zu einem angstvollen Sich-Verschließen, und da wie dort zu dem Mörderdenken, ob nicht doch eine "erlösende Spritze" für "diese unglücklichen Armen" angebracht sei. –Bestenfalls dann die Haltung des Pharisäers im Tempel. –"So eine Schande, so eine Schande", hat die Dame im schwarzen Fellmantel gemurmelt, da sie das vermummte Kind aus der Sprechstunde zu ihrem Volvo zurückzog. –Die Frage nach der Spritze wird öfter gestellt, als man glaubt, und – versteht sich – immer in einem Timbre, das der Frager für humanistisch hält: Er will ein vermeintliches Unglück enden, Richter über Tod und Leben von andren, und hat doch nur mit der eigenen Not zu tun. Draußen, in der Öffentlichkeit, geht es dann robuster zu, es fällt sogar manchmal das Wort "vergasen"; zugleich mehren sich Beispiele guten Verstehens, im Bus, in den Läden, selbst in Restaurants.

Die andere Art, ein Verstehn zu verstellen, ist die Illusion der Heilen Welt, die geistig Behinderte als eine Art von rousseauischen Wilden ansieht, und auch die Bergpredigt preist sie ja selig und spricht ihnen das Himmelreich zu. Manchmal mischt sich beides: Schock und Illusion; ihre Mitte ist dann peinvolles Mitleid, die andre Art selektierenden Denkens, oder die Illusion wird zum Fluchtweg und der Schock bricht in die Heile Welt und zerstört den Ansatz zu einem Verständnis, darin dieser Abbruch schon angelegt war.

Heile Welt in der Arbeitstherapie: Plötzlich, wie ohne Grund, faßt Ingo einen Hammer und schlägt damit auf Thomas ein; plötzlich, nebenan, in der Leinenwerkstatt, greift sich Viola unter den Rock und beginnt heulend zu onanieren, plötzlich wird Patrick ein Bündel Wut, und in den stumpfen Augen Christophs, der draußen im Gang vor seinem Rollstuhl liegt und wartet, bis der Pfleger ihn aufhebt, sammelt sich jählings schwarzer Haß. –Und auf dem Hügel aus gefrorenem Sand wiegt, während ihm Speichel aus dem Mund rinnt, der junge Mann langsam den Kopf hin und her. –"Ach, wie sind diese Kleinen niedlich!"—die Besucherin einer Kinderstation, die solcherart erleichtert aufseufzt, ist vor einer Grupper jener geflohen, zu denen die niedlichen Kleinen werden.

Ich gestehe, daß mir jenes Erschrecken nicht—wie auch anders—erspart geblieben: Bei meinem ersten Besuch einer Psychiatrie geriete ich, das war nicht in Fürstenwalde, auf der Flucht vor einem Wolkenbruch in den Aufenthaltsraum geistig Schwerstbehinderte, die dort friedlich wie je ihren Tag verbrachten; ein kahler Raum, mit Schulbänken angefüllt, und Lallende, Sabbernde, ungeschlacht Gestikulierende, von denen einige sofort auf mich zukamen, mich zu umarmen, mich zu betasten, mir etwas zu sagen, mir etwas zu zeigen; ein grunzender Strudel; er sog mich ein. Plötzlich von Gebärden und Mienen bedrängt, die ich als Bedrohung nahm: sich krallende Finger, heranschwingende Fäuste, Zischen aus aufgeblähten Mündern; ich war auf den Anblick nicht vorbereitet und fühlte jäh meine Kräfte schwinden, da sah ich, nahe dem physischen Stürzen, vor mir Friedrich Hölderlin. Ein junger Mann, in einer Schulbank, ein wenig gedunsen, allein Hölderlins Züge, von der Nase über die Mundwinkel tiefe Falten, freies Lockenhaar, blond, die sehr hohe Stirne, Hyperions traurig schwärmende Augen, er starrte zum Peloponnes hinuter, und die Lippen bewegten sich unhörbar. Er lächelte; er schrieb mit dem Finger der Rechten auf seine Linke, an seinem Lächeln hielt ich mich fest und an der Schulter eines Schnappmäuligen, der meinen Ärmel umklammerte. Und an einer Szene der Brüderlichkeit: Ein alter Mann, am Fensterbord lehnend, mußte Wasser lassen und kam mit dem Problem nicht zurecht, seine Hose aufzuknöpfen, der Urin floß in seine Schuhe; er quietschte, und der neben ihm an der Wand kam zu Hilfe und knöpfte dem Alten die Hose auf. Der Strahl plätscherte frei, die beiden lachten, und Hölderlin schaute träumend zu. Dann kam mein Begleiter hereingestürzt und sah, erleichtert, mich in Gesellschaft und kümmerte sich um Wischlappen und Eimer; dann kam auch der Wärter und wurde unwirsch. –Mein Begleiter klärte mich dann über Hölderlin auf: Ein Oberschüler, hoch begabt, ohne erkennbare Konflikte, und jählings in völlige Verweigerung stürzend, von einer Minute zu der andern, und heute ohne jeden Antrieb, ohne Handlungsziele, schier ohne Begehren, auch die Sprache beinah schon abgebaut. –Ich sah nur noch, daß er träumte und schrieb: aus meinem Schock war Schauder geworden, und ich hatte mich so weit gefangen, die mich Bedrängenden als bedürftig nach Wort und Umgang zu verstehn. Der Schnappmäulige erzählte stolz, er sei allein ins Kino gegangen, er, ganz allein, hin und zurück, ohne sich zu verlaufen, hin und zurück, er habe ganz allein hin- und zurückgefunden, den ganzen Weg, ganz allein, ins Kino, und er war so besessen von seiner Leistung, daß er die Worte nicht bändigen konnte, sie überstürzten sich aus dem schnappenden Mund, der sie in Brocken Geräuschs zerhackte, und nur die stete Wiederholung und die lebhafte Gestik offenbarten den Sinn. –Mein Begleiter ging dann mit mir jenen Weg; vors Haus, rechts hinunter, und rechts um die Ecke über die Straße; Kolumbus war nur geradeaus gesegelt. –Ich fühlte plötzlich das Verlangen, in jenen Raum zurückzukehren und den Gereisten zu umarmen und mir seine Fahrt erzählen zu lassen, lange, so lang er zu reden begehrte, und ihm ohne Ungeduld zuzuhören und seinen Gefährten ohne Furcht zu begegnen; ich wußte plötzlich, daß ich ihnen vertrauen konnte, da sie sich mir so anvertrauten; eine Möglichkeit arglosen Lebens, und aus Schock und Schauder wurde Scham.

An diesem Tag zeigt man mir auch jene, die man früher "Tobsüchtige" geheißen und an Ketten oder hinter Gittern einem ergötzten Publikum vorgeführt; sie lagen in hellen, unverschlossenen Sälen unter breiten, unvergitterten Fenstern ungebunden in schneeweißen Betten und dösten, von Drogen betäubt, dahin; ein Tag, der nichts als dämmernde Nacht war, und eine Nacht, die den Tag weiterschleppte, und nur der Atemgang und kleine Reflexe zeigten, daß diese Körper lebten. –Mein Begleiter war stolz. –Er sprach bewundernd von der Macht der Chemie, den Triumphen menschlichen Fortschritts, der die "sanfte Zwangsjacke" konstruiert, die jene aus Leinen überflüssig mache. –Er strahlte, da er vom Fortschritt sprach. –Die Augen der Kranken waren glanzlos, und ihre Gesichter schienen mir plötzlich als Talg. –Man zeigte mir dann auch den mattgelben Raum, darin Elektroschocks ausgeteilt werden, ein wachstuchüber- zogenes Lager, flach, mit Lederriemchen an den Seiten, und auf einem Tischchen eine Art Kopfhörer, als Bügel eine durch Schrauben verstellbare Zwinge mit einer schwarzen Kabelschnur. –Die Prozedur, sagte mein Begleiter, werde nicht häufig angewandt, aber sie sei therapeutisch unentbehrlich; natürlich werde der Patient informiert und seine Zustimmung eingeholt, sofern das technisch möglich sei. –Seitdem, nach bestimmten Tageserlebnissen, sehe ich diese Kammer im Traum.

Photographien geistig Behinderter—: Man hat diesen hier vorgeworfen, zuwenig von jenem Unheilen zu zeigen, das den Pflegern, und mehr noch die Pflegerin, mitunter bis zur Verzweiflung bedrängt: Aggres- sion, Verweigerung, sexuelle Ausbrüche; man hat aber, etwa bei einer Gruppenaufnahme von Kindern, diesen Bildern auch vorgeworfen, zu kraß vordergründig zu sein.

Ich halte Dietmar Riemanns Sehweise für hervorragend geeignet, den Weg zum Verstehen aufzutun.

Seine Bilder sind Porträts, oder sind es der Anlage nach; sie nehmen den geistig Behinderten als Menschen, nicht nur als Objekt, sondern auch als Person, sehn ihn also in einer Aura der Würde, und was die Kamera geführt hat, ist Ehrfurcht und Scheu. –Selbsverständlich ist solche Haltung nicht; Ethos ist mit Kunst deckungsgleich, ja, ihr Verhältnis ist ohne Berührungspunkt denkbar. –Es müßte für einen Photographen höchst verführerisch sein, hier eine Möglichkeit zu erproben, noch nie geschaute Bilder zu schaffen, ein Panoptikum des Häßlichschönen, bizarr und grotesk und faszinierend schockierend, kurzum, jenen Schock des Eingangserlebnisses ins Ästhetisch-Sensationelle zu heben; andrerseits wäre es ebenso verlockend, die Illusion als Idyll zu entfalten und einen Alltag im Bild zu verklären, der, das sei hier eingeräumt, nicht selten zur Verklärung einlädt.

Das Faszinierend-Schockierende: Diane Arbus etwa hat solche Bilder gemacht, im Alltag, auf der Straße, am Nacktbadestrand, in der Wohnung, auf dem Rummelplatz, in Hollywood, ein Panoptikum des Abnormen in einer Gesellschaft, die auf andere Weise abnorm ist; schließlich, um neue Modelle zu finden, hat sie eine Psychiatrie oder, so wäre hier exakter zu sagen, eine "Irrenanstalt" aufgesucht. –Ihre Bilder von dort sind unbetitelt geblieben: Nummern einer Schrenkensschau. Es ist gewiß nichts dagegen zu sagen, den Alltag in grausamen Bildern zu fassen, um sein Absurdes sehen zu lehren, allein ihr Gang in die Psychiatrie, und dort noch zu einem Maskenball, oder besser: einem Mummenschanz—; nein, ich wage doch kein Urteil, sie ist eine große Künstlerin und hat für ihre Kunst mit dem Leben gezahlt.

Hier also Ehrfurcht vor der Würde des Menschen, und daraus das Mühen um das Porträt, jene ästhetische Ausdrucksweise, die das Objekt auch als Subjekt braucht, ja sogar vorwiegend als Subjekt. Der Porträtist muß um Partnerschaft werben; er muß sich der Mithilfe des Aufzunehmenden versichern, da ohne sie kein Poträt gelingt. Diane Arbus hat sich über ihre Art, diese Hilfe zu gewinnen, in einem Interview so geäußert: "Wäre ich lediglich neugierig, dann wäre es es schwierig, zu jemand zu sagen, 'Ich möchte Sie besuchen, damit Sie mit mir reden und mir Ihre Lebensgeschichte erzählen können.' Dann würden die Leute bestimmt sagen: 'Sie sind ja verrückt!' Und die würden sich äußerst vorsichtig verhalten. Aber die Kamera ist eine Art Freibrief. Es gibt eine Menge Leute, die sich ebendiese Art Aufmerksamkeit wünschen, und das ist eine Aufmerksamkeit in vernünftigen Grenzen."

Riemann macht von diesem Freibrief keinen Gebrauch; seine Methode ist die des Gesprächs, er versucht einen Prozeß sich entwickeln zu lassen, in dem sich das Wesen dessen entfaltet, von dem er ein Bild vermitteln will, und er fixiert dann jenen Moment, in dem dieses Entfalten gipfelt: Atom der Ewigkeit, nicht der Zeit. Dieser Moment ist verdichteter Alltag, allerdings nicht im naturalistischen Sinn: Solch ein Gespräch ist ja ebenso Alltag wie zum Alltag ein Anderes; es konzentriert, was der tägliche Hingang zerstreut. Der Alte in der Badewanne etwa: Wenn man einen Badeablauf filmte und Bild um Bild dieser Prozedur isolierte, würde man auf den Moment nicht stoßen, den Riemanns Photographie uns zeigt—; Er hat ihn aus dem Mythos gewonnen, der jede Alltagshandlung *auch* ist und der in deren Verdichten zum Wesen hervortritt: im Gehen, Stehen, Spielen, Tanzen, Schlafen, Wachen, Träumen, Lernen, Nehmen, Geben, Atmen, Singen, Schweigen, Lachen, Weinen, Feiern, Reden, Essen, Trinken, ja sogar noch bei der Defäkation. –Ich finde es seines Themas würdig, daß dieser Band eine Defäkationsszene zeigt: Menschentum gerade auch hier. –Und so ist denn auch Baden Alltag wie Mythos: Susanna im Bad, der Teich Bethesda, von dem das Johannesevangelium spricht, das Baden im Meer, das Baden im Ganges, das Bad des Täufers, das Bad Agamemmons, das Bad des Neugeborenen, und hier also, ein Neues, das Bad des Alten: nahe der Pforte des Todes das Sich-Zusammenkrümmen zu dem, als das man einst sein Dasein begonnen, und gleichzeitig Ansatz zum letzten Sich-Strecken; Fruchtwasser des Lebens, Fruchtwasser des Todes, und beide trüb: des Daseins Schmutz. –Man wäscht ihn ab, um darin zu verharren. –Die Hände, geöffnet, die Welt zu umfangen, können nur noch den Leib umfassen: Die Zehen, die der Säugling in den Mund gesteckt, um sie als Eigenes zu erkennen, man spielt mit ihnen wie mit etwas Fremdem, und zugleich klammert man sich an sie: die Grenze dessen, was noch zu fassen gewährt wird. So wird man allein. Alt; nackt; arm im Geist; hilflos in der Wanne, und dennoch hält das, was die Arme umfangen, die Person, das Selbst, dem Gegenüber stand: Da sind diese Augen, die dich anschaun, und vor ihnen hast du nun zu bestehn.

Ich bitte den Leser, auf die Hände zu schauen, diese Hände und diese Füße, und wenn er's nicht mehr erträgt, in die Augen, die ihm ruhig sagen: So wirst auch du.

Der Alte mit dem verdeckten Geschlecht, hinter ihm der dunkellichte Vorhang—: Ich kann diese Photographie nicht betrachten, ohne an Auschwitz zu denken: in Schläfenhöhe dieses Duschrohr, schwarz, drohend offen, ausgerichtet; es zielt an des Betrachters Augen vorbei. –Wer es gesehn hat, sieht es immer. –Es ist gut, ein MEMENTO AUSCHWITZ in einem Bezirk zu finden, darin Auschwitz immer wieder erinnert wird. Dieses Gespräch aus der Badewanne, das, jeder Skurrilität entbehrend, ein Gespräch aus dem offenen Sarg ist, wird durch das Rohr doppelt akzentuiert: als Gespräch aus der Wanne, und als Gespräch vor dem Tod.

Daß eine Photographie solche Last tragen kann, macht sie groß.

Diane Arbus hat viele Bilder Alter geschaffen, großartige Photographien, so auch eine "Frau in ihrem Negligé". Sie zeigt sie frontal, auf der linken Ecke des kissenlosen, mit einer Schutzdecke überspannten Doppelbettes sitzend, darauf rechts, hinter einer offenen Handtasche, ein vages Häuflein Wäsche liegt, dazwischen, undeutlich, ein Büstenhalter. Die Hände sind über die Kante gebreitet, an der rechten ist der Ehering sichtbar, doch nichts im Zimmer weist darauf hin, daß ein Partner es mitbenutzt. Das Negligé will verführerisch sein: Pantöffelchen von einer Art Schlangenleder, Strümpfe und Hemd aus hauchdünnem Nylon, darunter der schwarze Slip sich abhebt, doch die sich so darbietet, ist eine Greisin, und ihre Wäsche, Jungsein lügend, konterkariert dermaßen kraß das runzlige Angesicht und die welken, pigmentübersäten, krampfvenigen und behaarten Gliedmaßen, daß, bei stattlich wirkendem Wuchs, eine Monstrosität erscheint, Alltagsparaphrase des Aufschrei: "Wie eitel ist alles!" Eine Existenzerschütterung. –Je länger man dieses Porträt betrachtet, um so mehr tritt, ein riesiger Rochen, die geschwungen-dreieckige Bettwand hinten hervor und das schwarze Dreieck des Slips, und schräg am Rand die schwarze Tasche, offen, leer, eingestepptes Reklameschildchen, und weit im Hintergrund, verschwommen, auf einer Kommode ein schwarzes Telephon. Hinter ihm ein Fenster, Morgensonne, halboffener Vorhang, die Nachttischlampe, und das alles im Spiegel des Ankleideschranks. Das Frühlicht bricht in dies düstere Zimmer, und es blitzt im Auge auf, nicht dem der Alten, sondern dem des Rochens. Nur in einem, dem linken, das andere ruht. –Alle Kraft der Frau ist zu einem Sprung versammelt, dazusein, wenn das Wunder anhöbe, wenn das Telephon zu läuten begönne, wenn Einer in ihr Zimmer träte, darin sie im Negligé wartet, doch wer eintrat, war die Photographin, mit einer Kamera als Freibrief, und ihr Opfer war zur Preisgabe bereit. –Wie eitel ist alles. –Diesem Porträt, das Perfektion ist, fehlt nur Eines, ein Zug von Trauer, und dies Fehlen springt um in einen Spott, der die Erschütterung konterkariert.

Durch diese doppelte Brechung erfolgt eine dritte: Die bewußt- und betonte amoralische Haltung bringt, so merkwürdig sich das anhört, einen Zug billigen Moralisierens ins Spiel: Es drängt sich einem geradezu auf, vor dem Porträt dieser Wartenden zu versichern, daß man so im Alter nicht werden müsse; der Betrachter mit der Photographin verbündet im Spott. –Der Alte in der Badewanne sagt das Müssen im unerbittlichen Blick und stellt es auf andere Art in Frage: Das Müssen zum Greis-Sein ist unabwendbar, aber wird man die Würde wahren, die aus seinen Augen spricht? Und wenn dieser Alte dann rasiert wird, erhebt er durch sein Pullover-Lüpfen, das den Hals einer Klinge freigibt, ein triviales Alltagsgeschehen zu einem feierlichen Akt, einem großen Ereignis in seinem Leben, das sich als groß dem Betrachter mitteilt und, behutsam das Komische streifend, ebendadurch mit seiner Würde schockiert. In der Würde dieser Gebärde, in der Positur des Thronens im tristen Waschraum, liegt ein Zug von Senilität, doch er bleibt in der Alterswürde und macht auch einen Mythos sichtbar: Der Alte, der rasiert wird, ist ein König Lear. Im Akt der Zivilisierung wird er erniedrigt und sein König-Sein geschmälert, wenn nicht schließlich aufgehoben; da er aus der Badewanne redete, war er stopplig, und das gewiß nicht durch Zufallsfügung: Das Barthaar ist das zäheste Leben; es ist das, was im Sarg noch wächst.

Wie jedes gültige Kunstwerk sind auch Photographien von Rang als Träger eines Mythos verstehbar; sie halten jenen Ort und jenen Moment fest, da der Alltag transzendiert oder, um es noch einmal zu sagen, da ein Atom Zeit ein Atom Ewigkeit wird. –Der Junge, gefesselt hinter Stäben, "fixiert", wie die Fachsprache es nennt, da er, weitgehend schmerzunempfindlich, sonst gegen sich selbst zu wüten begönne, etwa sich die Haare büschelweis ausraufte oder sich Stirn und Wangen zerfleischte. Es ist die uralte Form schmerzlichster Klage, ritualisierte Form der Reaktion auf einen jäh ins Dasein gebrochnen Verlust, den dann, als die Heilung des Selbst, erst Trauerarbeit bewältigen kann. –Um wen klagt der Junge, wen oder was hat er verloren? Oder welch ein anderer Feind als der grimme Tod ist in sein Dasein und seine Seele gebrochen, gegen den, da er innen sitzt, der Junge als gegen sich selber schlägt?–Bei den Alten war jede mania, jeder Wahnsinneinbruch, wie jeder Antrieb von einer Gottheit bewirkt, in deren spezifischer Wesenssphäre, bei Ares etwa einer andern als bei Hera oder Apollon, und als die Krieger des glorreichen Aias ihren Feldherrn an Trojas Küste im Wahn sahn, auf einem Haufen zerstückter Rinder, gegen die er mit dem Schwert gewütet, da er sie für seine Feinde gehalten, die ihn um den höchsten Siegespreis, die Waffen des Achilleus, betrogen—: da seine Krieger ihren Feldherrn solcherart geschlagen sahen, begannen sie, laut Sophokles, als erstes die Frage aufzuwerfen, welche Gottheit diese mania gesandt, um, entsprechend dem Besondern der Gottheit, das Besondere des Wahns erkennen zu können. Hier ist es Athene gewesen, und man erfährt dann auch einen Seherspruch, daß Aias geheilt werden könne, wenn man ihn einen Tag lang vor sich selbst bewahre, einen Tag ihn bewache, ihn nicht aus seinem Zelt lasse, notfalls an einen Pfosten binde, dann sei der Zorn der Göttin vorbei. Dieser Tag wird versäumt, und Aias heilt sich auf seine Weise, in Hybris, ohne göttliche Hilfe, indem er den Träger des Wahns hinwegschafft; durch den Sturz seiner selbst ins eigene Schwert.

Der wahnsinnsgeschlagene, gebundene Aias als Knabe—ich kann diese Photographie nicht anders betrachten, und mich erschüttert dieses Knaben Alleinsein; vielleicht ist es gerade seine mania, daß er das Alleinsein nicht erträgt. Das Fixieren wird—in dieser Anstalt selbstverständlich—nicht als Therapie angesehen; es ist Ausdruck von Mangel an geeigneten Kräften, verständigen Freunden, die tagsüber, und dann auch des Nachts, so lange bei dem Kranken sind, bis ihm die Wohltat des Schlafs zuteil wird. Die Alten haben da viel gewußt; einem Schriftchen "Geisteskrankheiten im klassischen Altertum" von Prof. J.L. Heiberg (Walter de Gruyter & Co., Berlin und Leipzig 1927) entnehme ich diese Wiedergabe von Therapievorschlägen des syrischen Arztes Archigenes, im ersten Jahrhundert nach der Zeitrechnung wirkend: "Es ist wichtig, den Patienten bei guter Laune zu erhalten, deshalb sollten seine besten Freunde ihn besuchen und ermuntern durch Erzählungen und unschuldige Gespräche. Die Krankheit bringt oft Schlaflosigkeit mit sich ... In solchen Fällen muß man kräftige Schlafmittel anwenden, Kopfbäder, Frottierungen unter den Fußsohlen, Krauen an den Schläfen oder hinter den Ohren (wie bei Tieren). Oft kann es auch helfen, dem Patienten die Verhältnisse zu verschaffen, worunter er gewohnt ist zu schlafen; den Seemann kann man in ein Boot legen, ihn von den Wellen wiegen, den Geruch von See und Schiff merken, die Brandung und das Sausen des Windes hören lassen; der Musiker soll durch Spielen und Singen zum Schlafen gebracht werden, der Lehrer durch kindliches Geplauder." –Man ermesse den Verlust. –Eine der Fragen, die diese Photographie provoziert, auch über die Anstaltssphäre hinaus, läuft, wie bei jeder Freiheitsbeschränkung, in zwei Richtungen: Man kann danach trachten, die Fixierung zu perfektionieren, oder aber nach Mitteln suchen, sie endlich überflüssig zu machen.

Dieser Junge müßte jemand haben, der ausschließlich ihn betreut; er hat ihn nicht; sehnt er sich nach ihm? Ich habe ihn nicht mehr kennengelernt; so halte ich mich an die Photographie: Welch ein technisches Aufgebot wider den Einen, der da von den Stäben zerschnitten wird. –Woher kommen die Schatten, die um seinen Kopf ziehn, seltsame Meridiane des Wahns, und Partien des Körpers liegen im Finstern, mit dem linken Arm auch das linke Bein. –Die Fixierung bewahrt vor Schäden; welche Schäden erzeugt sie, wer zöge Bilanz? –Ich will keinen Unmut gegen diese Anstalt wecken, sowenig wie Riemanns Bild es will; man weiß in Fürstenwalde um die eigenen Mängel, so um den nicht (oder kaum?) behebbaren des fehlenden Pflegepersonals—dabei hat die Samariteranstalt, von der Kirche getragen, ein weit größeres Reservoir selbstlos hilfswilliger junger Menschen als jede staatliche Schwesteranstalt, und sie erfreut sich auch noch des Vorteils, schwer Aggressive in geschlossene Heime überweisen zu können. –Dennoch; und ich finde es gut, daß man Grenzsituationen nicht aus dem eignen Bewußtsein verdrängt.

Dies gilt auch für eine andere Photographie, die ich, vor die Qual einer Wahl gestellt, als erschütterndste dieser Folge ansähe: das Gruppenporträt der Kinder im Schlafraum, das den Bildteil dieses Bandes eröffnet. Es sagt auch einen Mythos, den vom Einbruch des Geschlechts ins heranreifende Leben, den Mythos von Kore, der Tochter Demeters, die Hades in sein Unterwelt-Reich zog; er lebt in manchen Märchen weiter: Erinnert man sich des vergeblichen Mühens, Dornröschen vor der Spindel zu schützen, die sie unerbittlich einmal bluten macht?

Fünf Kinder, etwa zehnjährig, zwei Mädchen, drei Jungen, in Unterwäsche, Leibchen und Schlüpfer, eines an seiner Schlüsselschnur kauend; drei, linker Gruppenflügel, eine Hand am Geschlechtsteil; eines den Kopf in die Hand gestützt. –Das sorgende Kind. –Das Mädchen im Hintergrund lacht, der Junge vorn lächelt, doch auch im Lachen und Lächeln ist wenig Heitres; in der Miene des lächelnden Jungen liegt Trotz, im Lachen des Mädchens Einfältigkeit. –Das Mädchen mit dem Schlüssel blickt prüfend; der Junge links am Rand weiß viel. –Ringsum die Betten; sie umzingeln die Kinder; die Wand dahinter ohne Fenster, eine Schrankwand, Schlieflack, Betten spiegelnd, und durch die spaltoffene einzige Tür, davor der sorgende Junge sitzt, Finsternis und darin zwei Schlitze, Augen eines dämonischen Wesens; es sind Klinken, die in einem Licht aufgleißen, dessen Herkunft man hier nicht erkennt; auch die Funktion dieser Tür im Alltag ist unklar, im Bild schaut durch sie Zukunft herein.

Das Geschlecht ist eine schwere Bürde, in der Welt der geistig Behinderten nicht anders als in der Welt ringsum, nur daß ihm hier eben das versagt ist, was man "normale Erfüllung" nennt. Eheschließungen wären rechtlich möglich, die Behinderten sind nicht entmündigt; bislang ist kein Wunsch danach geäußert; man weiß nicht, wie man sich entschiede, würde er laut. –Zu intimeren Bindungen zwischen den Geschlechtern wird keine Gelegenheit gegeben; die äußerste Form eines Partnerverhältnisses zeigt sich beim allwöchentlichen Tanzabend als bescheidenes Schmusen: Händehalten, Untergehakt-Sitzen, Einander-über-die-Haare-Streichen, eine sich scherzhaft gebende Umarmung, schon nicht mehr ein erotischer Kuß. Was bleibt, sind homosexuelle Kontakte, die man nachts auf den Stationen duldet, ohne groß Aufhebens davon zu machen, und die Masturbation, die man als natürlich ansieht, in bestimmten Fällen auch tagsüber; man schickt den Pflegling dann auf die Toilette und läßt ihn, so lang er es braucht, ungestürt. –Triebdämpfende Mittel sind verpönt; man ist überhaupt sparsam mit Medikamenten, gibt Seditiva nur in dringenden Fällen (auch dies ein Vermächtnis der Antike), besitzt kein Elektroschockgerät und lehnt strikt die "weiße Zwangsjacke" ab, das Unterbinden von Aggressionen durch narkotisierende Pharmaka.

So weit, so gut; nicht allerorts solche Einsicht, vor allem zum homosexuellen Verkehr (über dessen Praktiken, da man ihn nicht belauert, man nichts Näheres weiß noch wissen will); und abermals dennoch: hinter der spaltoffenen Tür die Finsternis mit den zwei Augenschlitzen. –Wer sieht ihre Gestalt ganz? –Man sollte ihr frei ins Gesicht blicken dürfen, und ein Weiterdenken sei geboten, ob mit den geschilderten Formen der Duldung alle Möglichkeiten erschöpft sind. –Aus einer ändern Anstalt etwa kenne ich das Beispiel einer Art Ehe bei mindestens einseitiger Sterilisation; oder für ein heterosexuelles Paar die Gelegenheit gegenseitigen Masturbierens. –Nur Probleme der Anstalt? –Auch in der Welt draußen ist Allzuvielen die Geschlechtserfüllung, die sie sich ersehnen, versagt; hier aber springt diese Not ins Auge: Das individuell Ungemäße wird von vornherein, und dies chancenlos, Norm. –Draußen ist immerhin Hoffnung, und daraus ein Mühen, die anlagegemäße Befriedigung zu finden; die Möglichkeit zu ihr ist draußen gegeben, hier drinnen herrscht Unerbittlichkeit, und man sagt, man muß sich mit ihr so abfinden wie mit seiner

Behinderung. Doch die ist im Geist, der Trieb im Fleisch, und wo der Defekt auch im Physischen liegt, wie bei manchen Spastikern, kann das Fleisch dem eigenen Fleisch nicht helfen, dann ist auch die Selbstbefriedigung verwehrt. Sollte da jede Hilfe versagt sein? Beschwichtigende Worte gehn rasch vom Mund, daß "die" es eben nicht so spürten und daß es auch draußen solche Notfälle gebe. Das letzte stimmt schon, und es ist gewiß auch richtig, die Sexualität im menschlichen Leben nicht dann und dort zur Hauptsache zu machen, wann und wo sie eine solche Rolle nicht spielt.

Dennoch.

Man betrachte Riemanns Photographie.

V   Die Frage nach der "erlösenden Spritze" ist, will man sie objektiv nehmen, die Frage nach dem Sinn in der Psychiatrie. Sie wäre dreifach aufzuwerfen: als Frage nach dem Sinn des geminderten Daseins, also wesentlich unter sozialem Aspekt; dann in metaphysischer Hinsicht, als Frage nach dem Sinn der Minderung selbst (in diesem Wort seien hier einmal vereinfacht Krankheit und Behinderung zusammengefaßt, die ja nicht miteinander identisch sein müssen), und schließlich als die Frage nach dem Sinn ärztlichen und pflegerischen Wirkens, dies ihre wissenschaftlich akzeptable Gestalt. Die Antworten auf diese Fragenbündlung wären dann wieder zu scheiden in jene, die, falls sie es ermöchten, die Geminderten selber gäben und die man überraschend oft als "Glück" deuten könnte; daneben stünden die Antworten derer, die sie betreuen, und schließlich die der Gesellschaft, darin beide leben. All diese Fragen verknäulen sich, mühsam entwirrbar, ihre Aspekte gehn ineinander über, ohne je ganz identisch zu werden, und die Antworten haben im geschichtlichen Ablauf mannigfache Gestalt angenommen, vor allem in sozialer Hinsicht, sie reichen da vom "Heiligen Narren" als Sprachrohr göttlichen Offenbarens bis zum Lustobjekt der Schau, da führte man die an Leib oder Geist Geminderten oder Andersgearteten wie Tiere einem Publikum vor, das, sich an ihnen delektierend, die Wonnen seines Normalseins genoß. Danach sah dies Normalsein in den "Irren" Objekte, die es bändigen mußte, sie verwalten zu können; der Nationalsozialismus schließlich hat den Sinn solchen Daseins entschieden verneint, und die Schlote der Krematorien rauchten.

All diese Antwortfiguren dauern noch an: nachts in unseren Träumen, und nicht nur dort.

Um diese Fragen zu konzentrieren und ihr Wesen in der Essenz zu fassen, sei ein extremer Fall erörtert, einer, wo der Gauärzteführer ohne Zögern "ins Gas!" entschieden hätte. Also: Welchen Sinn hätte ein Menschendasein als Dasein Eines, den man nach einem Sinn nicht einmal indirekt fragen kann, da er willen- und antriebslos dahinlöst, kaum noch grunzend oder lallend, unfähig, Kot und Urin zu halten, unfähig auch, sich zu erheben, den man füttern und töpfen und säubern muß, ohne auch nur den Schein eines Lächelns als Lohn solcher Pflegemühen zu ernten? Nun, just solch ein Fall ist noch vor drei Jahren Peter gewesen, ein absoluter Pflegefall, Langdon-Down-Syndrom mit geistiger Behinderung dritten Grades, jenes äußersten, schwersten, den man früher "Idiotie" genannt hat, und dieser Peter ist eben zu dem geworden, der heute mit Ball oder Püppchen in der Werkstatt erscheint, um, wenn es ihm gefällt, ein Täschlein zu nähen, und beim Spaziergang fährt er den Spastiker Ulli im Rollstuhl, draußen freilich stets unter strenger Aufsicht: Peter hält die Autos für freundliche Wesen und steuert, wenn er eins erblickt, Freund Ulli im Rollstuhl darauf zu.

Auch diesen Peter von heute, dessen Entwicklung nun wohl abgeschlossen ist – es gilt, sein Errungenes zu wahren anstatt weitere Forderungen zu stellen, an denen er entweder scheitern oder deren Erfüllung ihn nur drillen, also in seiner Persönlichkeit mindern würde—: auch diesen Peter von heute hätte der Gauärzteführer mit einer lässigen Geste ins Gas gesandt; und der Autofahrer, auf den Peter zusteuert, wird wahrscheinlich wütend den Unsinn beschimpfen, "solche" auf der Straße sich bewegen zu lassen. Allein für jemand, der Peters Entwicklung kennt, tritt der Sinn therapeutischen Mühens leuchtend hervor, auch dort, wo solch ein Erfolg versagt ist: seine Möglichkeit bleibt existent, und zum Verwirklichen dieser Möglichkeit gehört auch das Bewegen in der Umwelt. –Die dies stille Wunder menschlichen Entfaltens wesentlich mitgewirkt hat, Gabriele D., die Betreuerin beim Ausflug, ist mit Peter im Bild auch festgehalten, da sie ihm fröhlich einen Gute-Nacht-Kuß gibt. Sie hat ihm diesen Kuß auch früher gegeben; allabendlich, auch in jener Zeit, da Peter ein hoffnungsloser Fall schien, und es ist die Zuwendung von Liebe und Wärme, von Hoffnung und von Sinn gewesen, die Peters Menschenwürde geweckt hat: Der Sinn des Menschen ist der Mensch.

Der metephysische Sinn-Aspekt, jener, der ganz aus der Wissenschaft fällt, ist für den religiös gebundenen Menschen überwältigend im Johannesevangelium, Kapitel 9, Vers 1-3, beantwortet: "Und im Vorbeigehen erblickte er einen Menschen, der von Geburt an blind war. Und seine Jünger fragten ihn, 'Rabbi, wer hat gesündigt, dieser oder seine Eltern, daß er blind geboren wurde?' Jesus anwortete: 'Weder dieser hat gesündigt noch seine Eltern. Vielmehr sollen die Werke Gottes an ihm offenbar werden.'"

Für einen Christen ist dies Wort wohl die Sinn-Offenbarung schlechthin, allein es läßt auch manchen nicht los, der sich nicht im Glauben weiß, und er muß die Frage zu Ende denken, ob und wie dieses Wort auch für ihn gelte.

Die Auffassung vom Sinn einer Krankheit als göttlicher Strafe oder als Mahnung für andre, Böses zu meiden, oder als Antrieb zum Bußetun ist alt; die Frage der Jünger wächst ebendaraus, und den Sinn der mania des großen Aias sahn die Zeitgenossen als Strafe für seine Hybris an, einst den Beistand Athenes verschmäht zu haben, um allein, ohne Gottheit, im Kampf zu bestehn.

Bei Sophokles liest sich das so:

Als ihn die Göttin Pallas einst zum Kampfe trieb,

Damit er tauche seine Hand in Feindesblut,

Da rief er ihr in frechem Übermute zu:

Den andern Griechen, Herrin, stehe schützend bei,

Hier aber, wo ich stehe, bricht kein Feind hindurch.

Durch solche kecke Reden zog er sich den Zorn

Der Göttin zu, die solcher Hoffart widersteht.

Doch wenn er diesen heut'gen Tag noch überlebt,

So könnt ihr ihn mit Gottes Hilfe retten noch.

Allein Aias, konsequent bis zum letzten, schlägt ebendiese Hilfe aus; er gäbe sich in einer Heilung selbst auf, und so fällt er durch eigene Hand. –Eine gnadenlos feste, logische Kette. –Auch Jesu Jünger denken noch ganz in der Tradition einer Kausalverknüpfung von Sünde als Ursache und strafender Krankheit als Folge, erschauernd vor dem Zorn eines Gottes, der da straft bis ins siebente Glied: "Denn ich, Jahwe, dein Gott, bin ein eifernder Gott, der die Schuld der Väter ahndet an den Kindern, Enkeln und Urenkeln derer, die mich hassen", wie es der Dekalog, im 2. Buch Mose, verkündet. Rabbi Jesus zerbricht diese Kette: Weder der Blinde noch dessen Eltern hätten gesündigt, der Sinn der Krankheit liege vielmehr darin, daß Gottes Macht sich offenbare. –Worin? –In der Macht, Menschliches zu zerstören? Die Antike hat dies so gesehen.

"Ich kann mit Blindheit schlagen auch den Sehenden", sagt in des Sophokles "Aias" Athene von sich, und Odysseus beeilt sich, ihr recht zu geben: "Der Götter Macht kann freilich alles, was sie will."

Die Offenbarung göttlicher Macht durch Zerstörung von Menschlichem, so wäre jene Stelle kaum aufzufassen; ihre Folge, die Heilung, verweist ja auf das Andre: Entfaltung geminderten Menschentums. Jesus "spie . . . auf den Boden, machte einen Teig aus dem Speichel, strich ihm" (dem Blinden) "den Teig auf die Augen und sagt zu ihm: 'Geh, wasche dich in dem Teich Siloach' . . . Er ging also hin und wusch sich und kam sehend zurück."

Dies war ärztliche Arbeit, sie geschah am Sabbat, und darauf stand die Todesstrafe. –Dennoch. –Jeder Kommentator dieser Stelle, der heilige Augustinus, etwa, sieht die Offenbarung der göttlichen Macht in der Heilung des Blinden, und in der Heilung eines Blinden die Offenbarung göttlicher Macht. Doch auch der gläubige Christ wird die Säkularisierung dieses Gedankens nicht als blasphemisch empfinden können, daß in der Heilung, in ihren verschiedenen Graden, sich die Kraft des Menschseins entfaltet, des Genesenden wie des Heilenden.

Der Sinn einer Minderung läge—die Fragestellung einmal akzeptiert—dann darin, daß sich auch in ihr und daß sich an ihr die Kraft des Menschentums entfalte, für den Geminderten wie für dessen Betreuer, die beide der Gattung Mensch angehören, mag man den als Geschöpf und Gehilfen Gottes oder nur auf sich selbst gestellt sehn. Dieser Sinn muß freilich gegeben werden, er ist nicht in der Minderung selbst, er wird in sie hineingebracht, und wenn die Wissenschaft ihn als Frage auch abweist—die Frage, welchen Sinn etwa Epilepsie habe, ist wissenschaftlich gesehen sinnlos—, so steht er ihr doch als ein Wert gegenüber, den, wenn schon nicht die Wissenschaft, so in ihr jeder annehmen sollte, dem es um den Geminderten als Menschen und nicht bloß als Objekt seines Fachgebiets geht.

Einen Andern aber als Menschen zu nehmen heißt zunächst, ihn als Menschen wie sich selbst anzuerkennen; da wird sehr schnell mit dem Kopf genickt, doch ist die Frage dahin gestellt, sich selbst auch als Menschen wie ihn anzusehen, sich der eigenen Minderung bewußt zu werden, die jeglichem von uns zuteil ward, und sich auch vorstellen zu können, an Stelle seines Betreuten zu stehn, dann geht das Nicken in Kopfschütteln über, und im Geist tippt der Finger gegen die Stirn. Doch ebendarauf käme es an: Daß man nicht nur den Geminderten zu geben, sondern auch von ihnen zu nehmen bereit ist.

Wir, die wir uns in Arbeit wie Freizeit zerstreuen, uns so schwer konzentrieren können, so schnell von Einem zum Anderen springen, wir könnten von Heike und Monika lernen, was Hingabe an eine Arbeit heißt, und wir, die uns in der Arbeit wie in der Freizeit verbiestern, Beruf wie Hobby und über den Kopf wachsen lassen, Sklaven statt Herren unseres Tuns sind, wir könnten von Bernd und Peter lernen, gelassener mit uns selbst umzugehn. –Gelassen ist nicht zerstreut, und konzientriert nicht verbiestert. –Der Autofahrer, der Peter beschimpft, soll gewiß nicht von ihm übernehmen, auf einen anderen Wagen zuzusteuern, aber einander als Freund statt als Feind zu begegnen wäre die schlechteste Lehre nicht. Wem von uns ist es gegeben, sich so zu freuen wie Willi oder Jürgen, sich so offen zu seinem Gefühl zu bekennen, so arglos sein freies Gesicht zu zeigen? Man sage nicht, das sei eben die Einfalt der Armen im Geiste, man frage vielmehr, ob ein Geist nicht beschränkt sei, der solche Beschränkung vom Menschentum fordert, wie es etwa der Geist des "keep smiling" verlangt: alle Mienen uniformiert zu der einen, und ihr Konfektionsoptimismus löscht mit der Vielfalt der Emotionen auch alle Bekundung von Zuversicht aus. –Jede Gesellschaft macht da ihre eigene Erfahrung, und offenbar lernt keine aus ihr. –"Wer schaffen will, muß fröhlich sein!" –mir schaudert vor diesem Imperativ. Ich sehe sein Bild; so sieht man Volk: emsig und sich vor Lachen ausschüttend, wenn der Meister einen Witz erzählt. In den Fürstenwalder Werkstätten wird nicht oft gelacht, die Grundstimmung ist gesammeltes Mühen, und daraus wächst, ohne verordnet zu werden, die stille Freude gewonnenen Sinns.

Was aber wäre von Peter zu lernen gewesen, als er willenlos auf seiner Bettstatt lag? Von der Gestalt, die er damals verkörpert, noch nichts, doch alles von dem, was ihm geschah: Werden. Im Werden entfaltet sich der Sinn, und dies in wechselseitiger Hinsicht: in der Sache, in die er eingebracht wird, wie in Jenem, der ihn eingebracht hat.

Ist es der Sinn von Gabrieles und all der andern Betreuer Pflege gewesen, daß Peters Menschentum sich entwickle, so hat auch die Entwicklung Peters auf die Gemeinschaft seiner Betreuer gewirkt: Sie sind durch ihn nicht nur bestätigt, sie sind durch ihn auch gefördert worden, durch seine sinnvolle Existenz. Zu ihr muß heute auch gehören, daß er entscheidet, ob er näht oder Ball spielt, daß er die Autos für Freunde hält, daß er ständig ein Püppchen hätschelt, daß er nur schwarze Hunde malt, mit übergroßen Köpfen und meist zwei oder drei stets waagrecht auseinandergespreißten Beinen, die mit ihren scheibenförmigen Pfoten wie Geräte von Gewichthebern aussehn. Er hat ein Recht auf seine Persönlichkeit, und keiner denkt daran, ihn zu dressieren, einen Arbeitsgang hindurch nur Taschen zu nähen oder einen "richtigen Hund" zu malen statt des Geschöpfs seiner Mythologie. Sie wäre leistbar, diese Dressur, allein sie würde nichts mehr entfalten, sie würde Peters Persönlichkeit mindern, von der andern, der gesellschaftlichen Seite her, und damit schadete man nicht nur Peter, man schadete damit auch sich selbst: Dressur dressiert auch den Dresseur.

Zuchtmeister zu sein ist kein guter Beruf.

Den Behinderten als Menschen zu nehmen heißt, ihn als Persönlichkeit zu nehmen, um ihn als Partner anerkennen zu können. Die gültige Antwort auf die Frage nach der "erlösenden Spritze" liegt nicht in einem warmherzigen Appell an humanes Verhalten gegenüber "auch solchen" oder schlimmer noch "selbst sochen", denen man damit jene nutzlose Existenz unterstellt, die anderswo "lebensunwertes Leben" genannt wird; sie kann, diese Antwort, nur ein Bekenntnis zu allen geistig Behinderten als der Gemeinschaft nützlichen Trägern sinnvoller Existenzen sein.

Darum ist es so bedeutungsvoll, daß Heike ihr Brett mit Steinchen füllt, sie baut damit ein Stück Kultur, das wertvoller ist als so manches Erzeugnis in Schaufenstern oder Galerien, das unter Anspruch auf Eigenleistung nichts als Reproduktion reproduziert. Was Heike zeitigt, ist Schöpfertum, und es beweist sich als solches darin, daß es auf andere ausstrahlen kann: Nicht nur Heike wächst an ihnen, sie wachsen selbst auch durch Heikes Tun. Und die Ärztin, die nach hartem Tagwerk jeden Feierabend noch eine Stunde mit einem autistischen Kind verbringt, es ermunternd, ein konisch zulaufendes Hölzchen in ein Brett mit Löchern zu stecken, nur dies, nichts als dies: "Steck hinein!" und ein Streicheln, wenn dieses schwierige Werk gelang, und – über ein Versagen ohne Aufhebens hinweggehend—die Aufforderung zu erneutem Versuch: "Steck hinein!"; jeden Abend, eine volle Stunde, und der Erfolg von sechs Wochen wäre, daß diese Arbeit viermal hintereinander ohne eine Fehlleistung gelingt—: diese Ärztin, sich ausgebend, gibt nicht nur, sie nimmt auch etwas, und das Kind, im tiefsten Bezirk der Seele, fühlt sich auch als ein Gebender und kann also eine Partnerschaft aufbaun, das rettende Heile in seinen Sinnen, die das Außen als ein einziges Feindliches sehn.

VI   Photographien geistig Behinderter—; Sie haben mich in den Bann gezogen durch etwas, das beinahe schon als suspekt gilt: durch ihre Affirmation. Diese Bilder sagen ja, zu den Behinderten wie zu ihren Betreuern, und sie sagen ihr Ja aus doppelter Notwendigkeit: Riemanns Prinzip, seine Kameraobjekte in ein Partnerverhältnis zu stellen, ist hier einer Welt begegnet, deren Daseinsprinzip eben Partnerschaft heißt.

Dies Ja verklärt seinen Gegenstand nicht, es schließt auch schmerzliche Kritik ein und spitzt bedrängende Fragen noch zu: ein Ja, wie und wo es am Platz ist. Ich versuche mir ein Ja vorzustellen zu einer Anstalt mit Drogenzwangsjacke, mit schlagenden Wärtern und sich göttergleich wähnenden Ärzten, mit Elektroschocks, mit gedemütigten Seelen in verwalteten Leibern: Ein Ja zu ihr heiße Zynik oder Lüge, wobei Zynik als Boden von Kunst immerhin denkbar bleibt.

Ich will jetzt nicht von Ästhetischem sprechen, dazu ist hier der Ort nicht mehr. Ich nehme das Ja dieser Bilderwelt auf, um in ihrer Aura daran zu erinnern, daß von allen Opfern des nationalsozialistischen Mordens jene am wenigsten Anteilnahme erfuhren, die als erste ins Gas hatten gehen müssen:

die psychisch wie physisch Behinderten. Wir sind ihnen so gut wie noch alles schuldig. Ich kenne kein Mahnmal, das an sie erinnert, kein Werk der Kunst hat sie gewürdigt, sie sind aus der Literatur gefallen, keiner ihrer Lebenswege ist aufgezeichnet, als Gruppe Verfolgter sind sie nicht anerkannt, die Namen 'Hadamar' oder 'Grafeneck' oder 'Sonnenstein' oder 'Eglfing-Haar' oder 'Bernburg' oder 'Hartheim' sagen kaum jemand etwas, wiewohl dort die ersten Selektionen geschahen. Der Widerstand in den Anstalten ist wenig erforscht. Einige wenige, sehr verdienstvolle Dokumentationen über die—fälschlich so genannten—Euthanasieverbrechen der Hitlerära bestätigen als Ausnahme die Regel.

Die moralische Rehabilitierung ist wie die Auseinandersetzung mit den Theorien rings um die "gnädige Spritze" so gut wie ausschließlich bei Halbheiten stehengeblieben, bei einem "auch die" und "sogar die", bei Gegenaufrechnungen von Pflegekosten, beim Rekurrieren auf das Fünfte Gebot. Noch immer wird bei theoretischen Diskursen das völlig anders gelagerte Problem der Sterbehilfe mit dem des Mordes an geistig oder leiblich Behinderten zusammengezogen: Gerade an diesen Persönlichkeiten erweist sich das berühmte Marx-Wort, daß die freie Entfaltung eines Jeden die Voraussetzung der freien Entfaltung Aller sei.

Damit mich niemand mißverstehe: Ich will aus einer Plage keine Wohltat machen. Jede Minderung ist ein Übel, jeder Schritt zu ihrer Verhütung ein Wohltun, und jede Rehabilitation ein Segen. Der Sinn einer Krankheit sei ihre Heilung und die Tilgung dessen, was sie hervorbringt. Es ist dem Menschen gelungen, Weltseuchen zu bannen: Pest, Cholera, Tuberkulose; die mannigfachen Behinderungen werden nie auszumerzen sein. Solange sie aber unter uns sind, sind ihre Träger unseres- und wir ihresgleichen: Was ihnen geschieht, geschieht auch uns.

Die Entfaltung eines Jeden als Bedingung der Entfaltung Aller: Fürstenwalde ist dafür ein Beispiel. Diese Photographien machen es sichtbar. Ich habe eine aus dem Umkreis dieses Bandes gerahmt an die Wand des Raumes gehängt, in dem ich arbeite, esse und schlafe.

Es ist ein Porträt Monikas.

Ich lerne von ihr, auch auf Knien zu gehen.

DIE JÜNGSTEN / THE YOUNGEST

Photographs by Dietmar Riemann

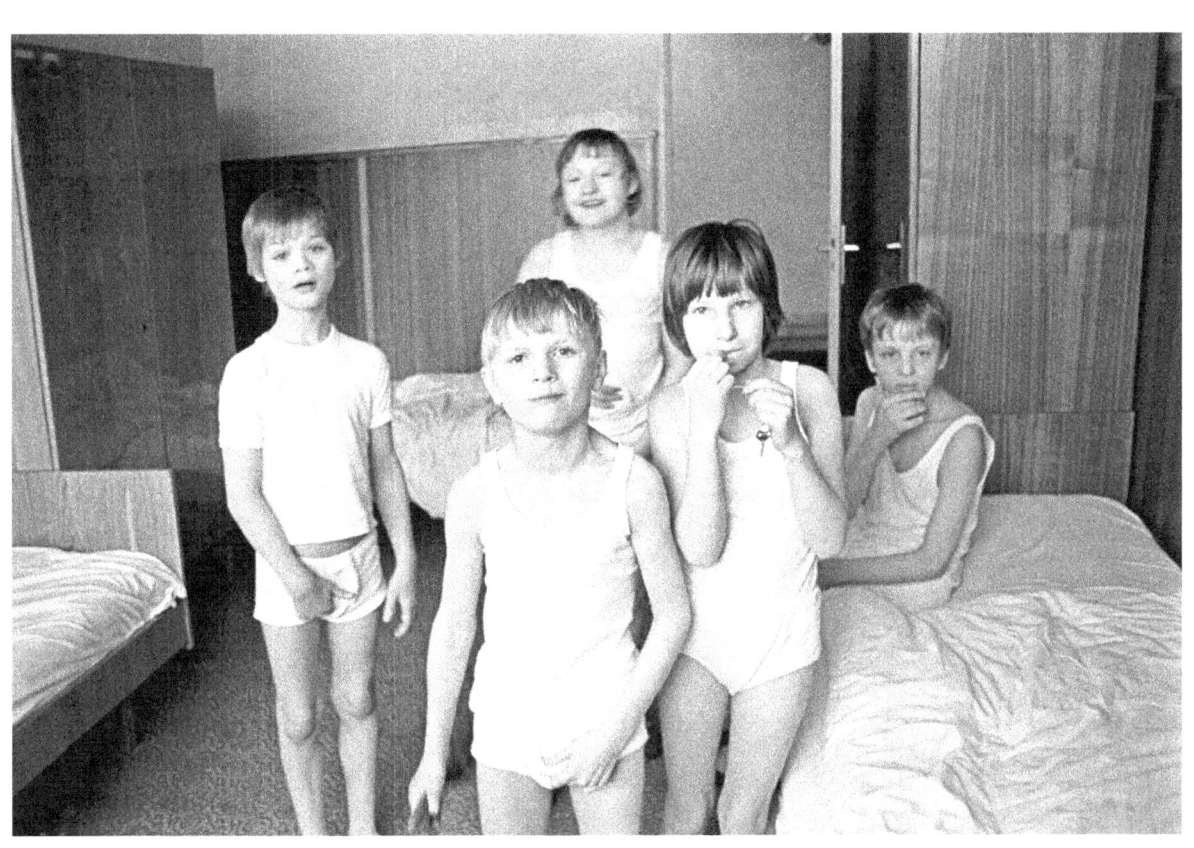

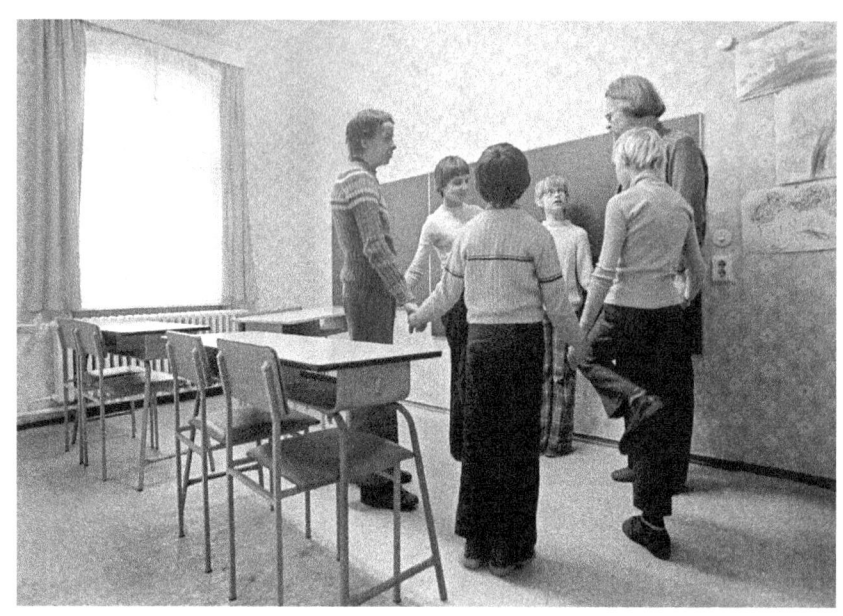

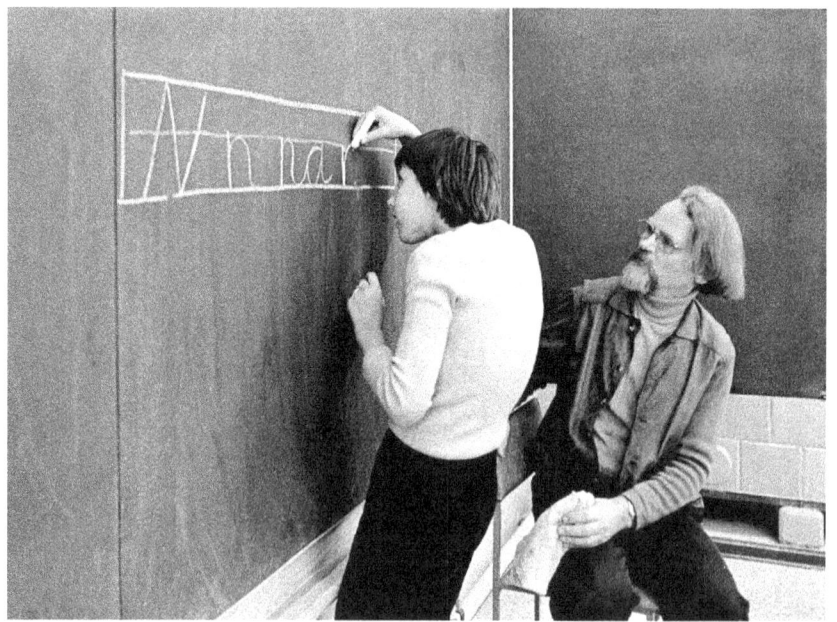

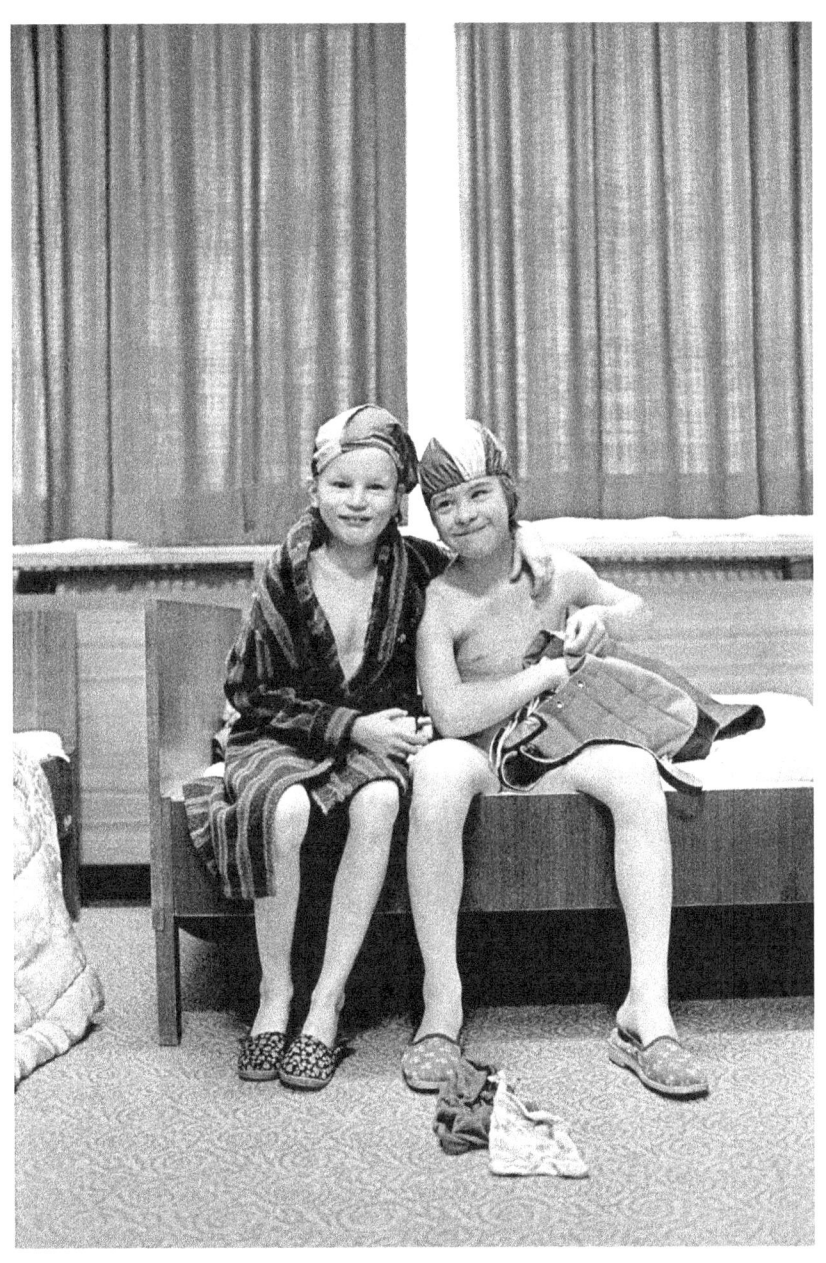

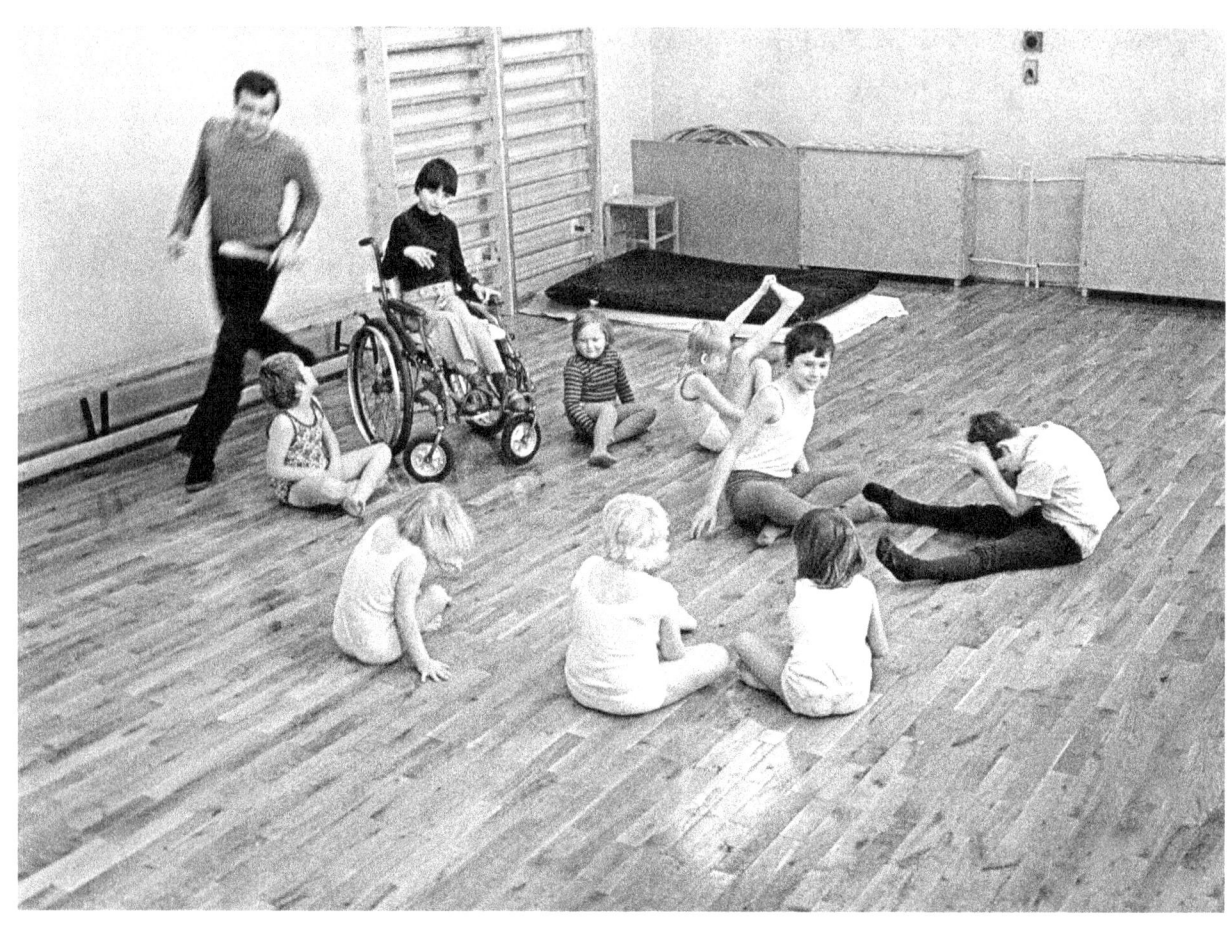

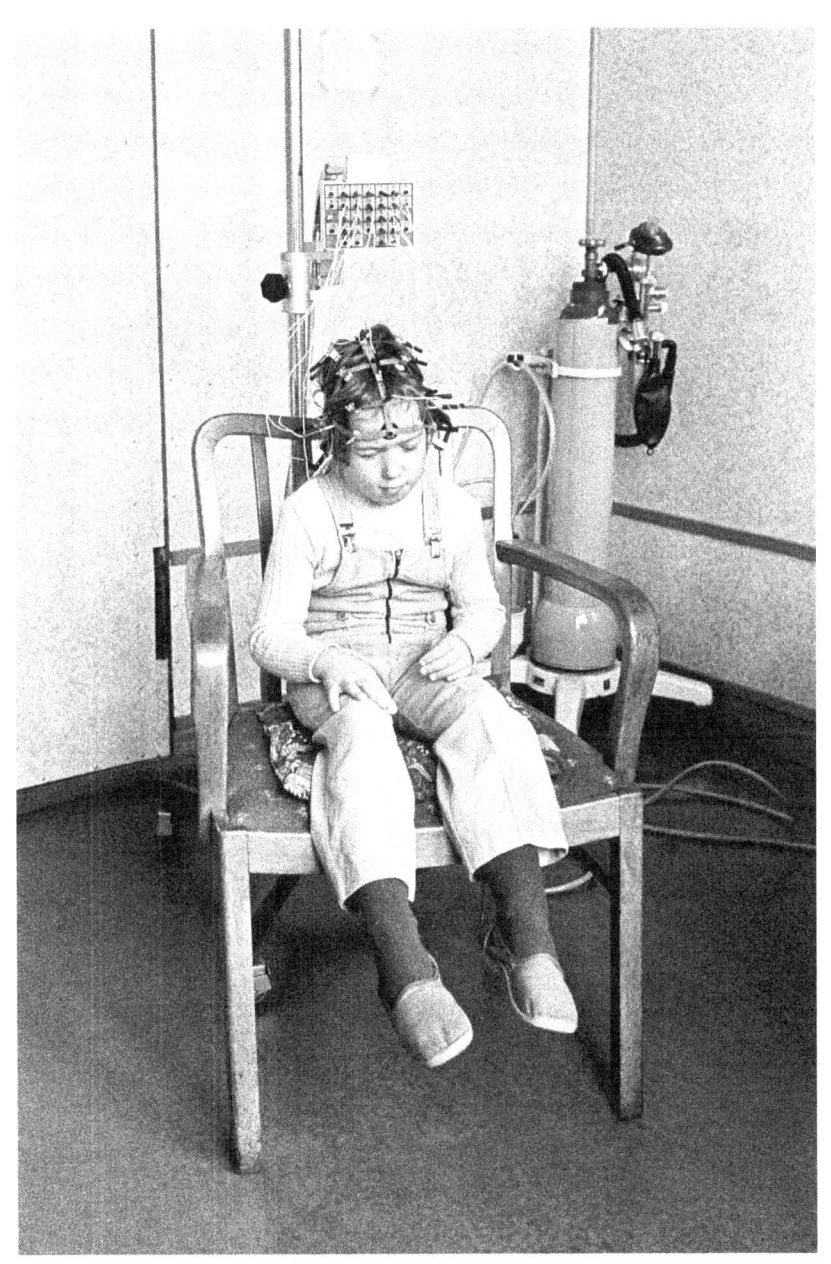

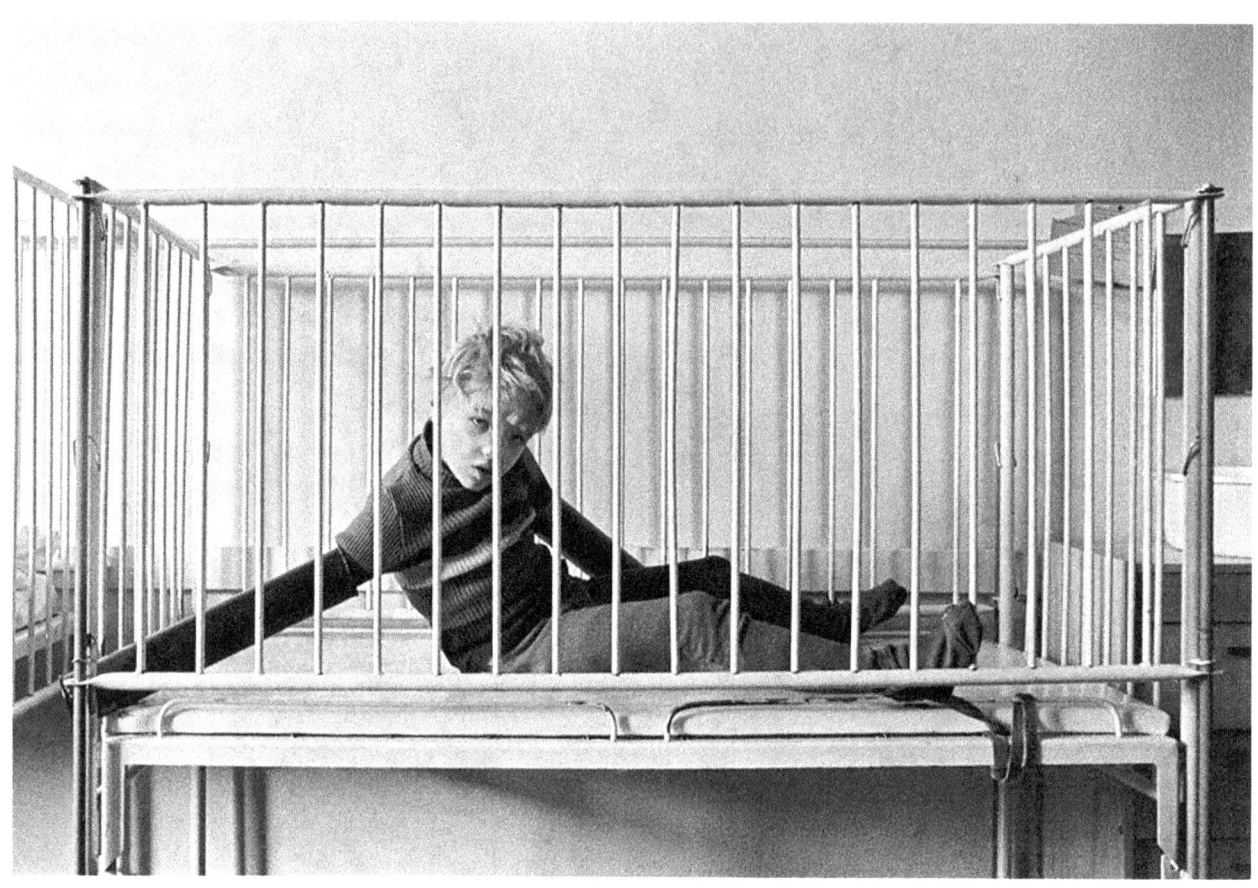

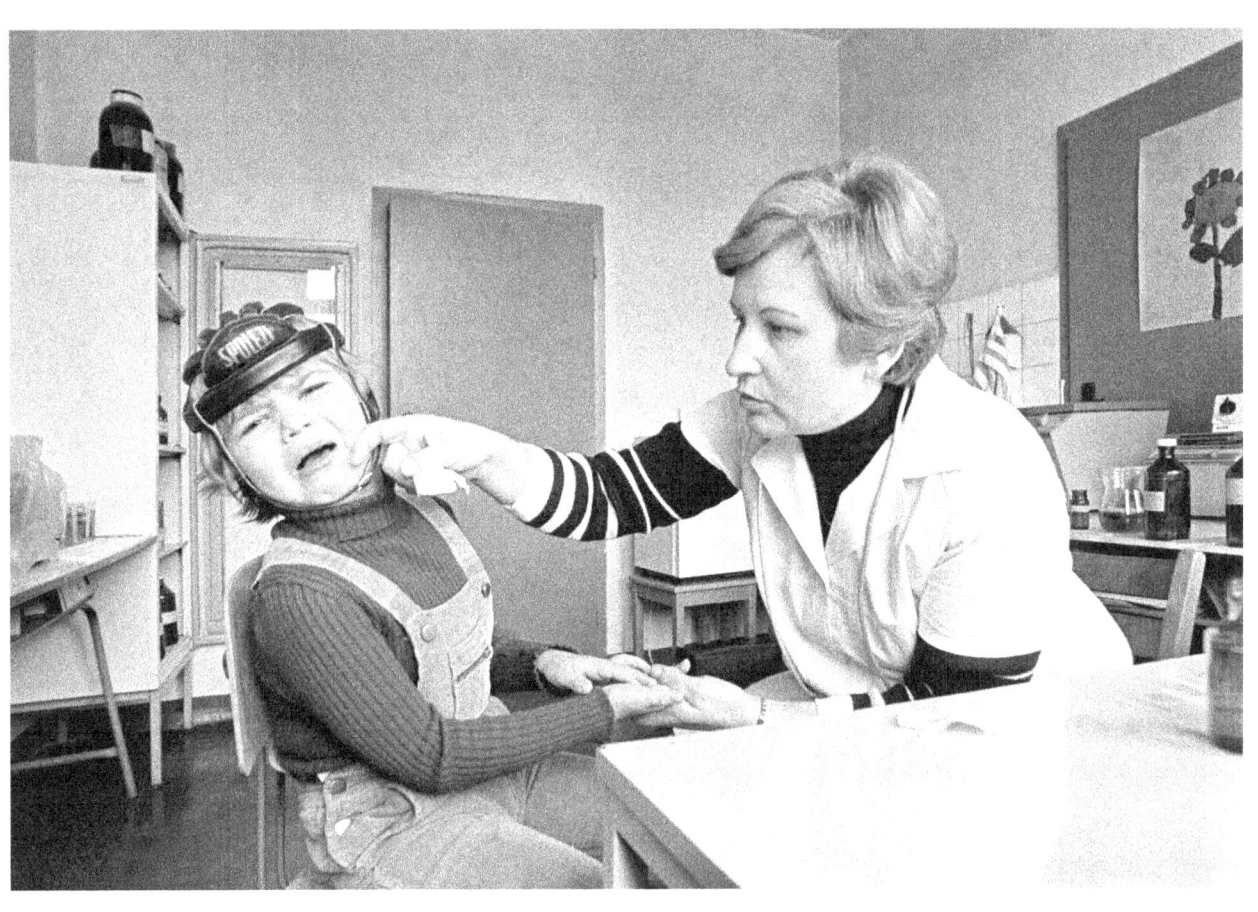

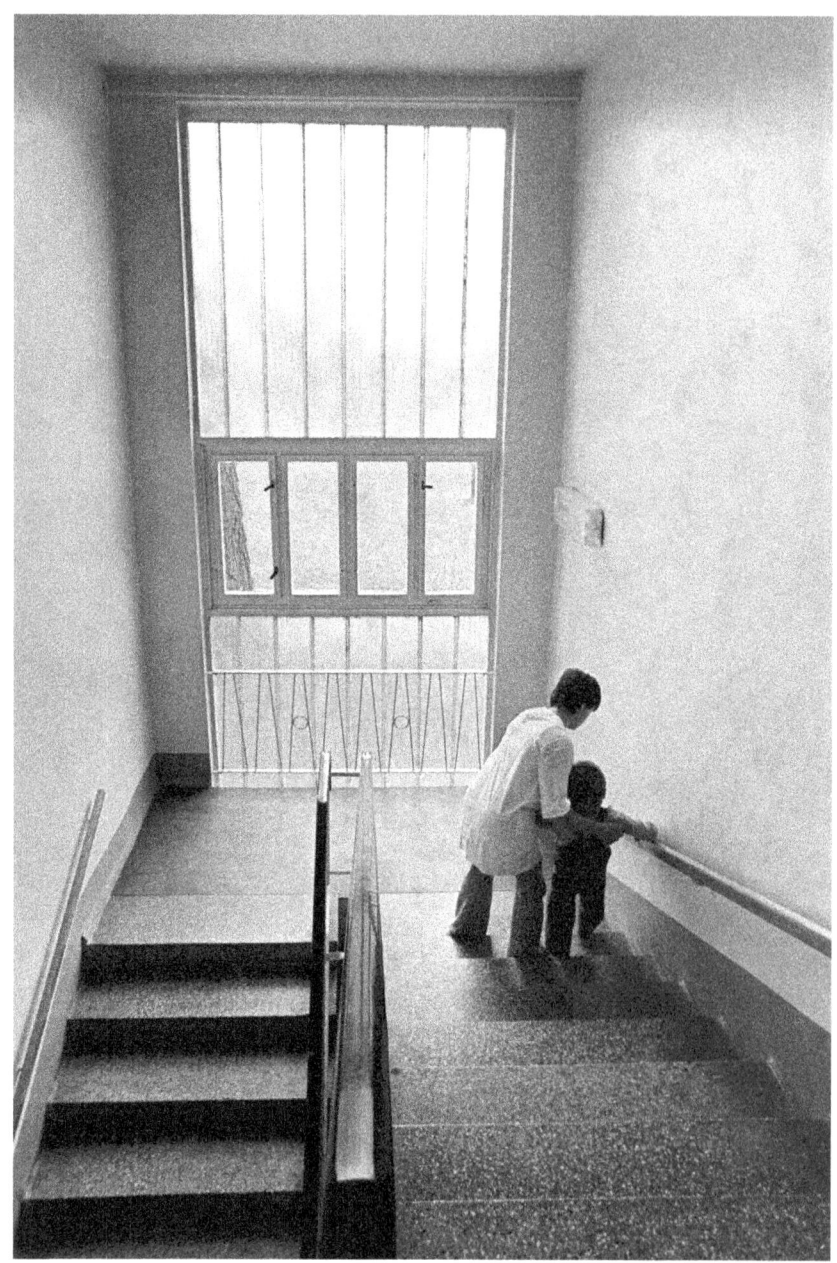

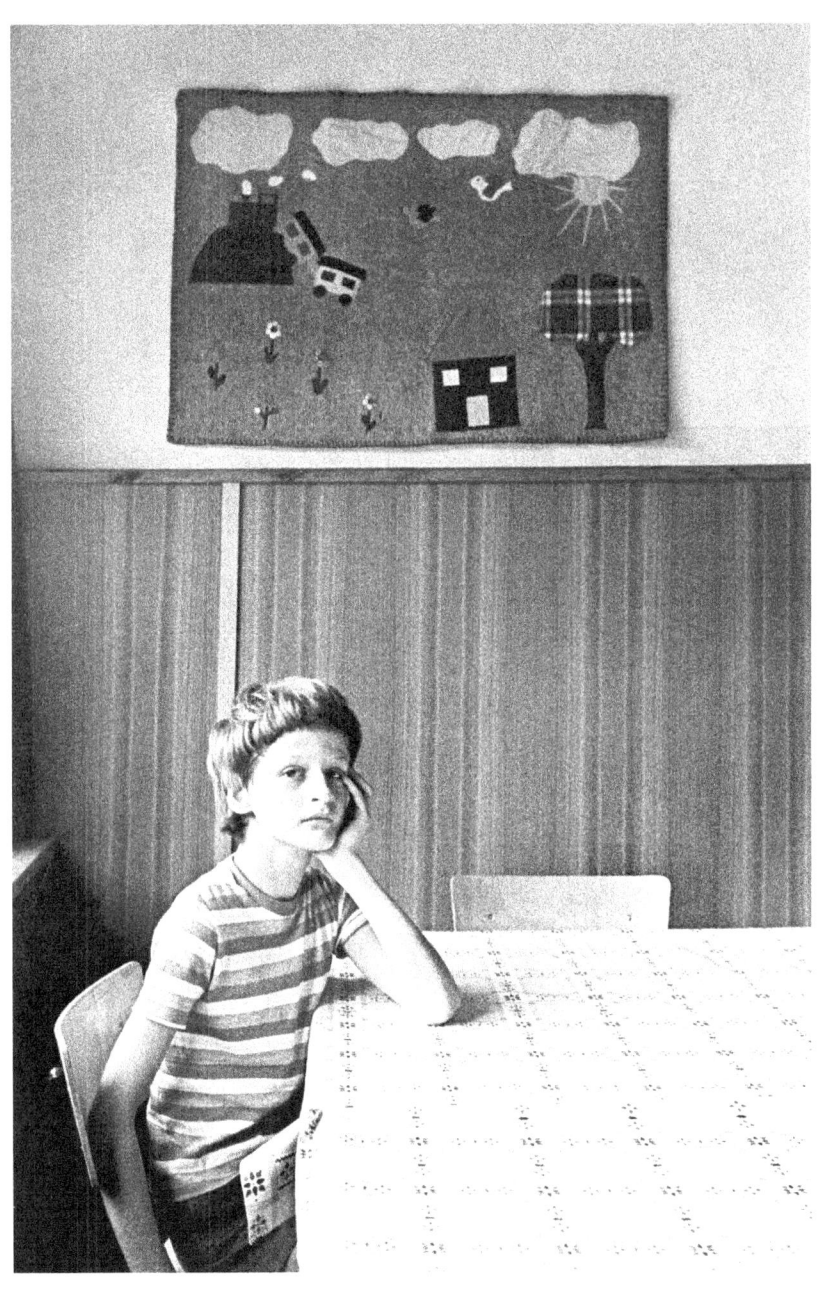

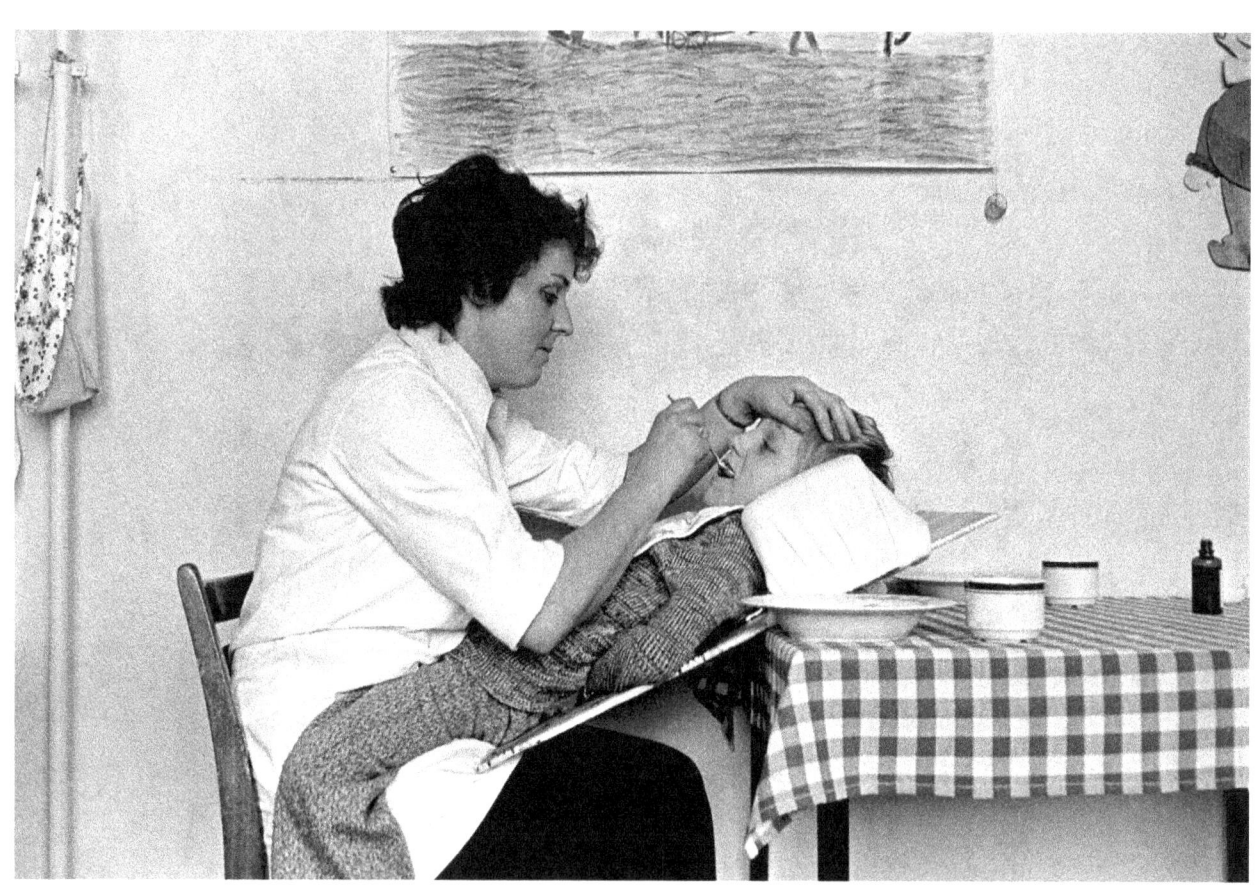

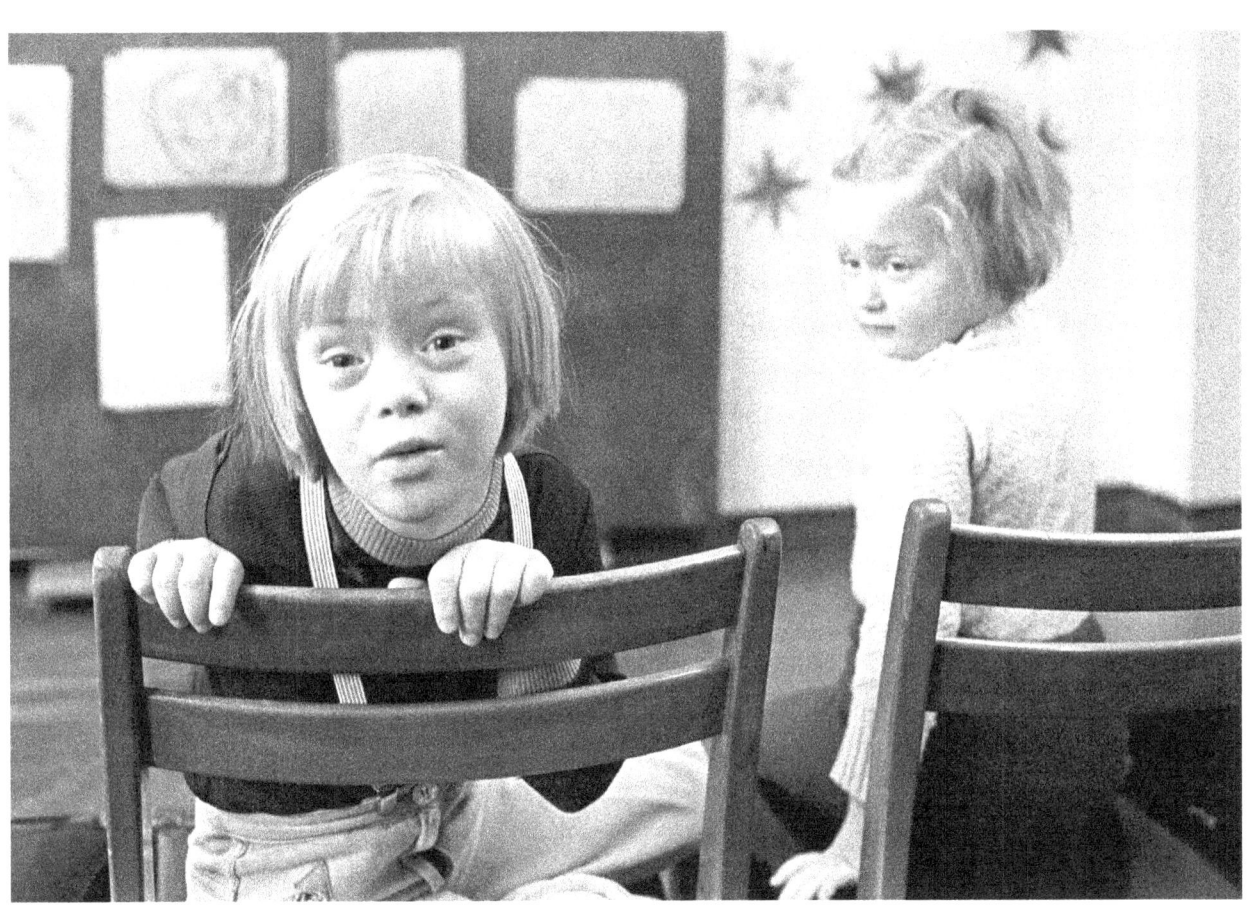

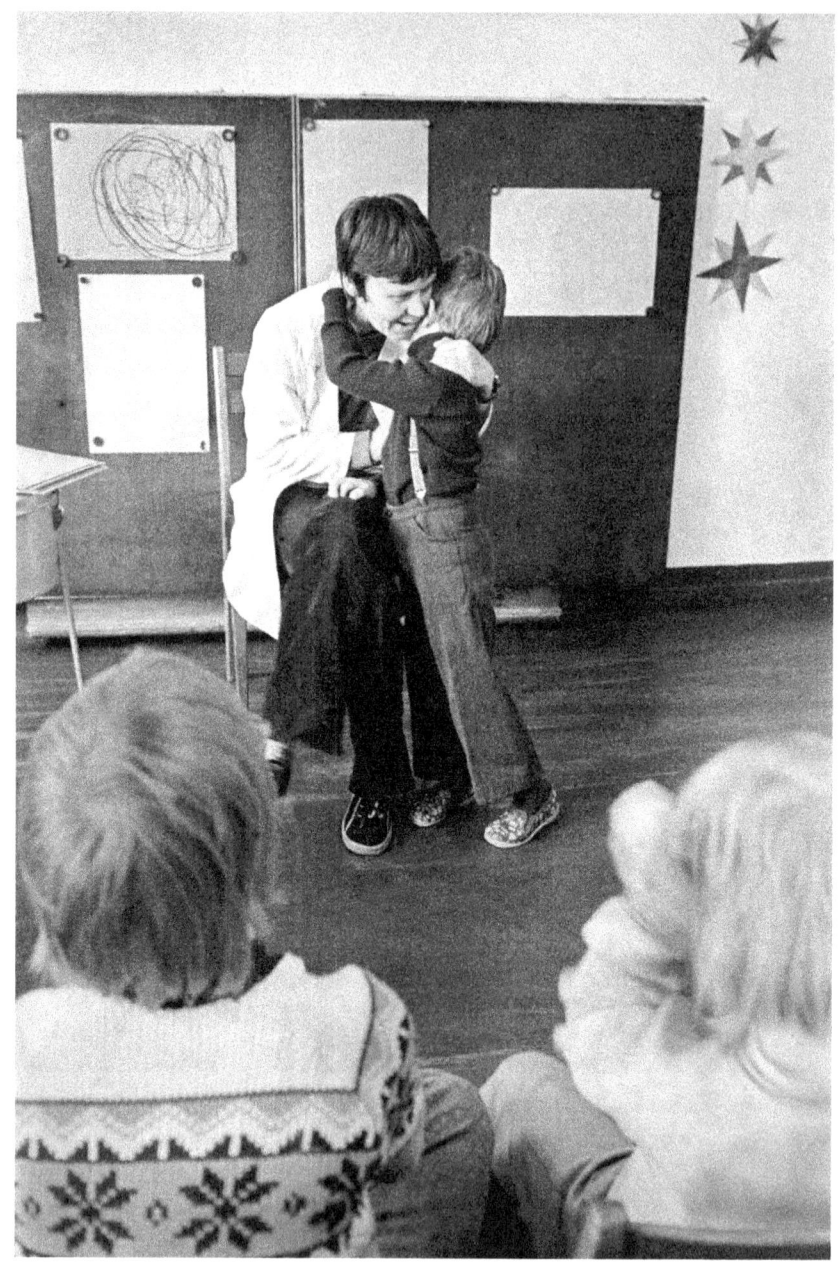

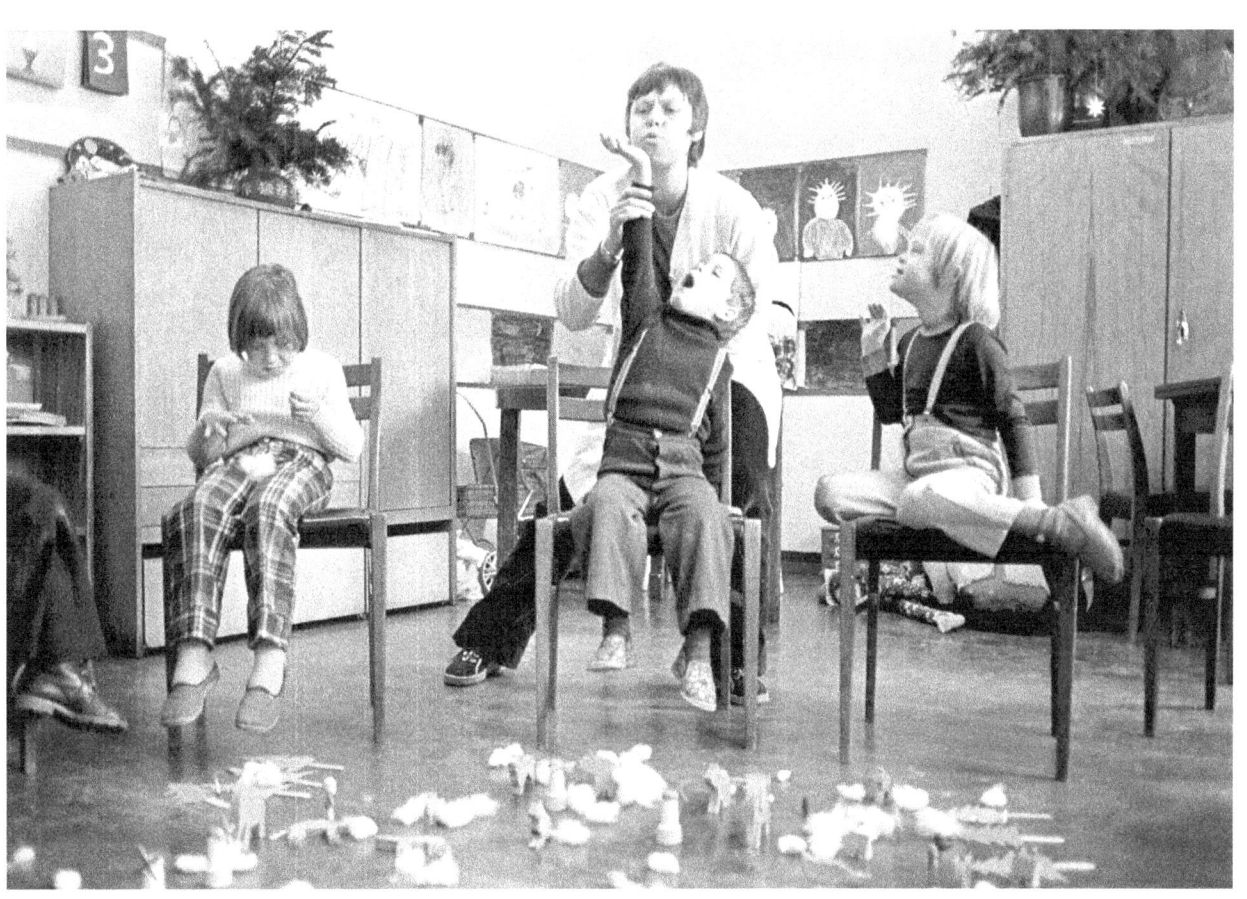

ALLTAG IM HEIM / EVERYDAY LIFE IN THE SAMARITANS' INSTITUTION

Photographs by Dietmar Riemann

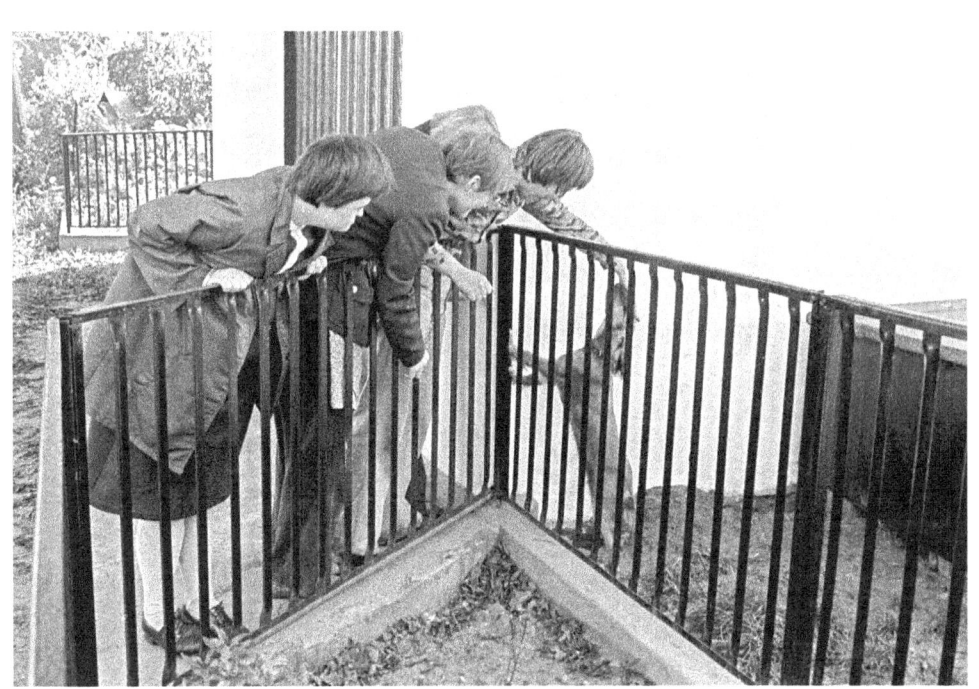

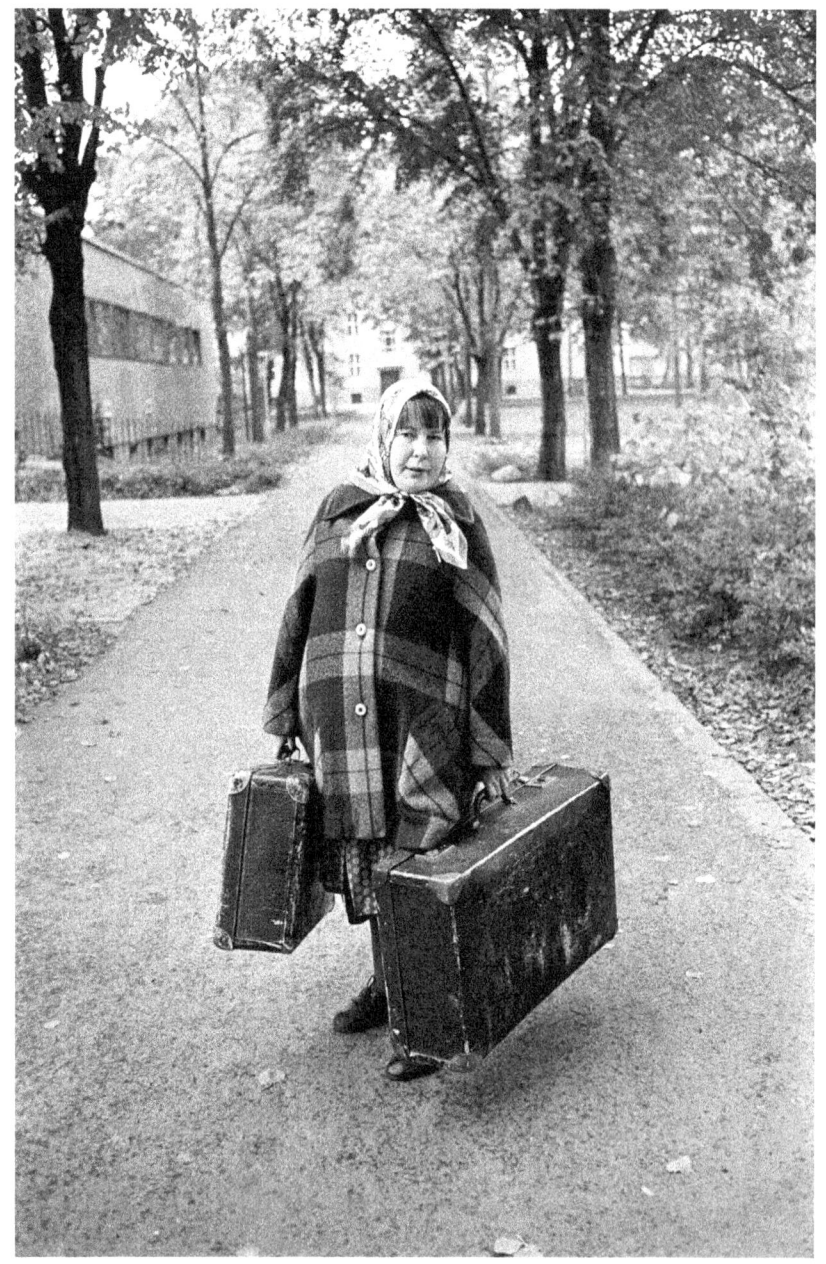

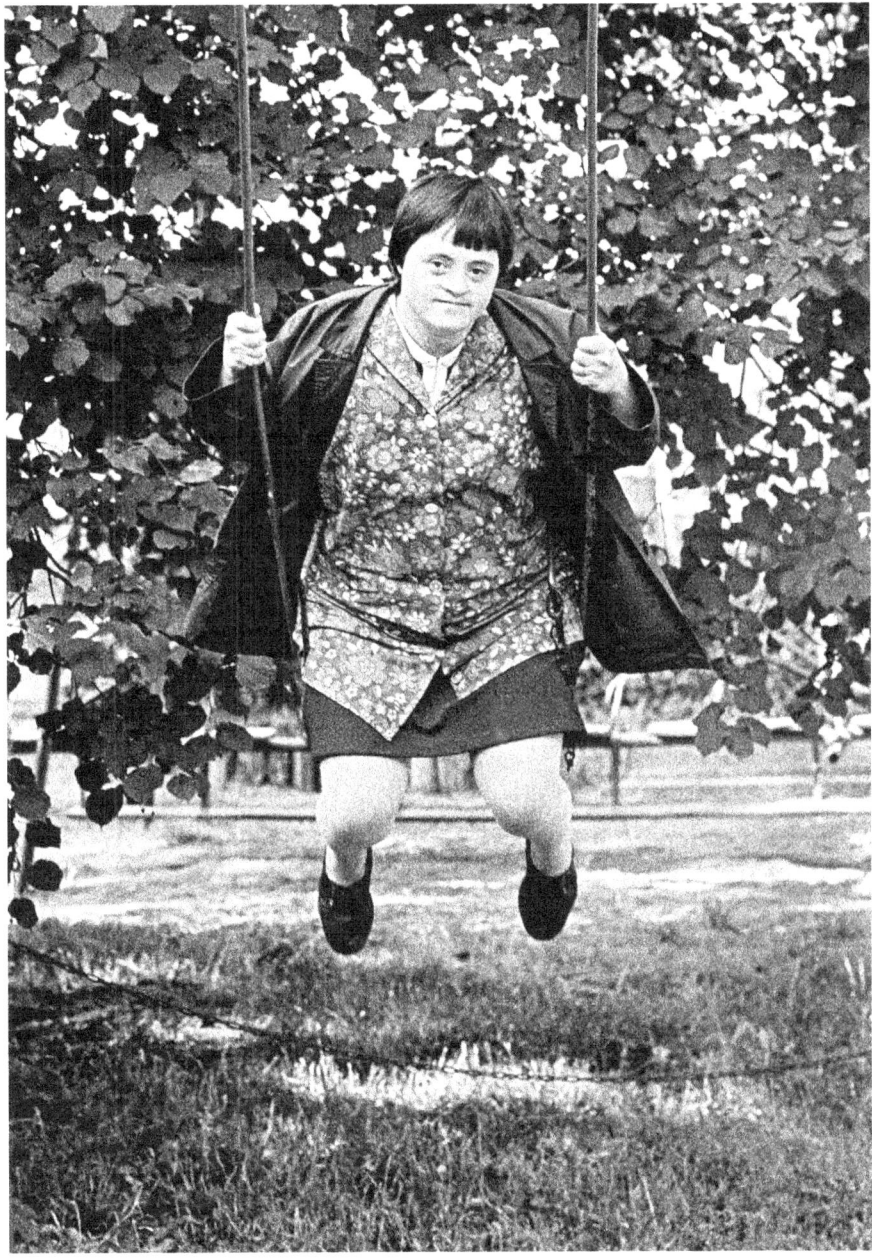

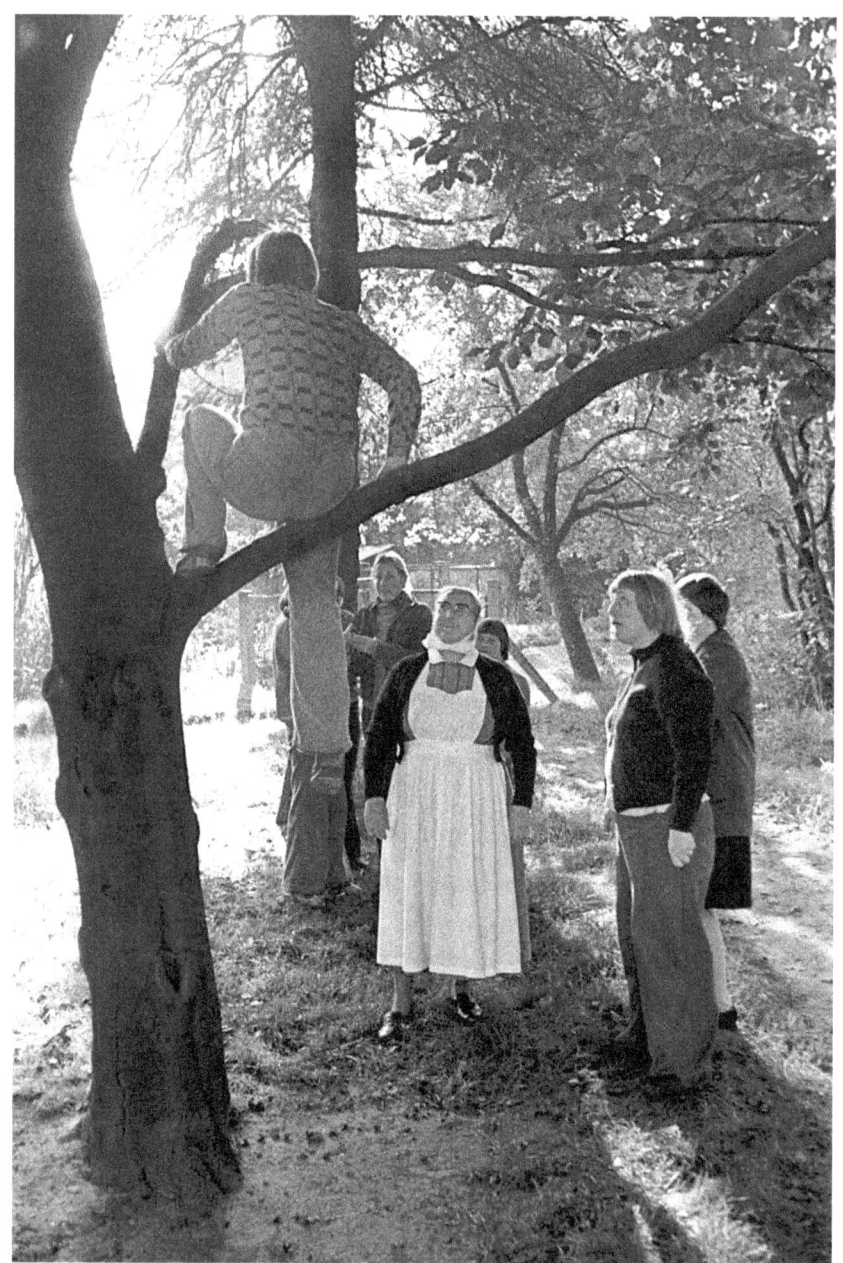

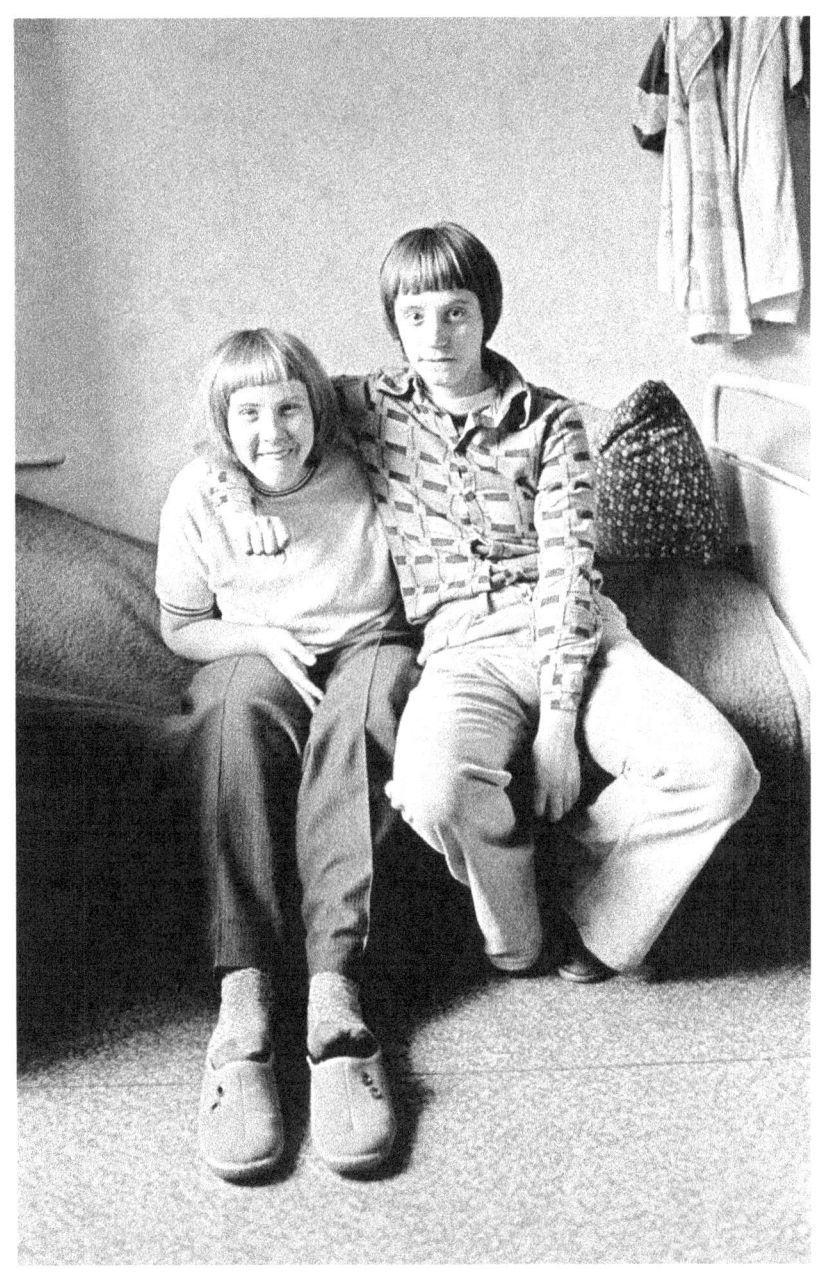

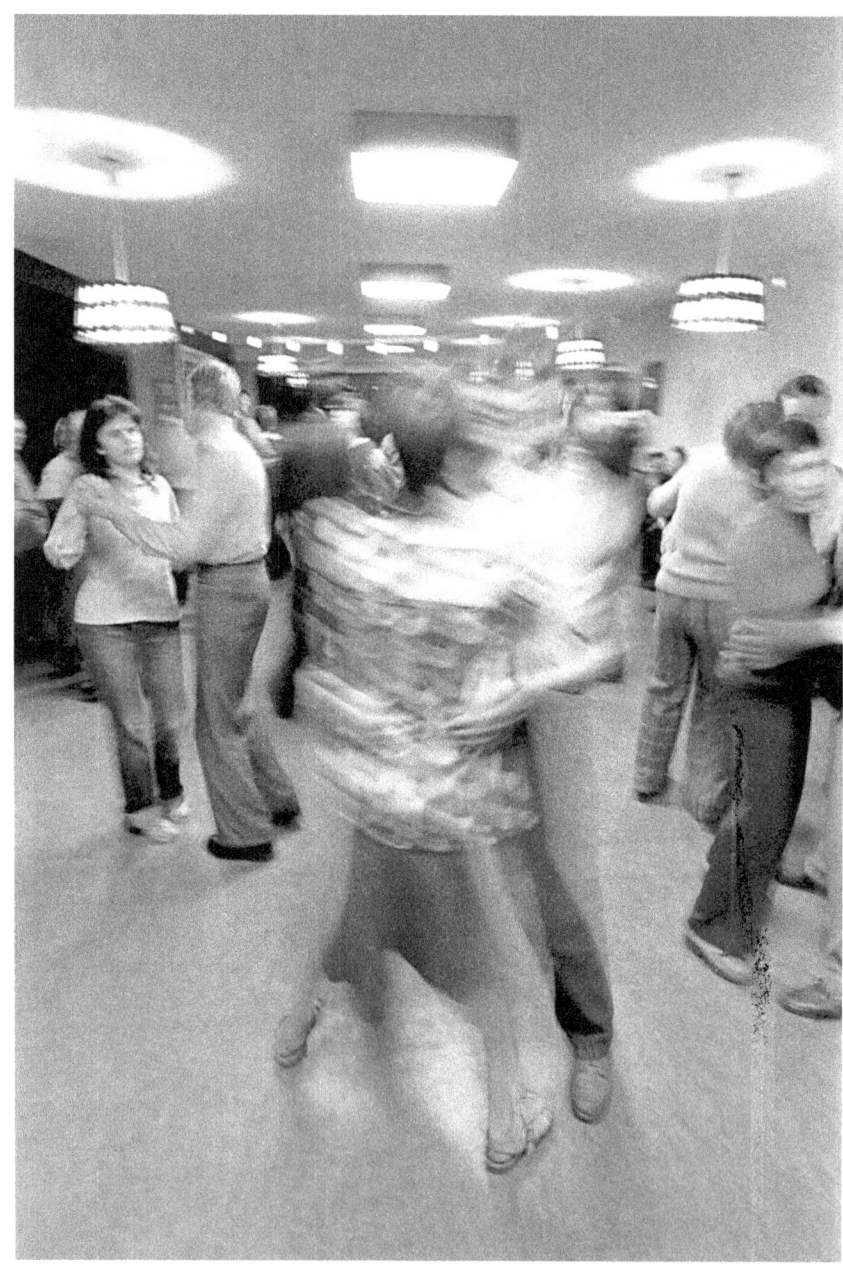

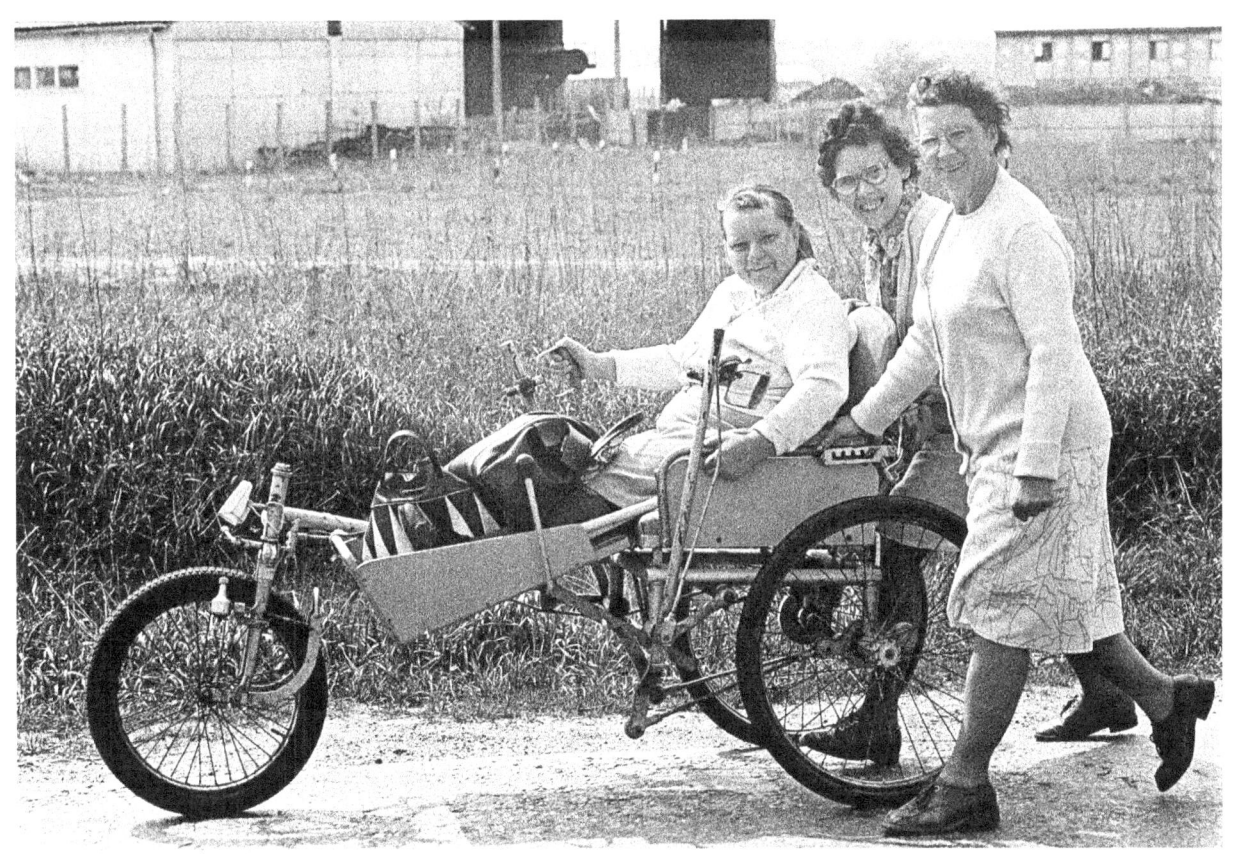

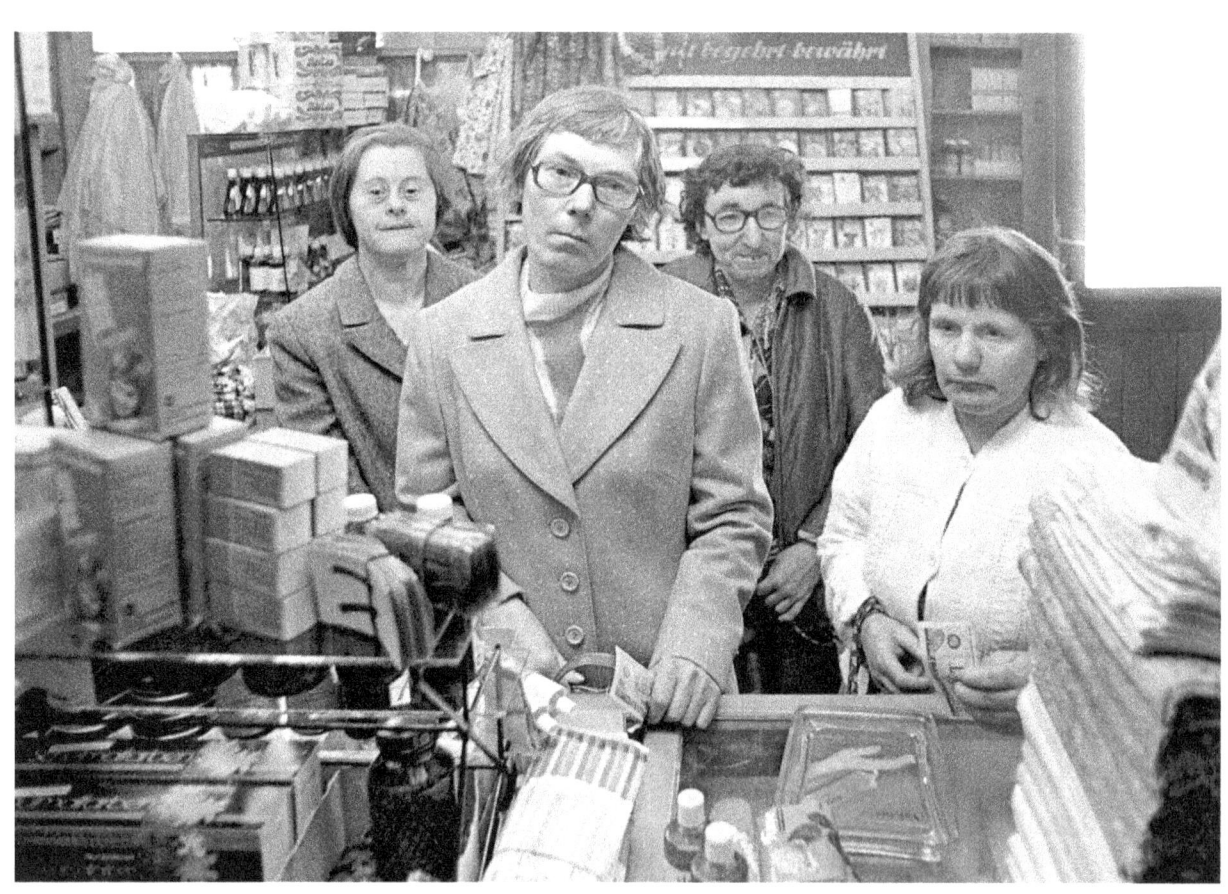

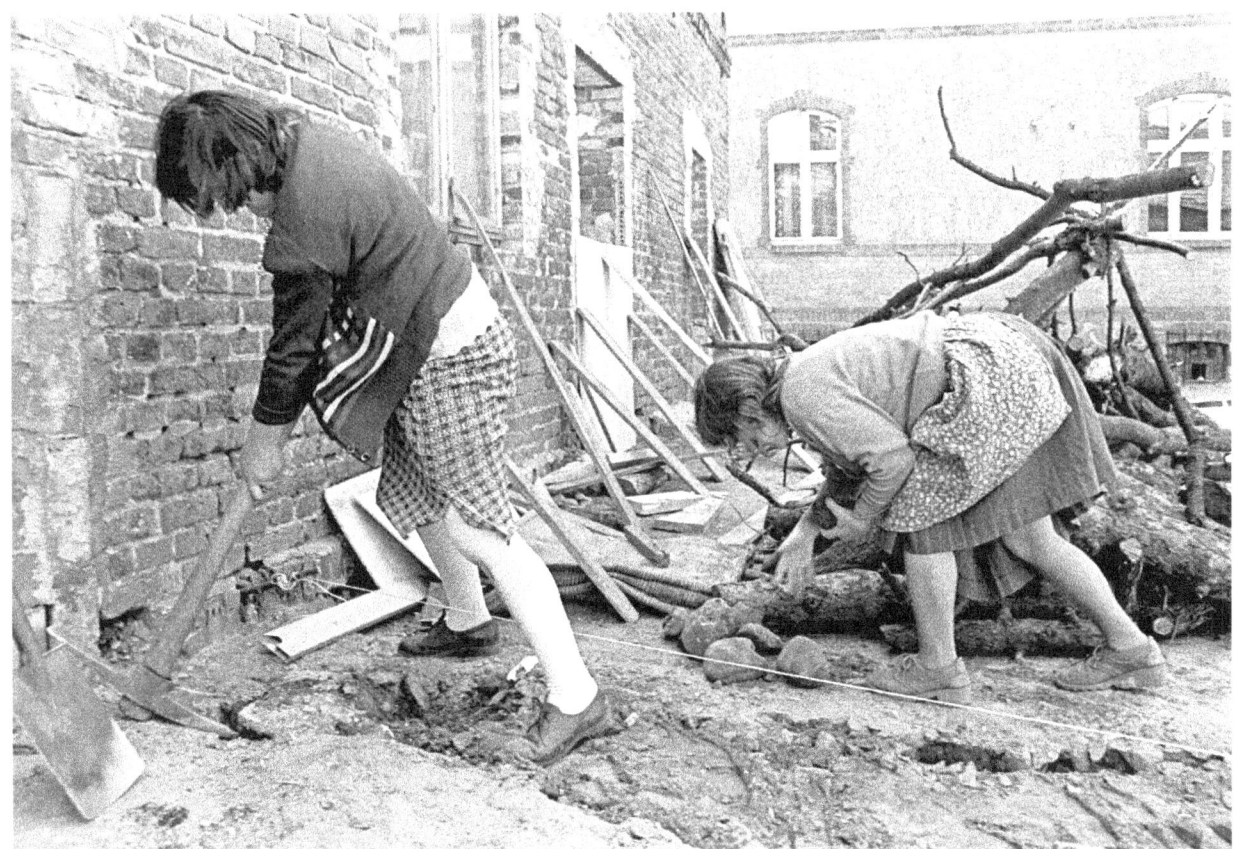

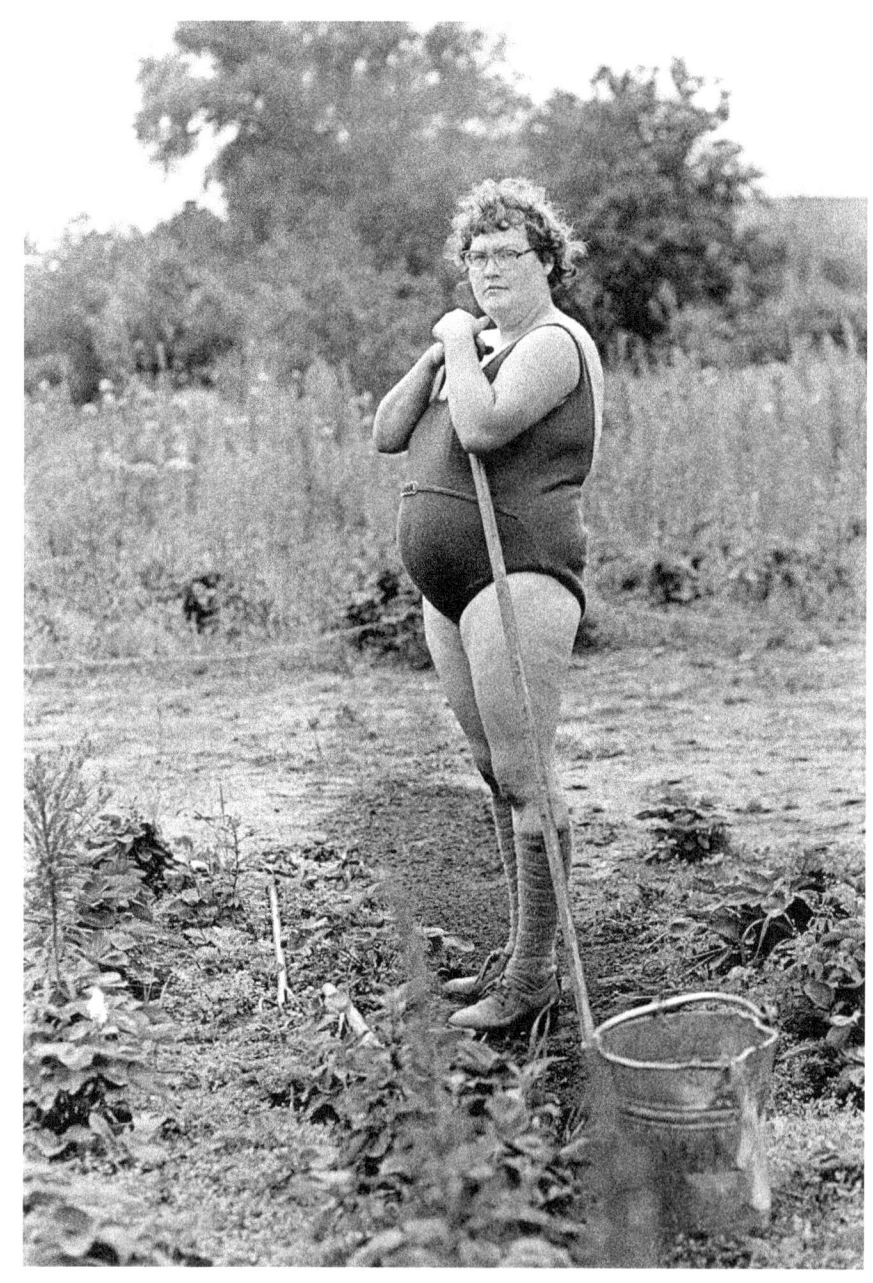

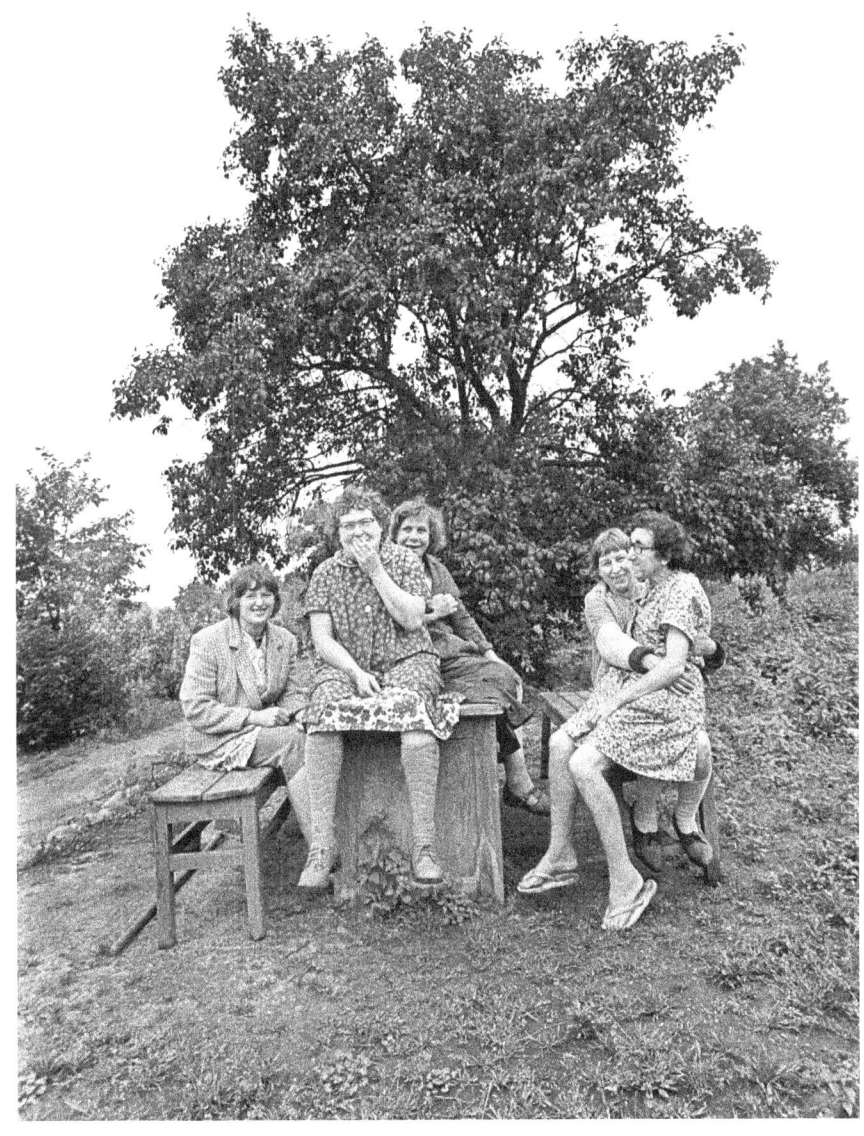

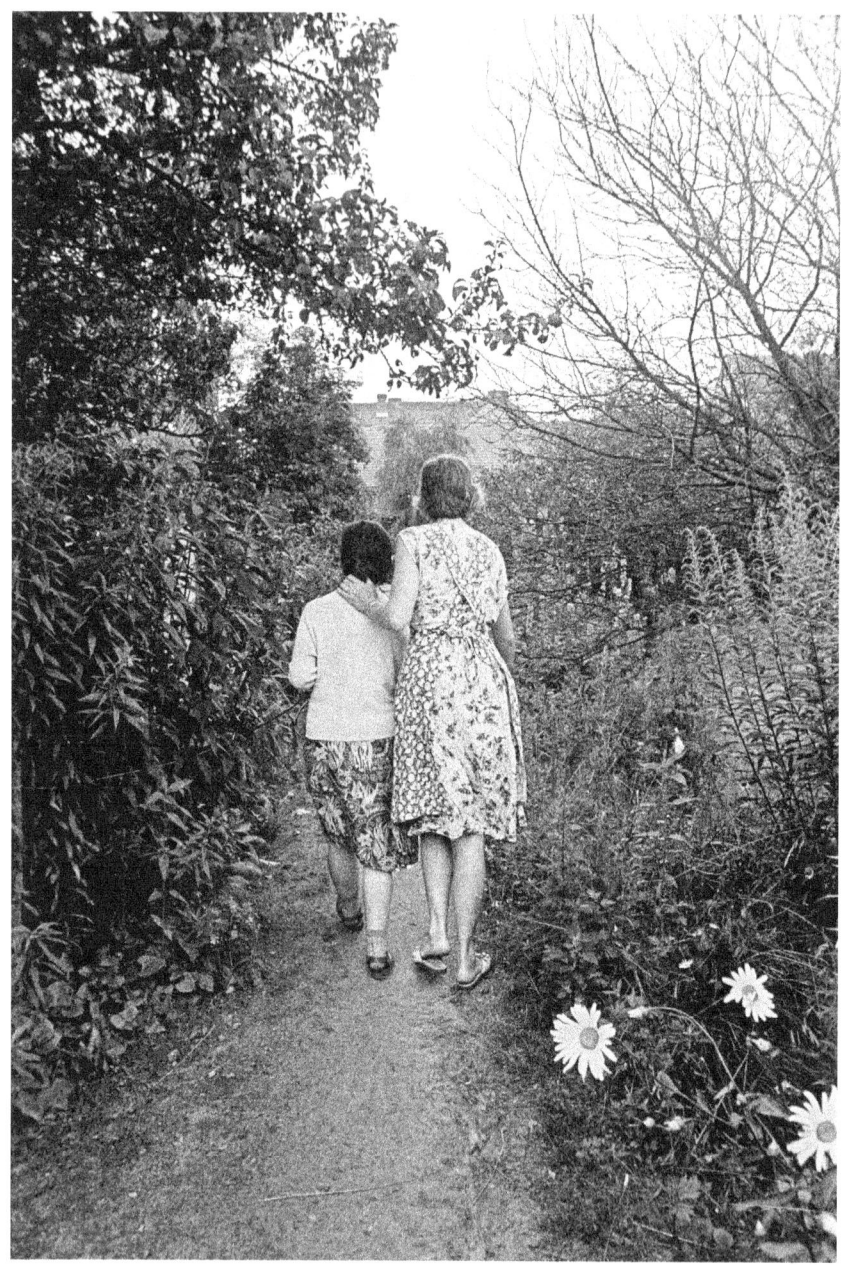

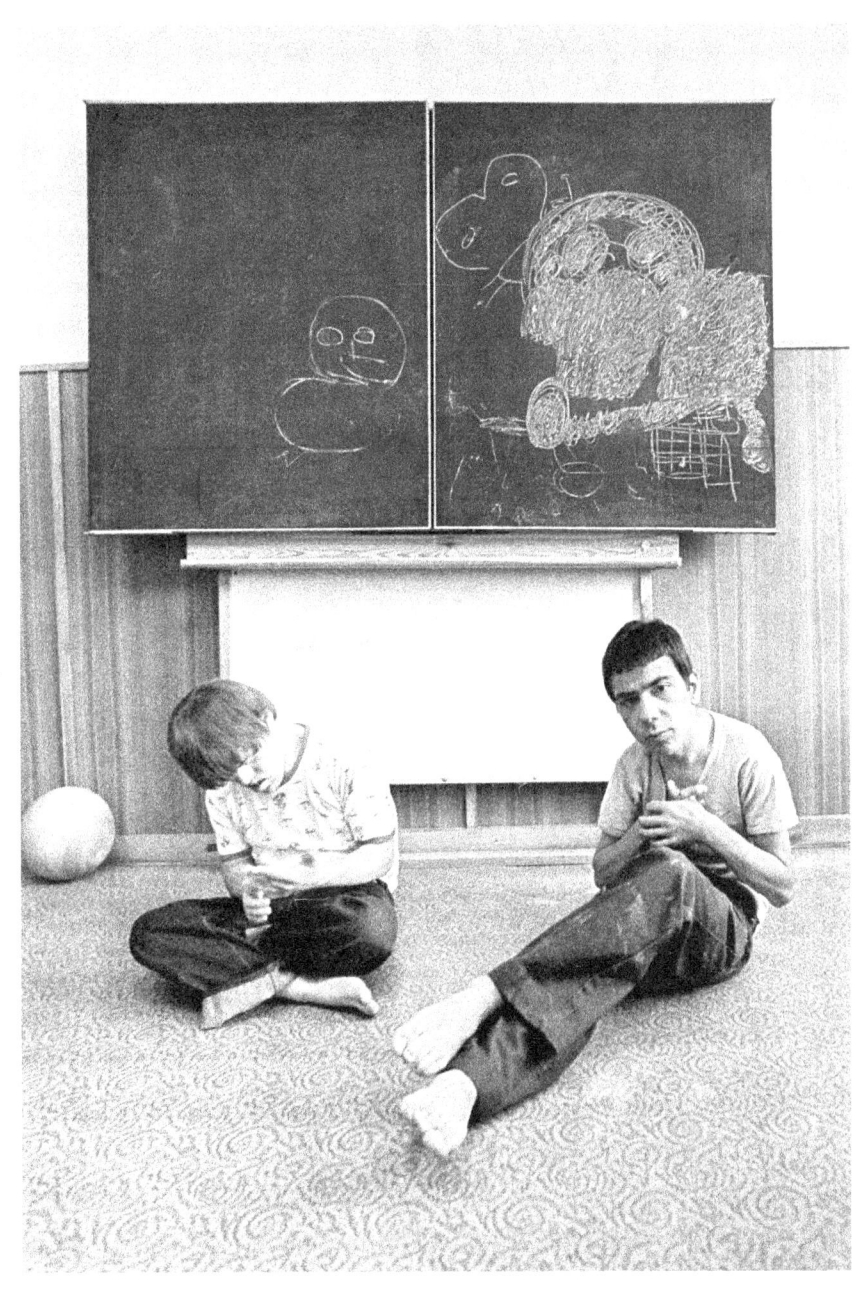

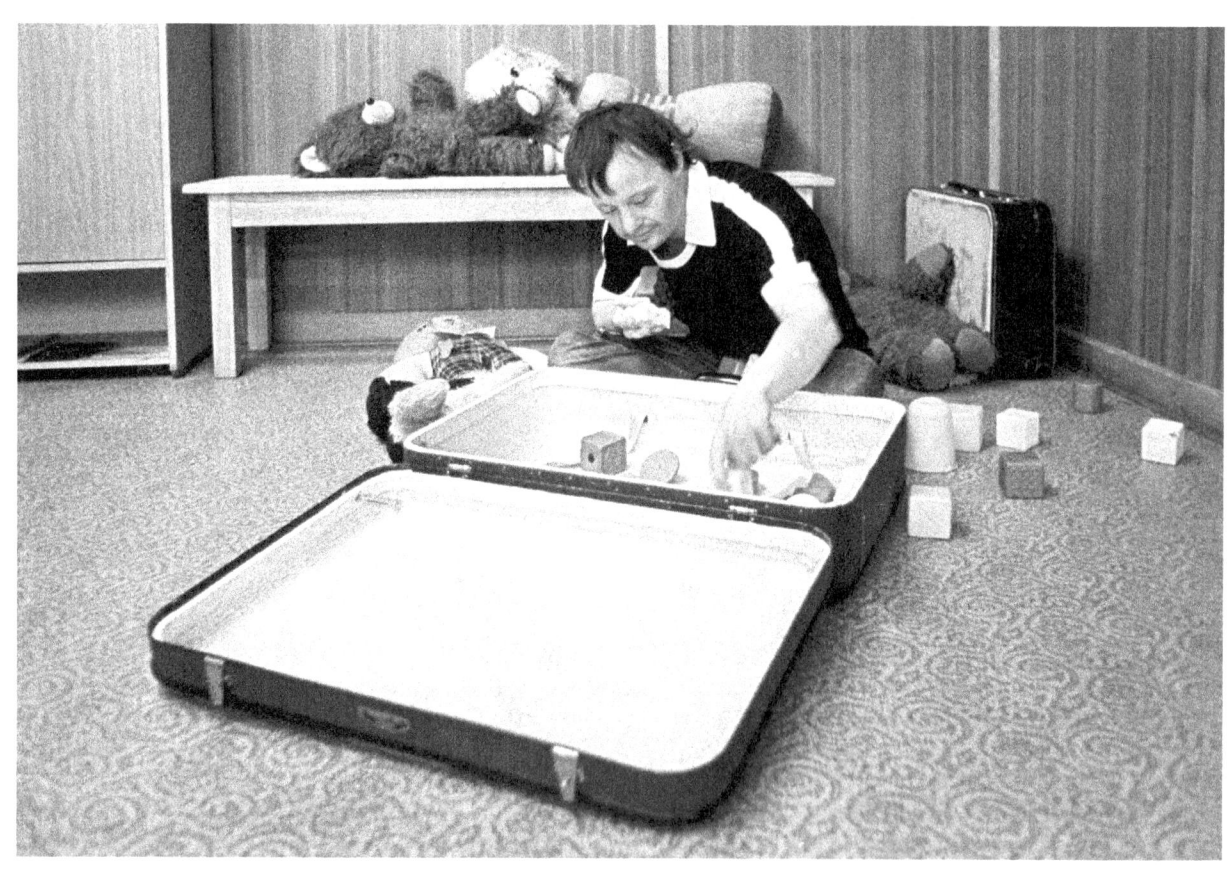

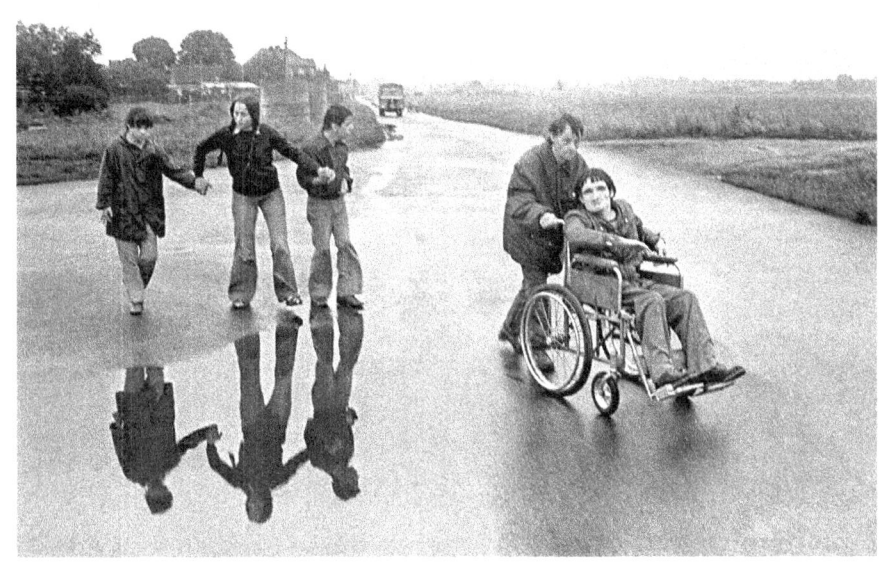

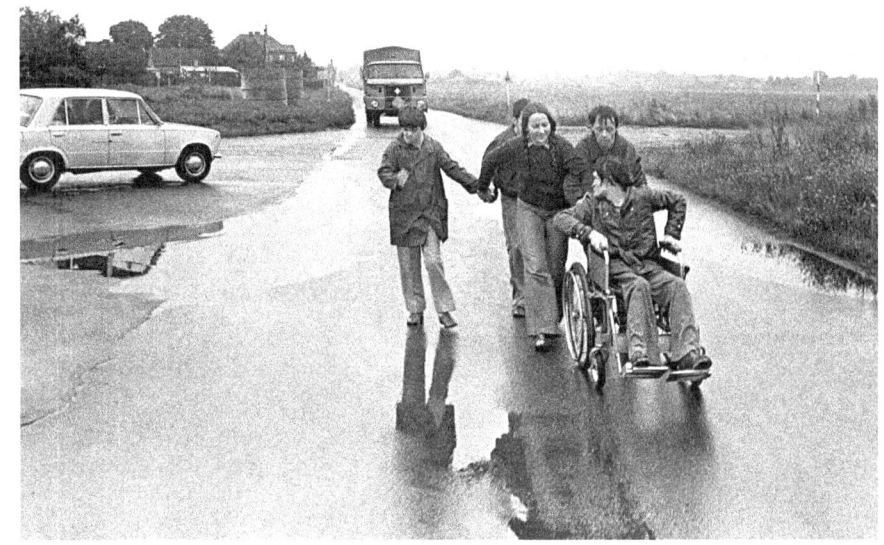

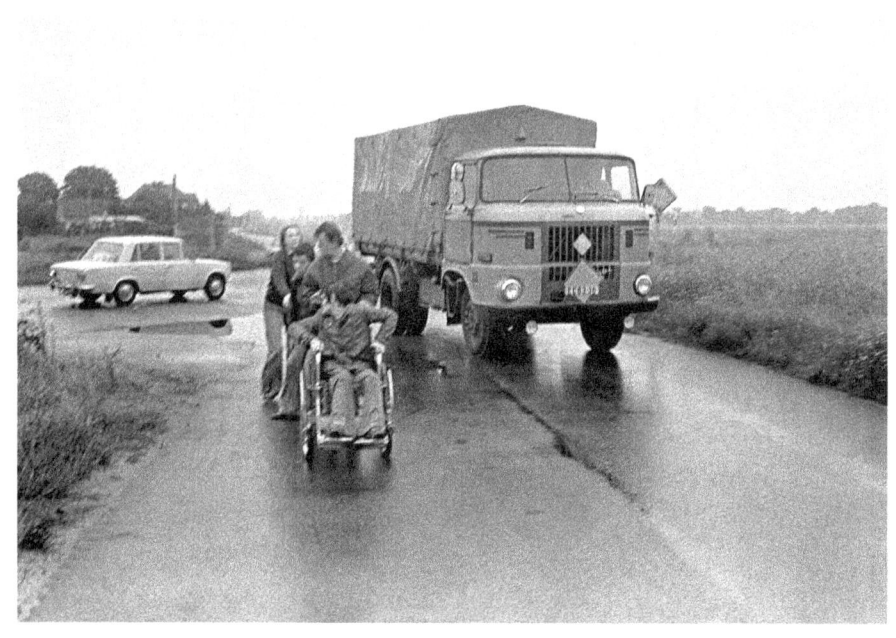

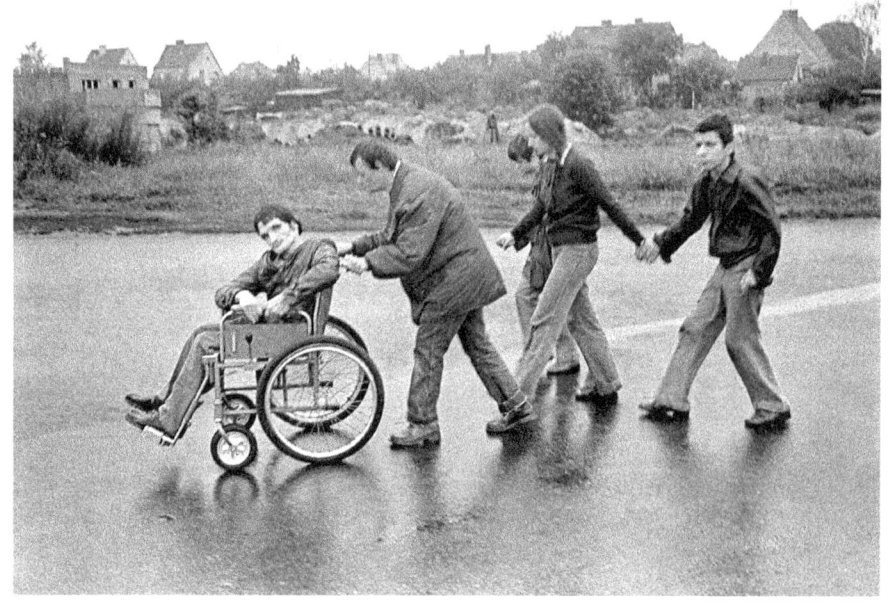

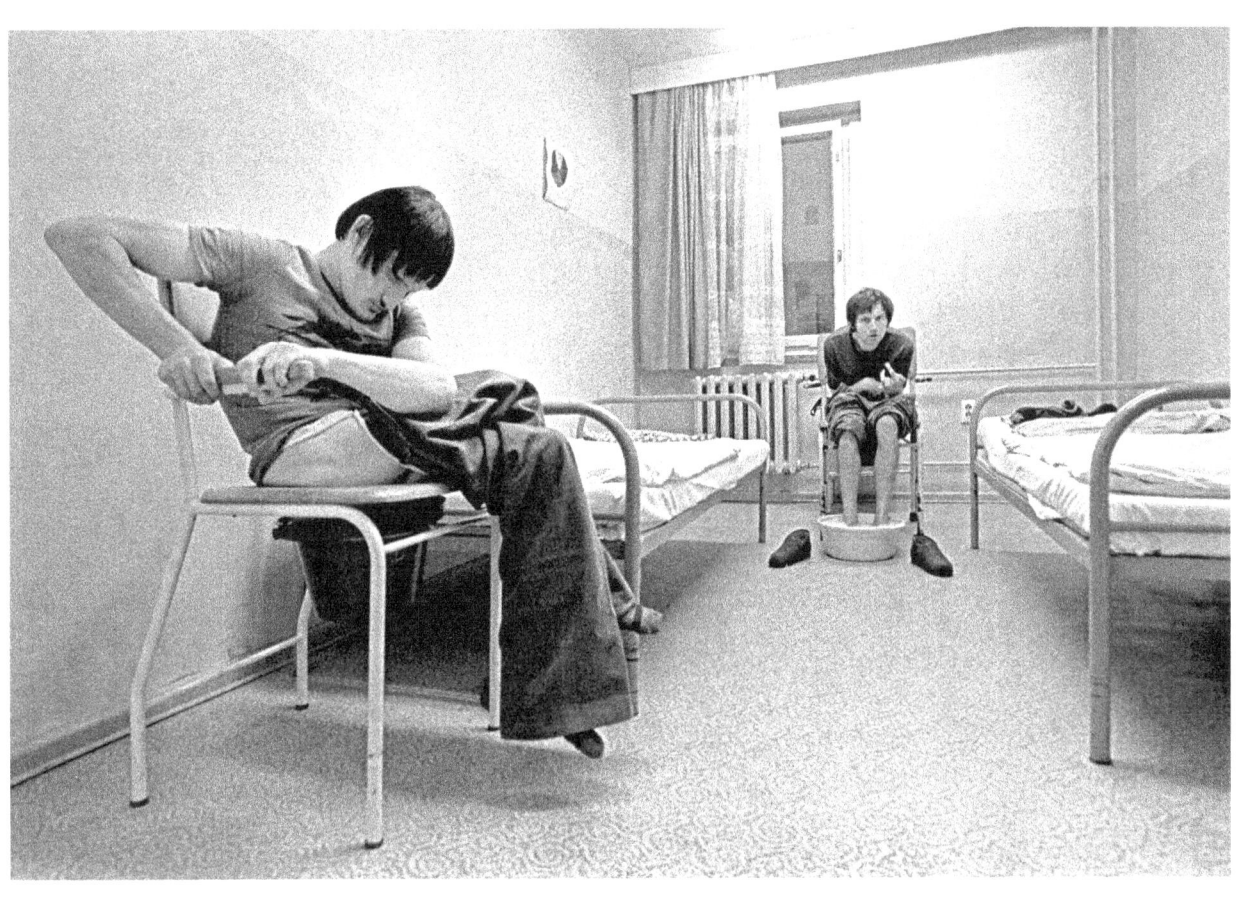

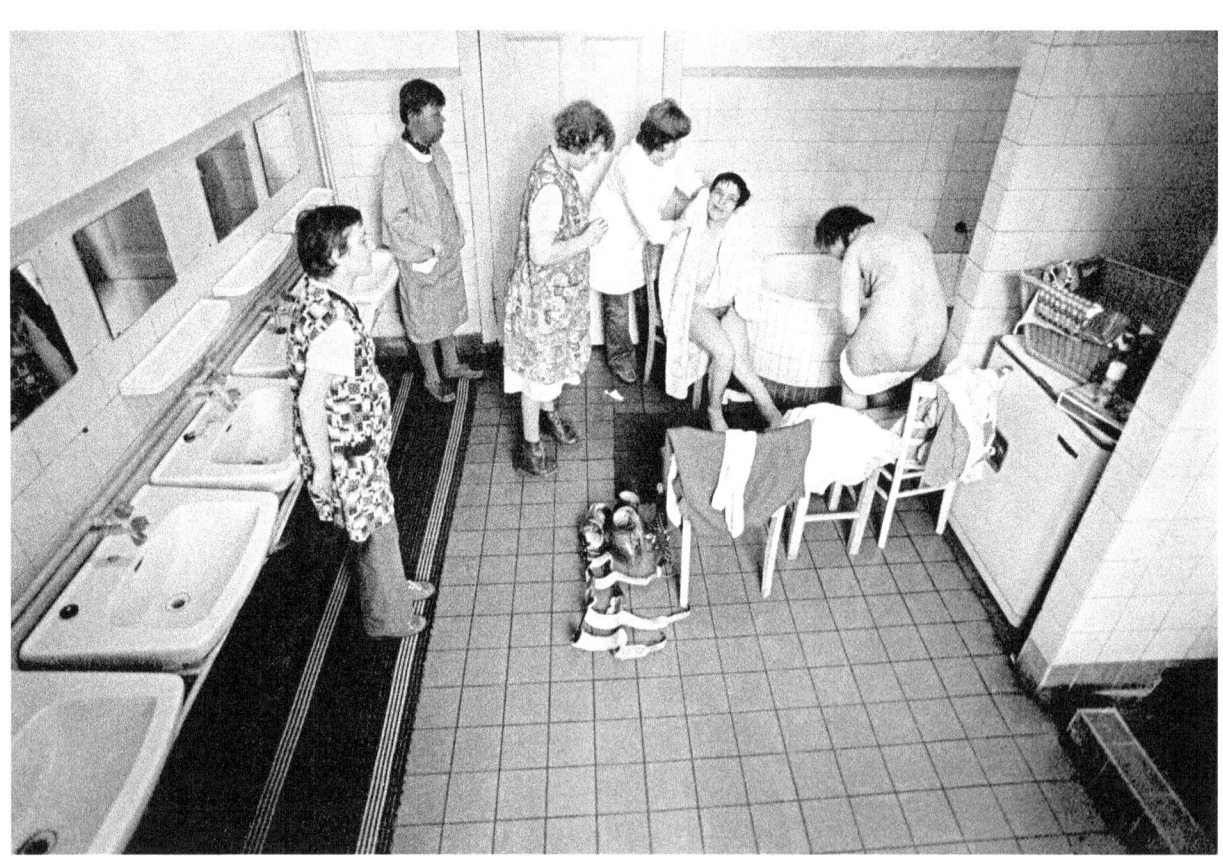

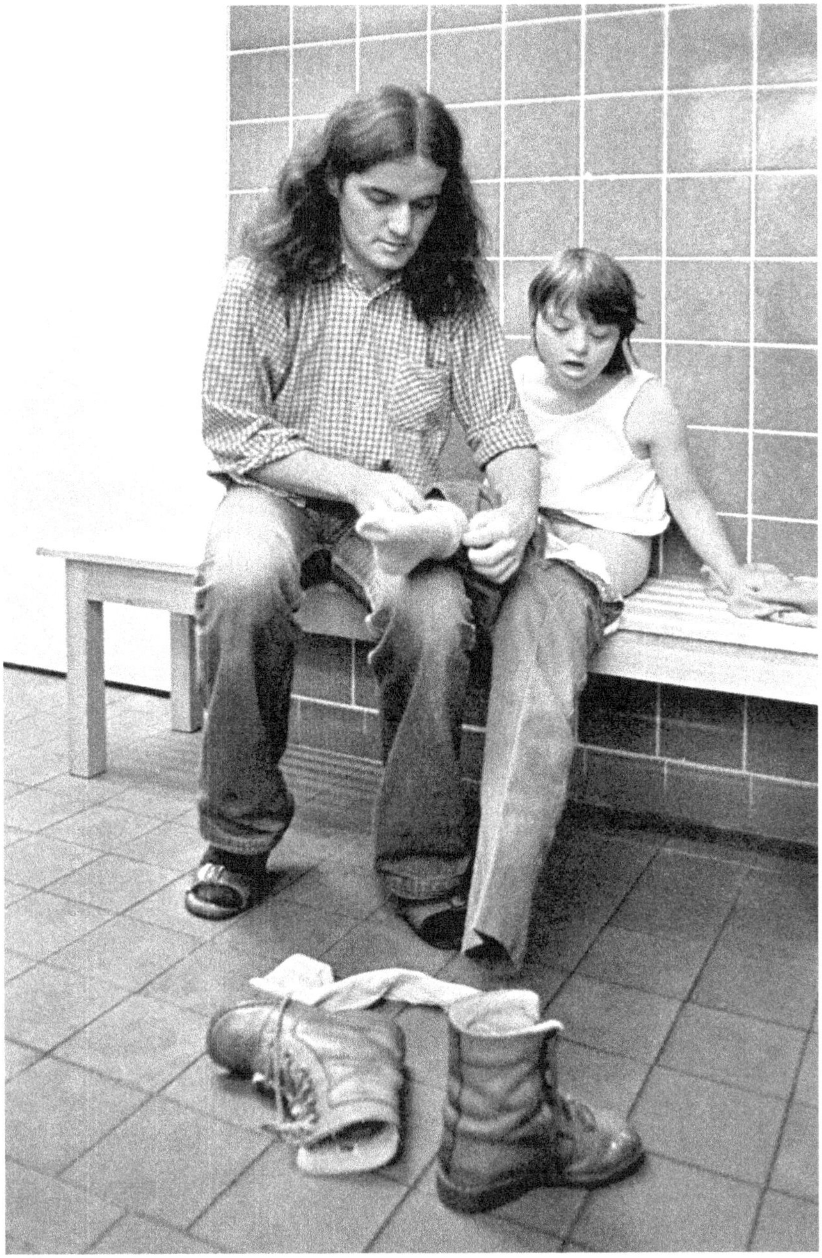

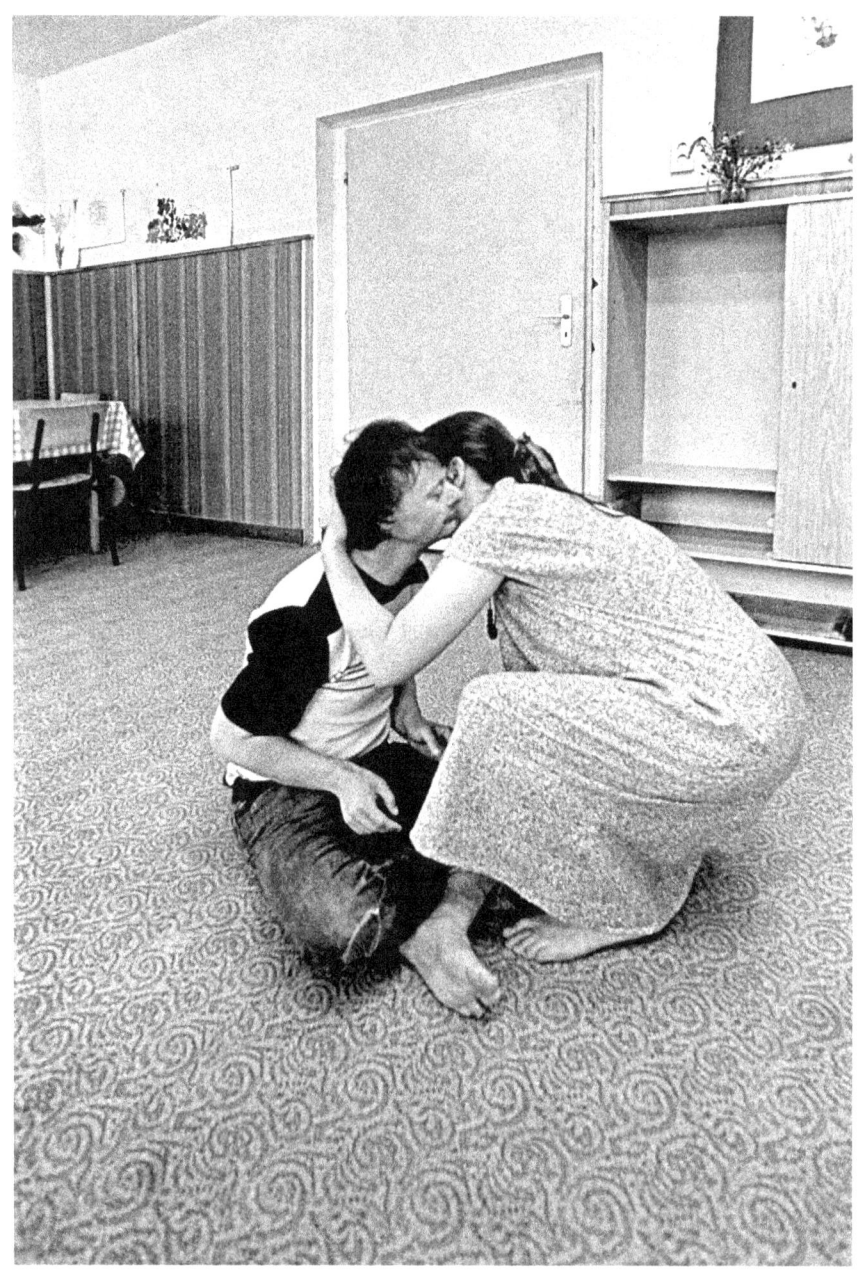

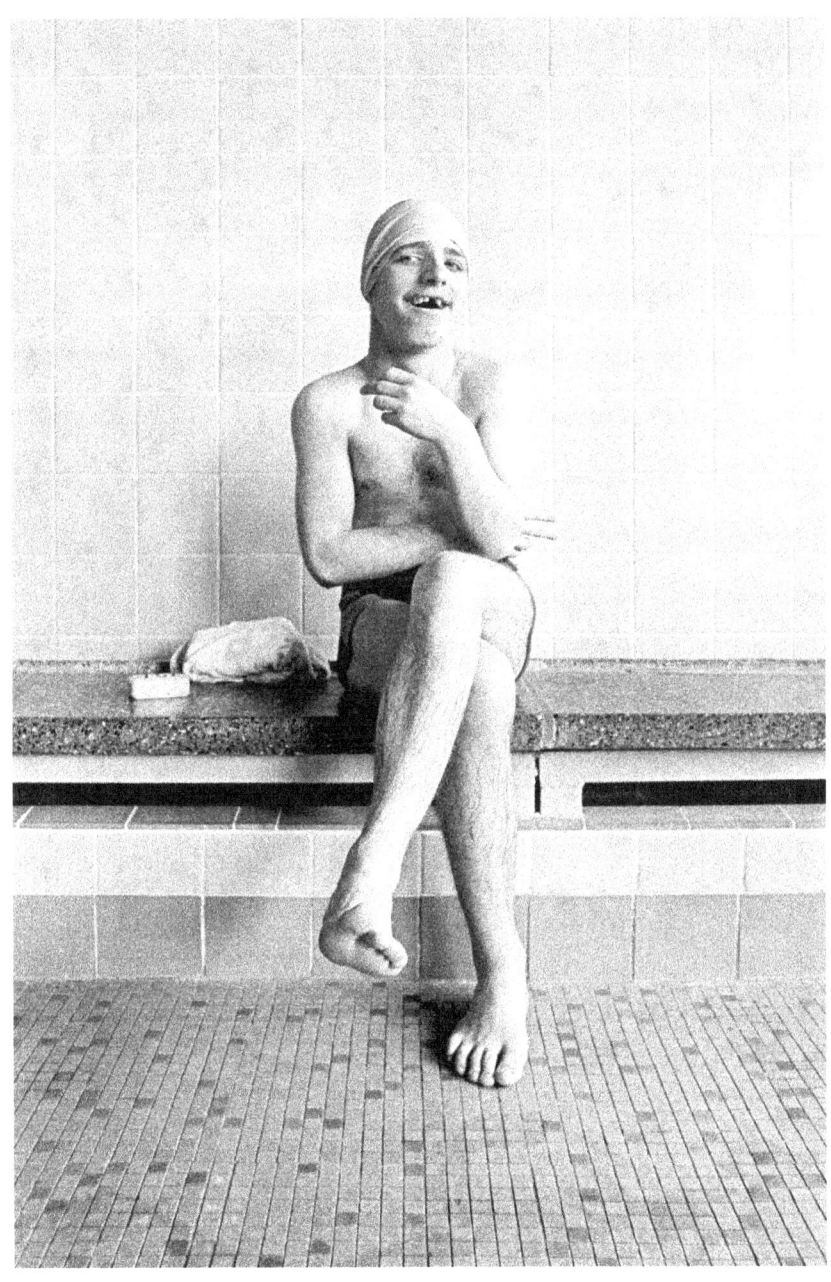

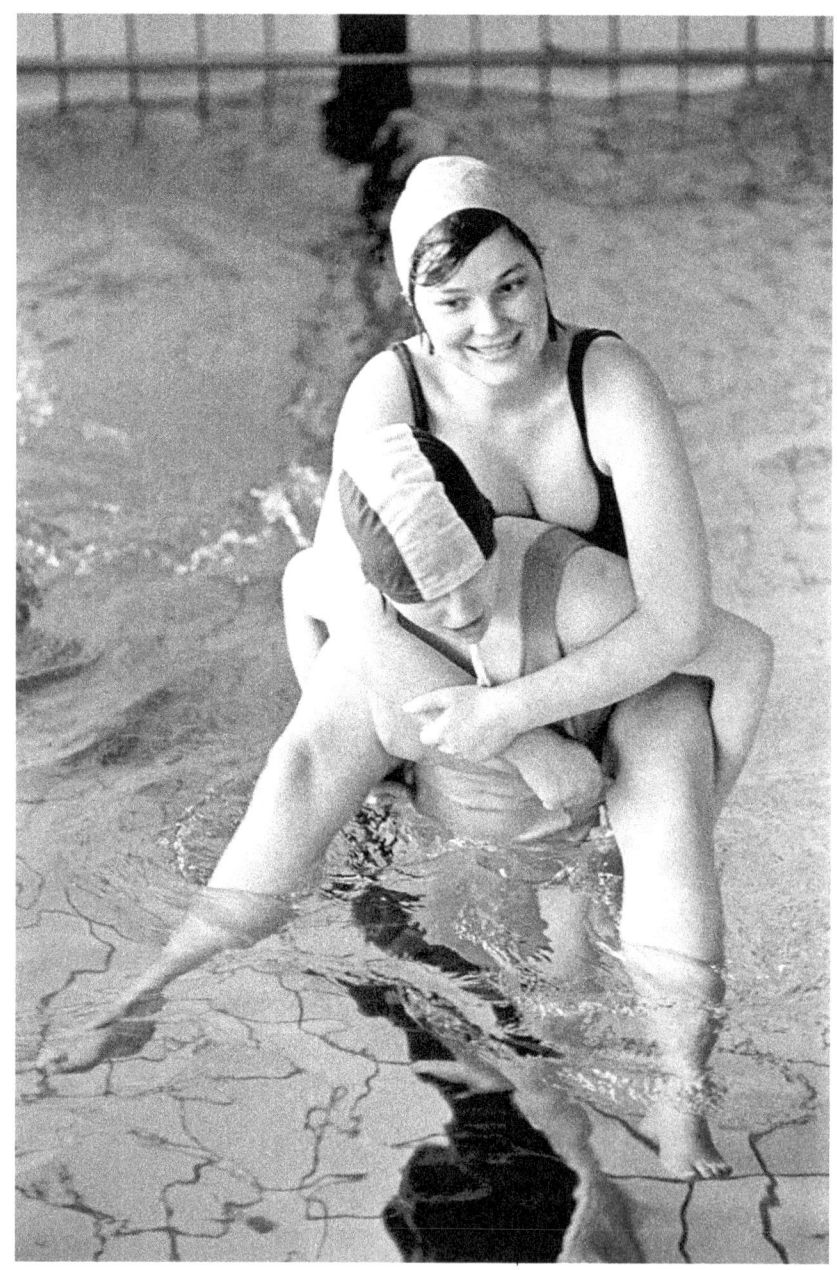

WHAT KIND OF ISLAND IN WHAT KIND OF SEA

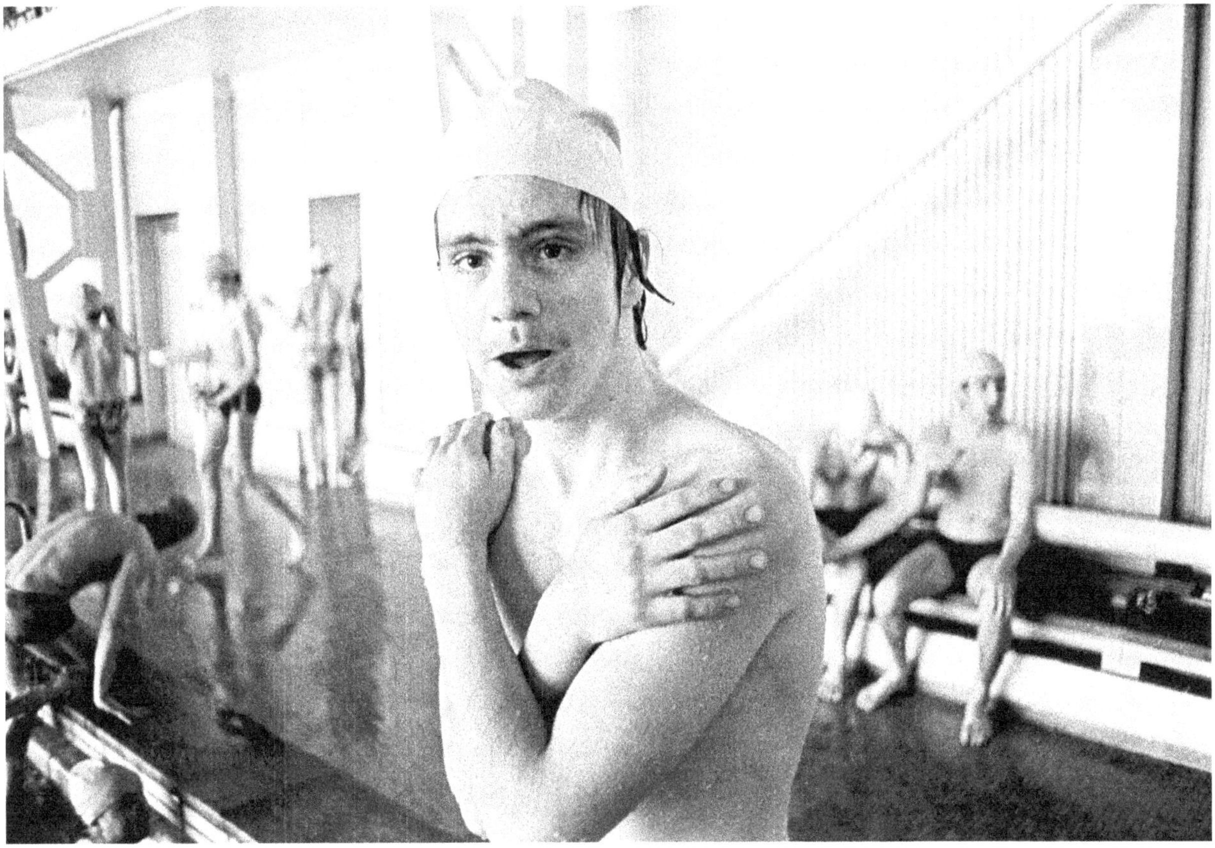

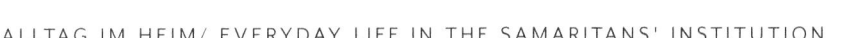

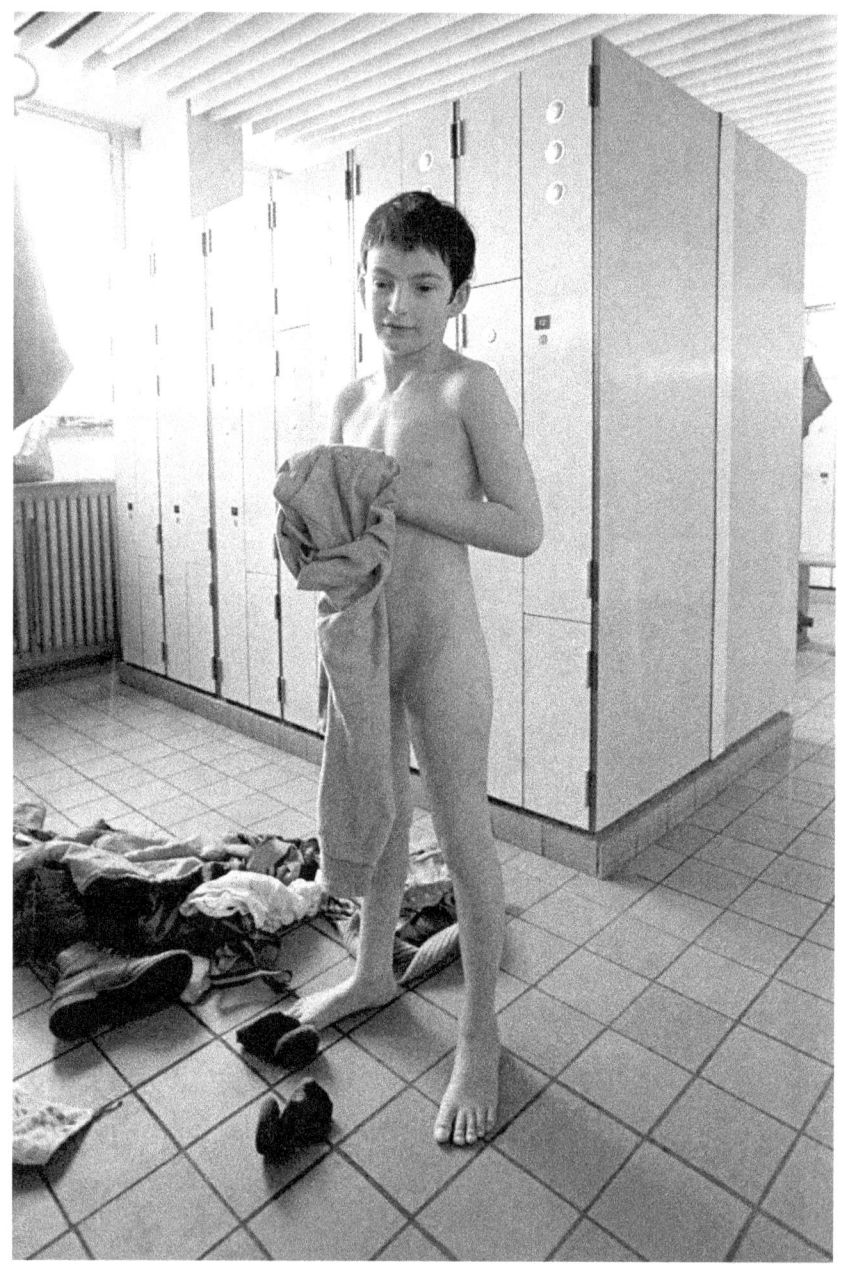

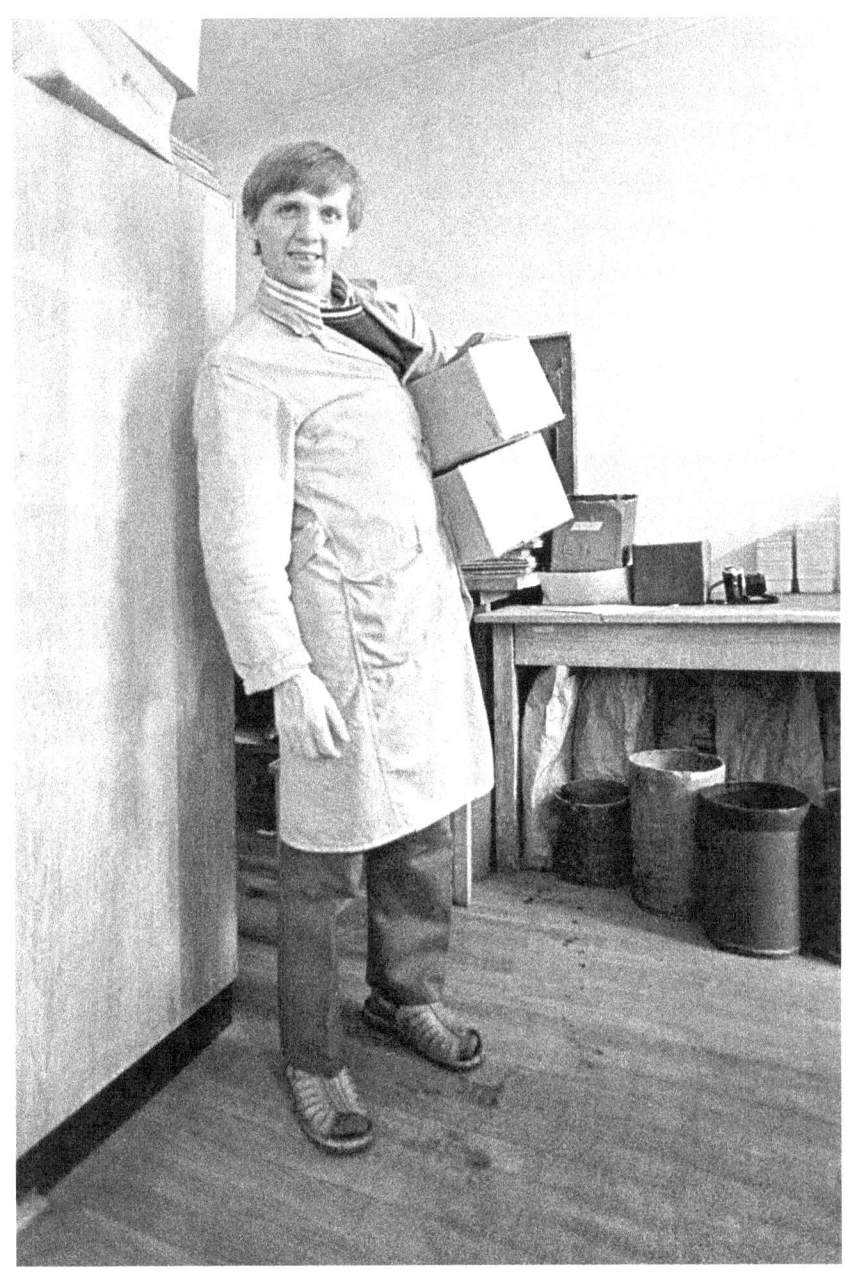

ARBEIT ALS THERAPIE / WORK AS THERAPY

Photographs by Dietmar Riemann

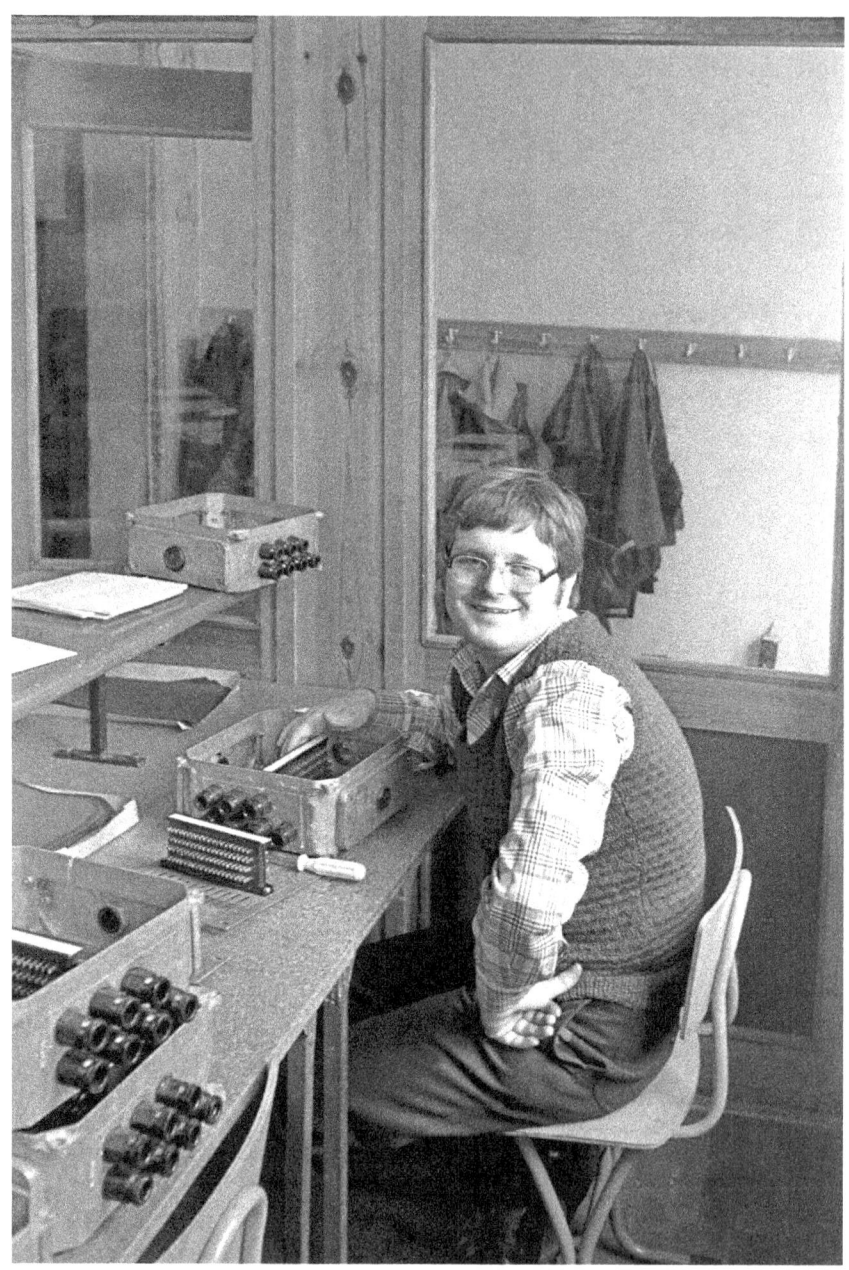

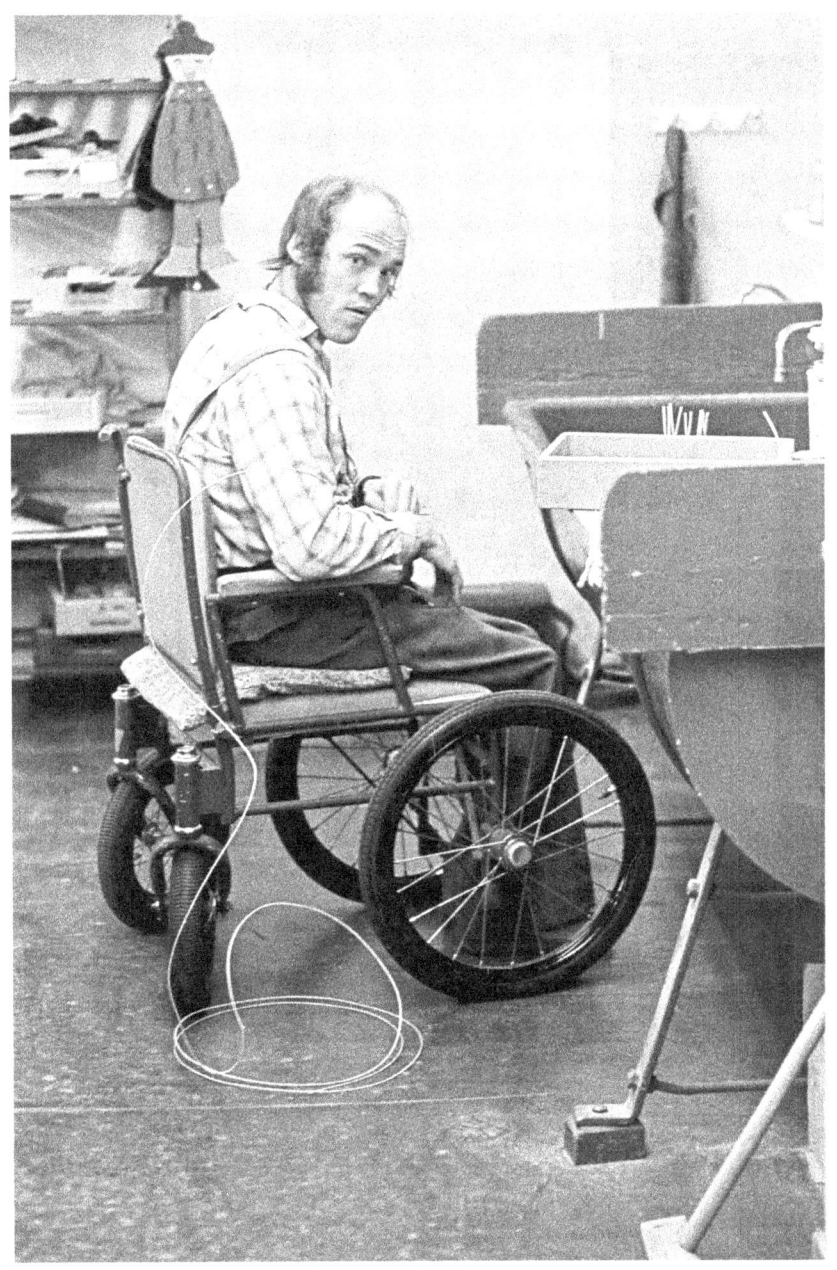

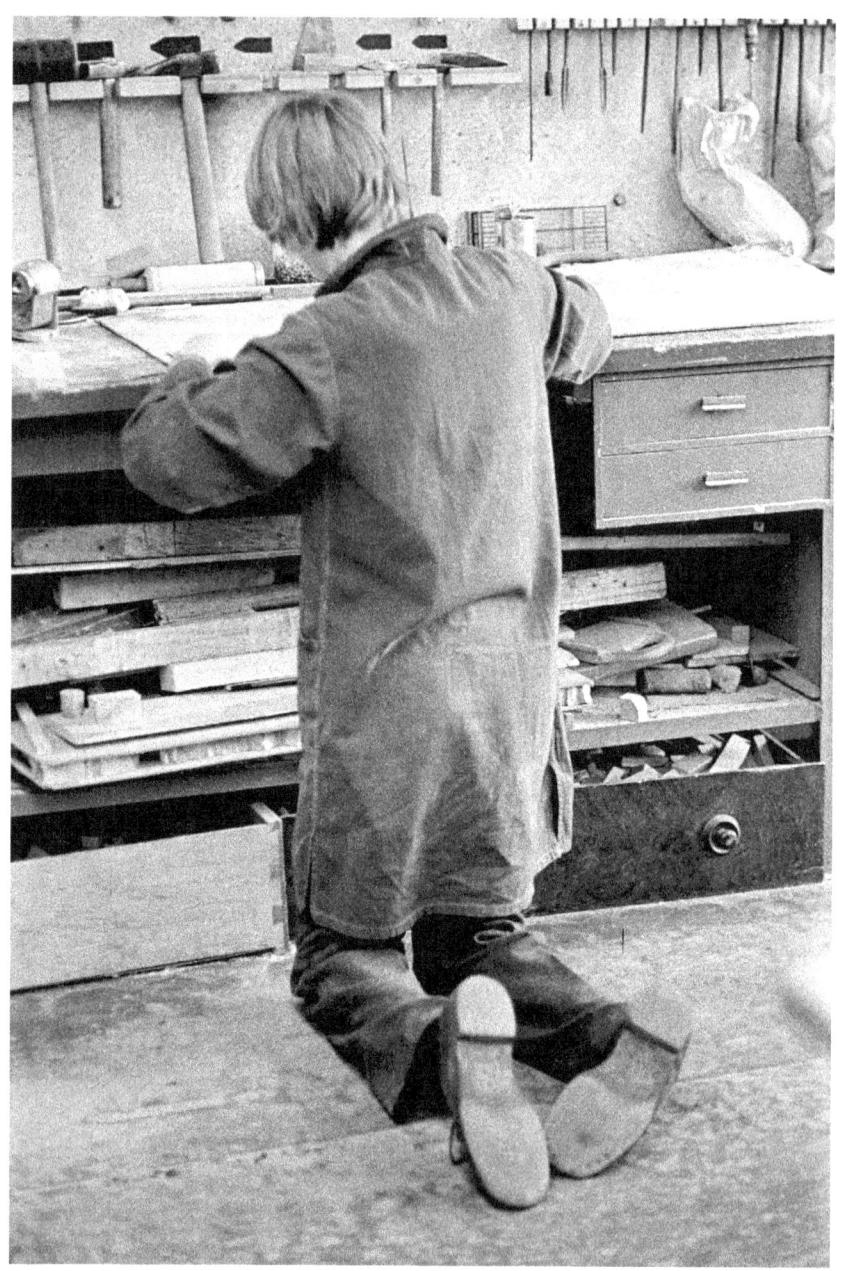

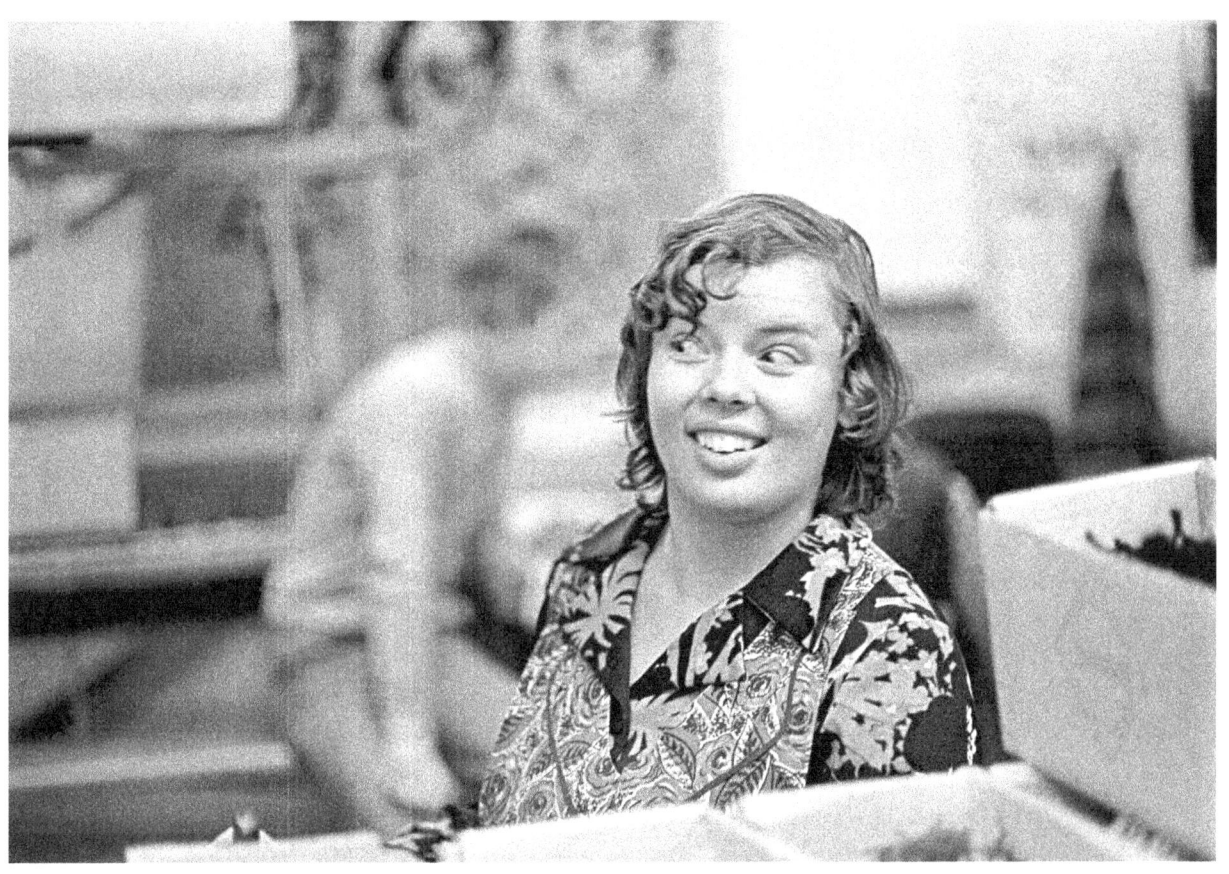

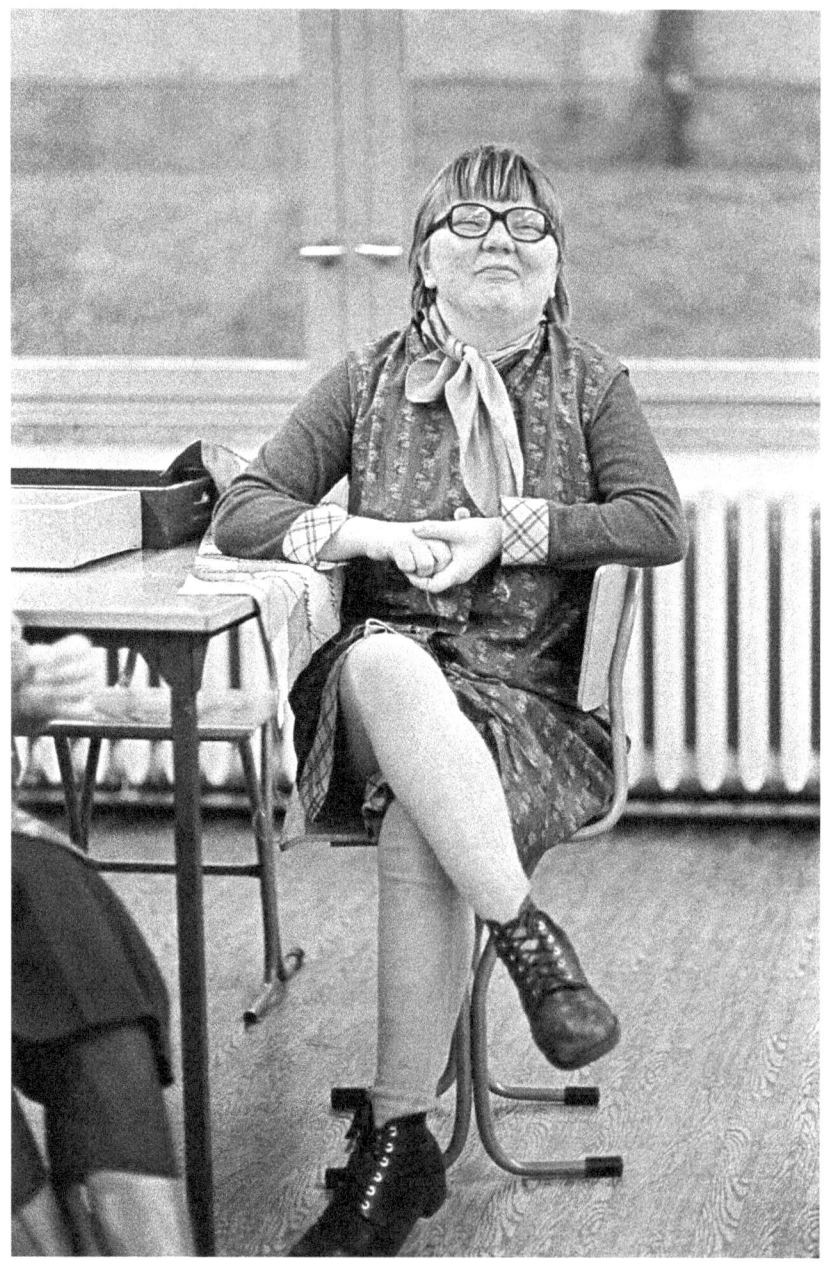

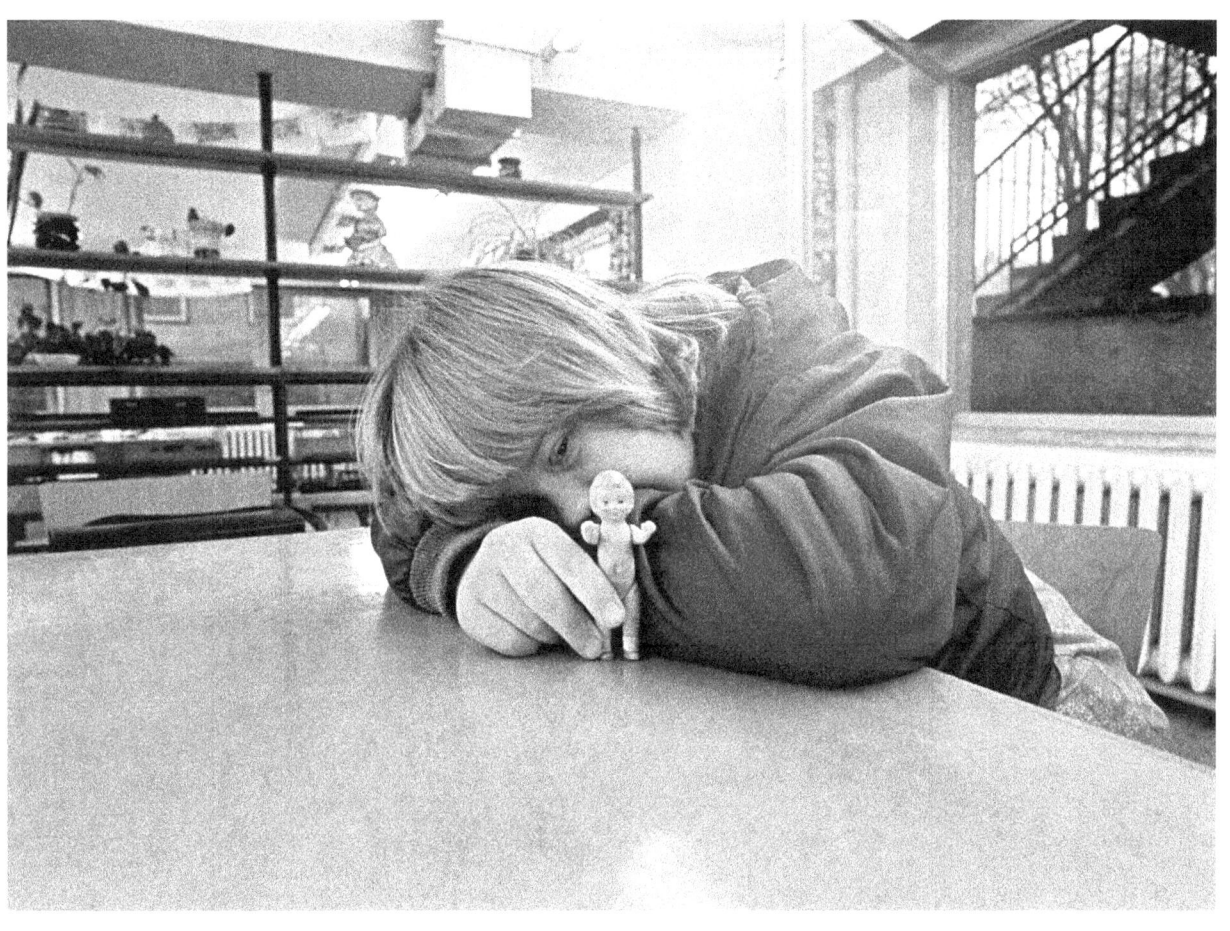

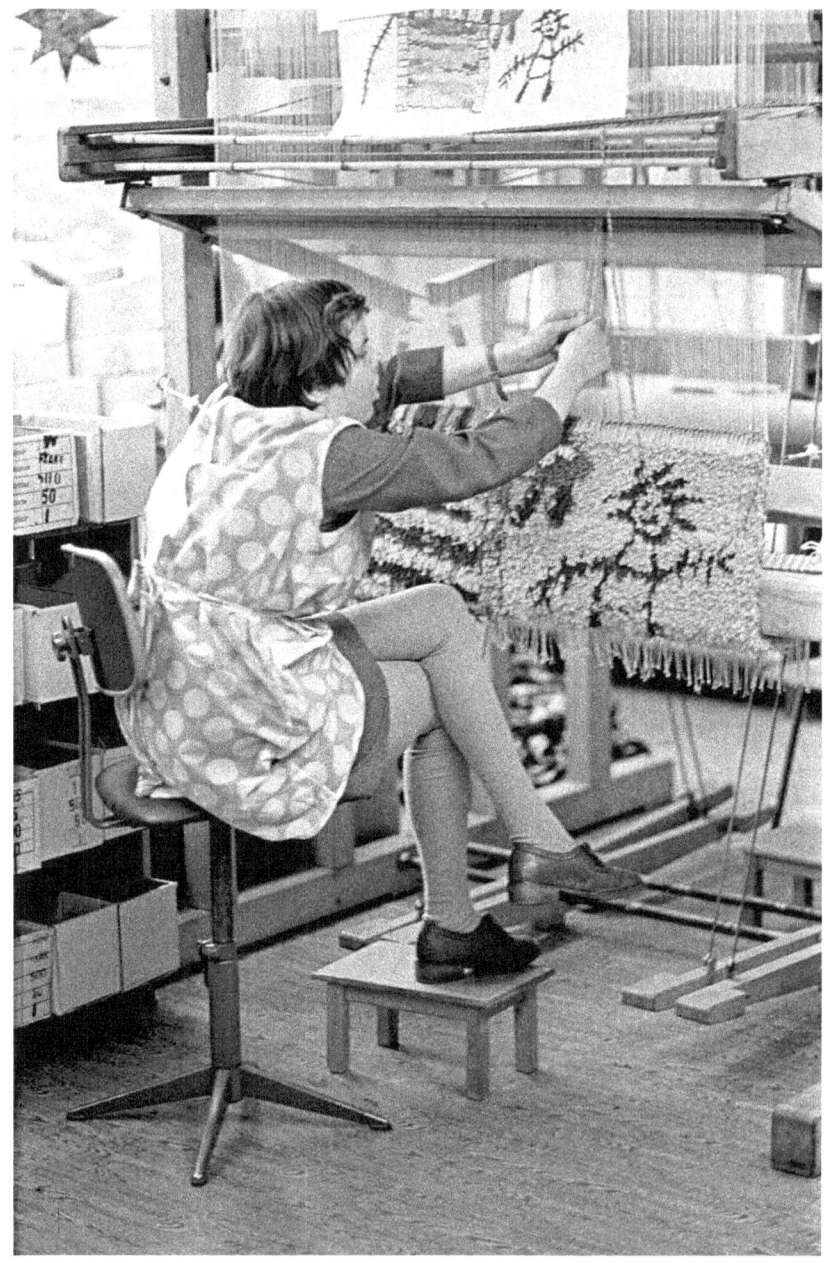

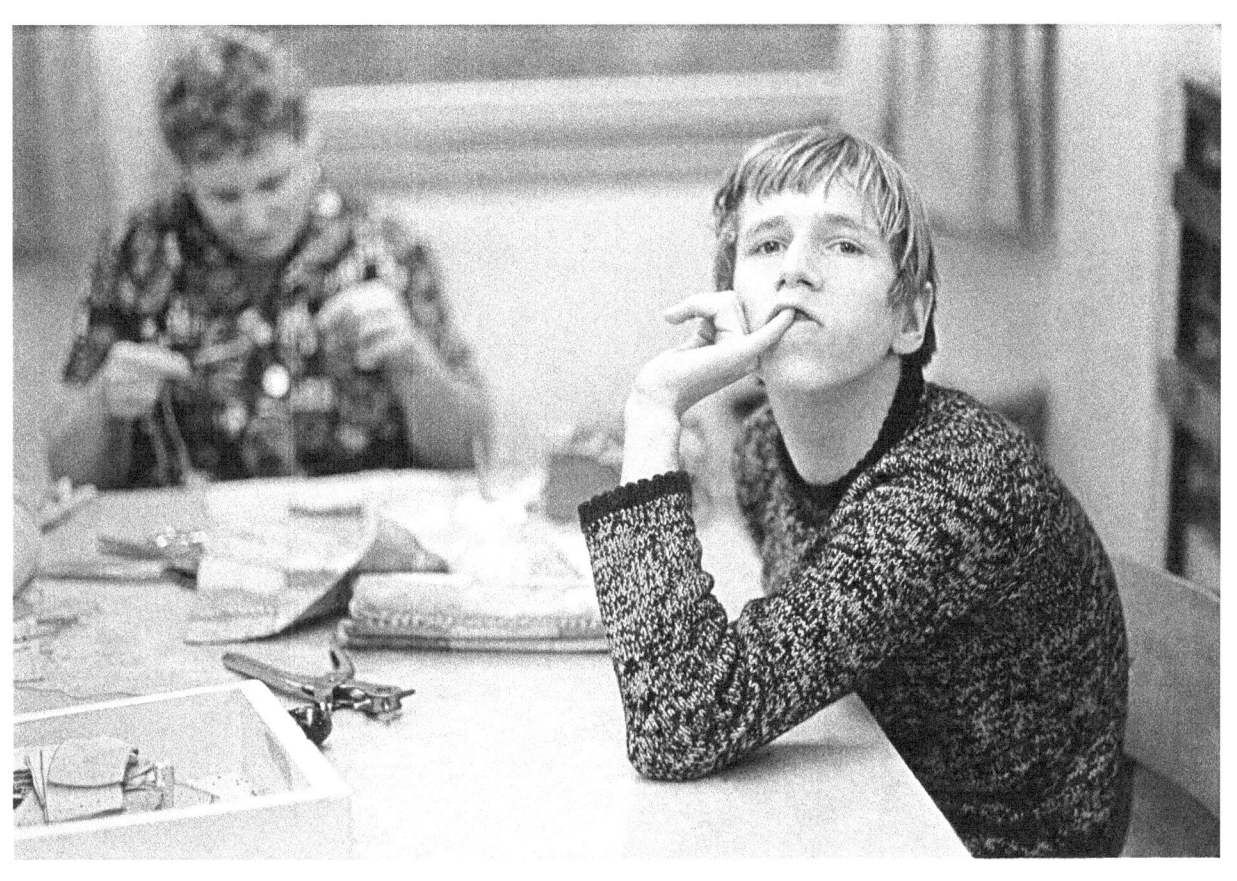

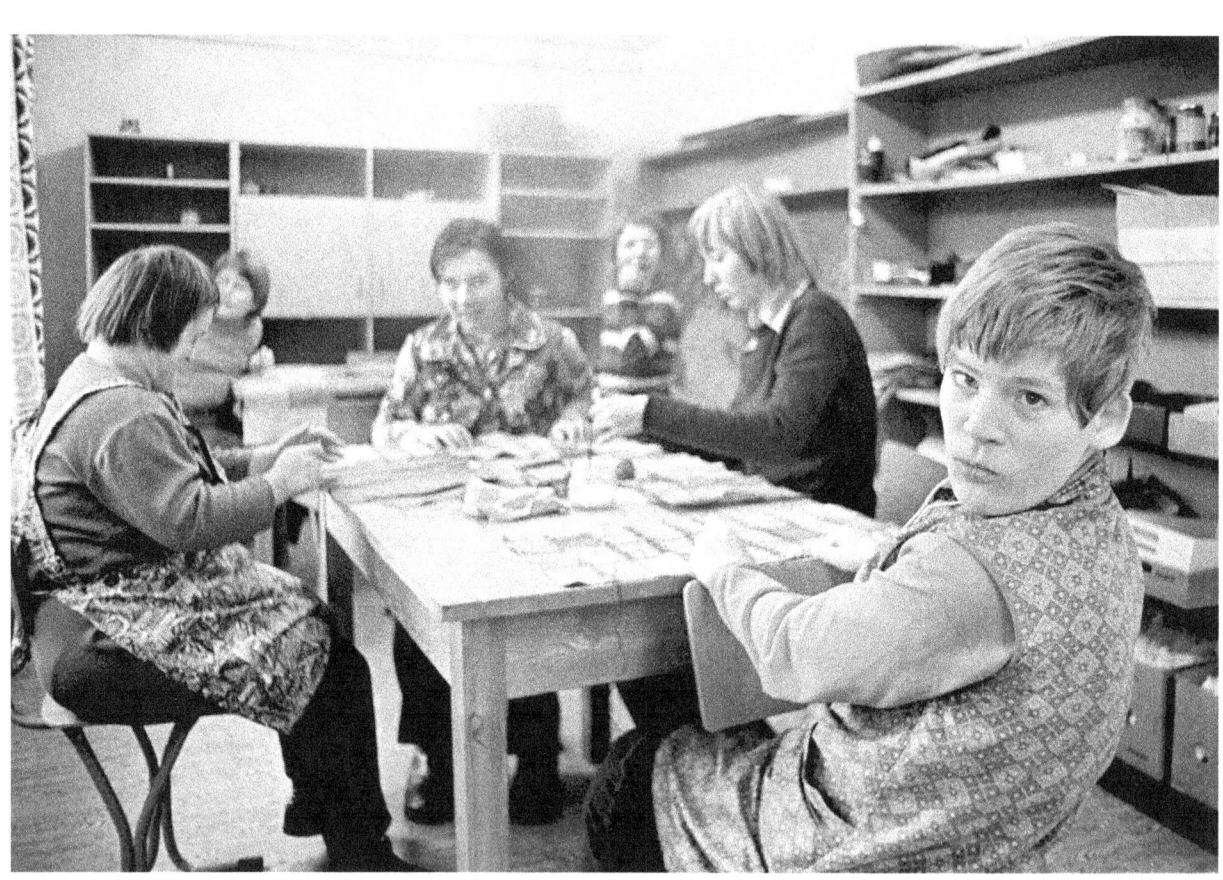

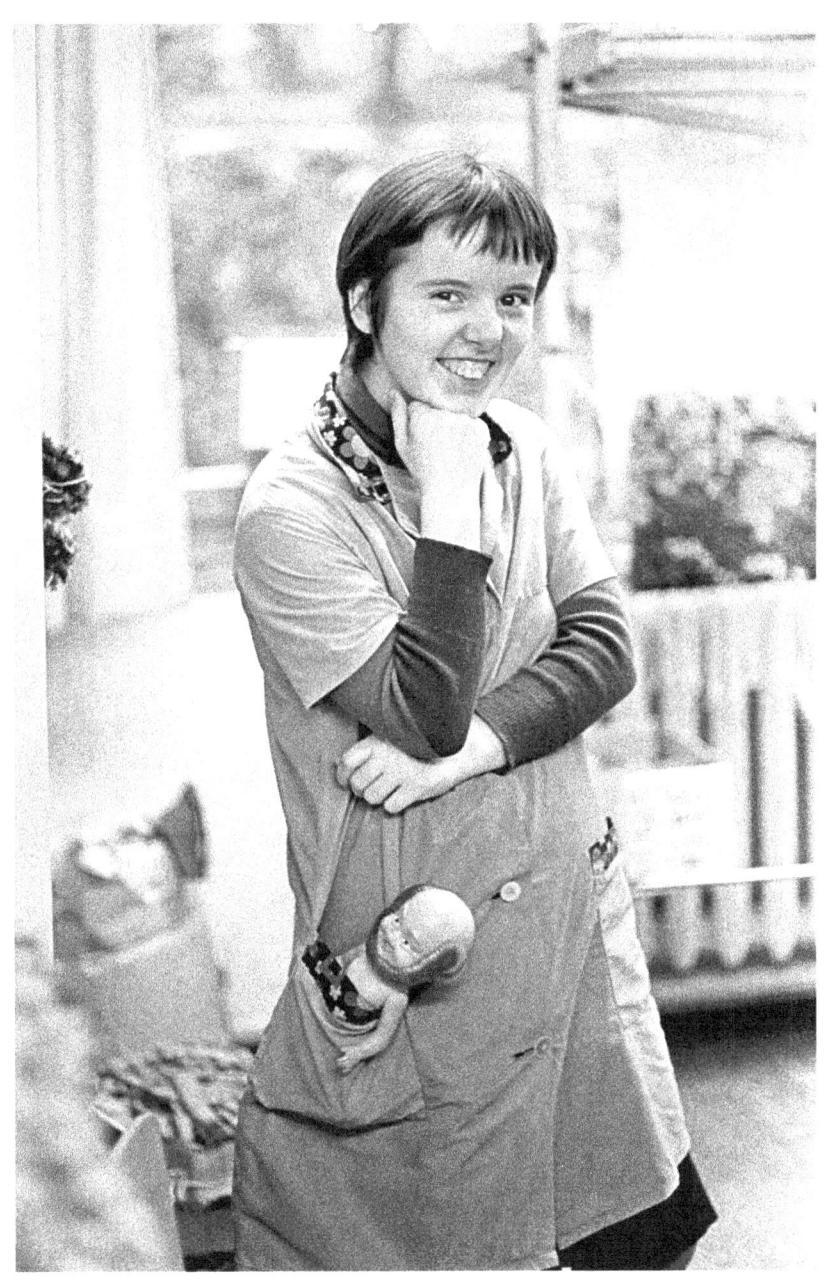

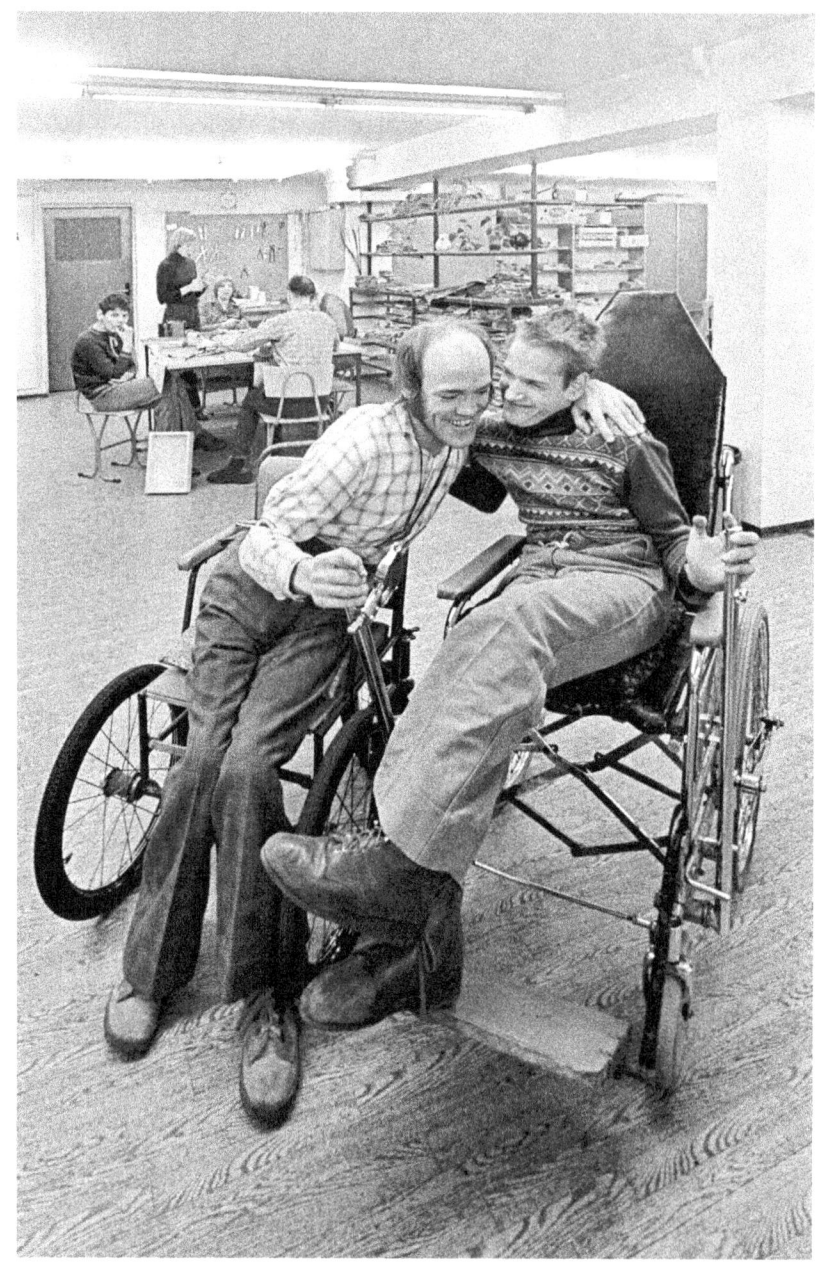

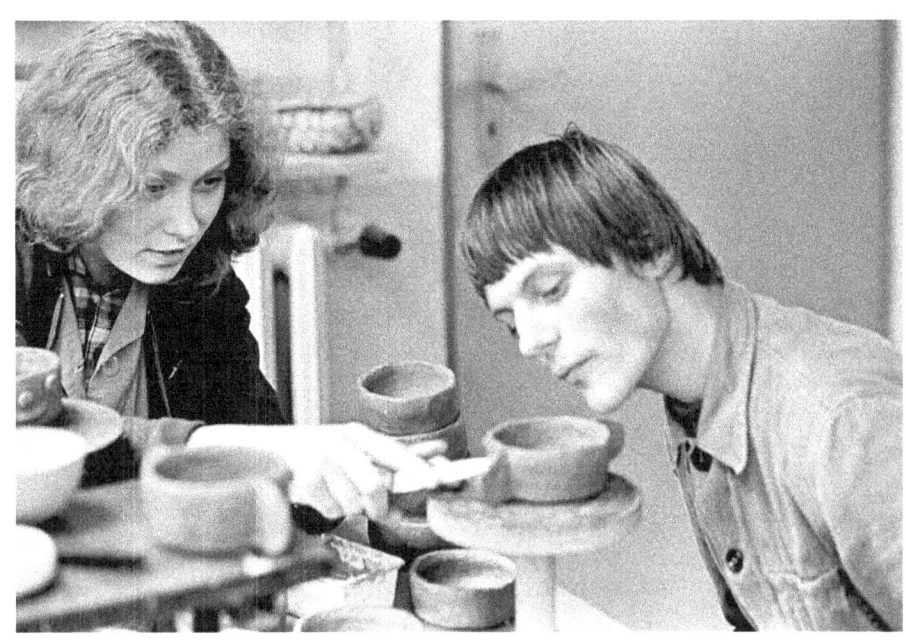

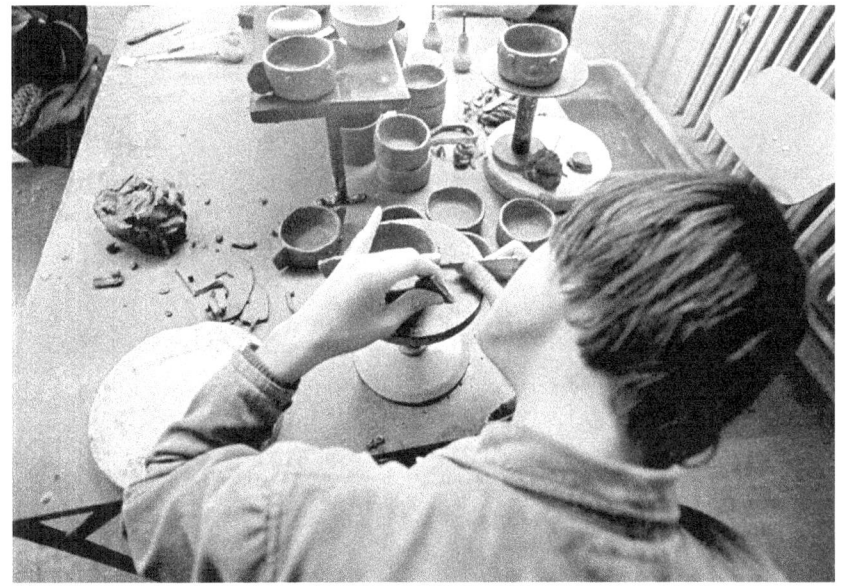

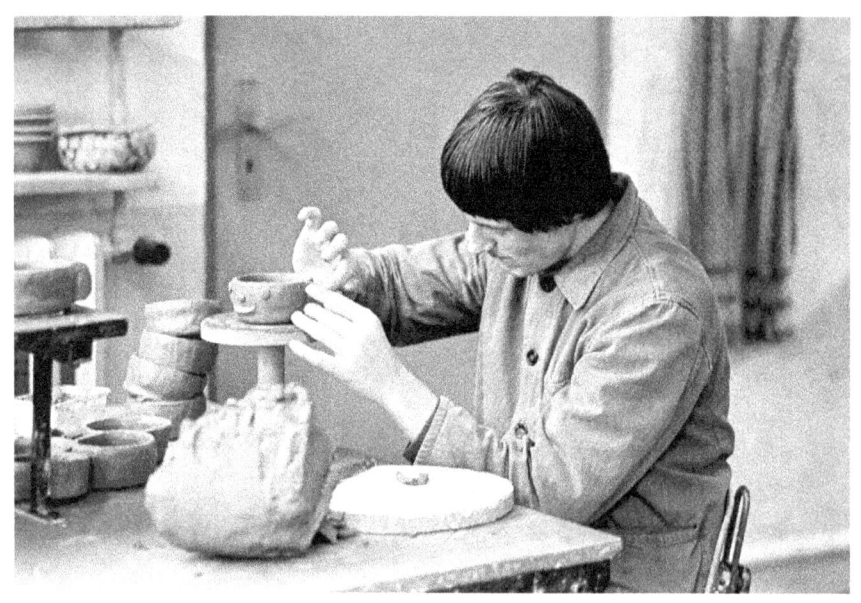

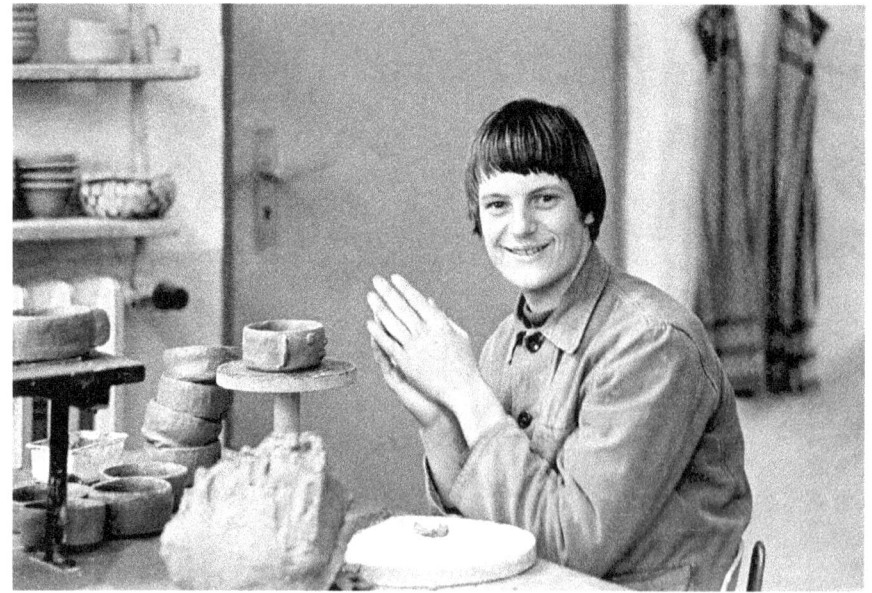

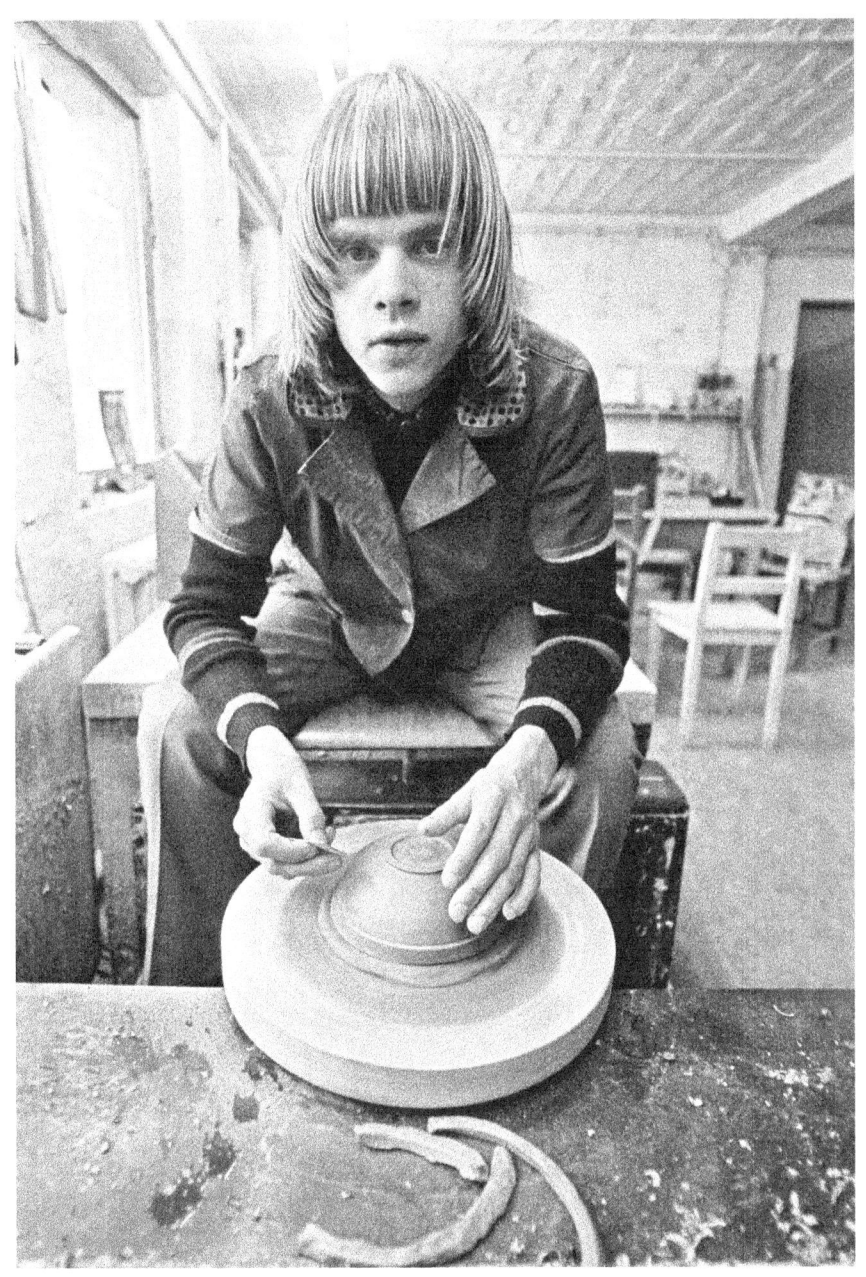

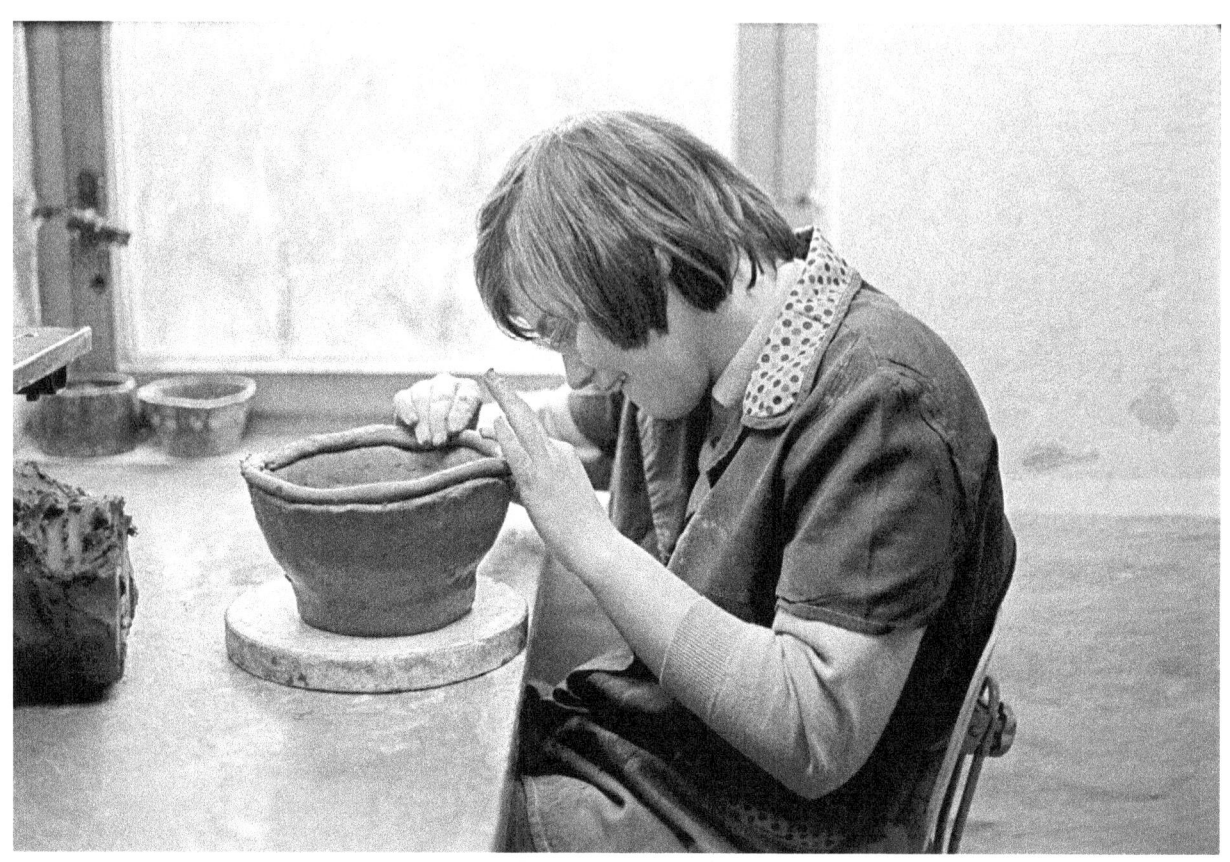

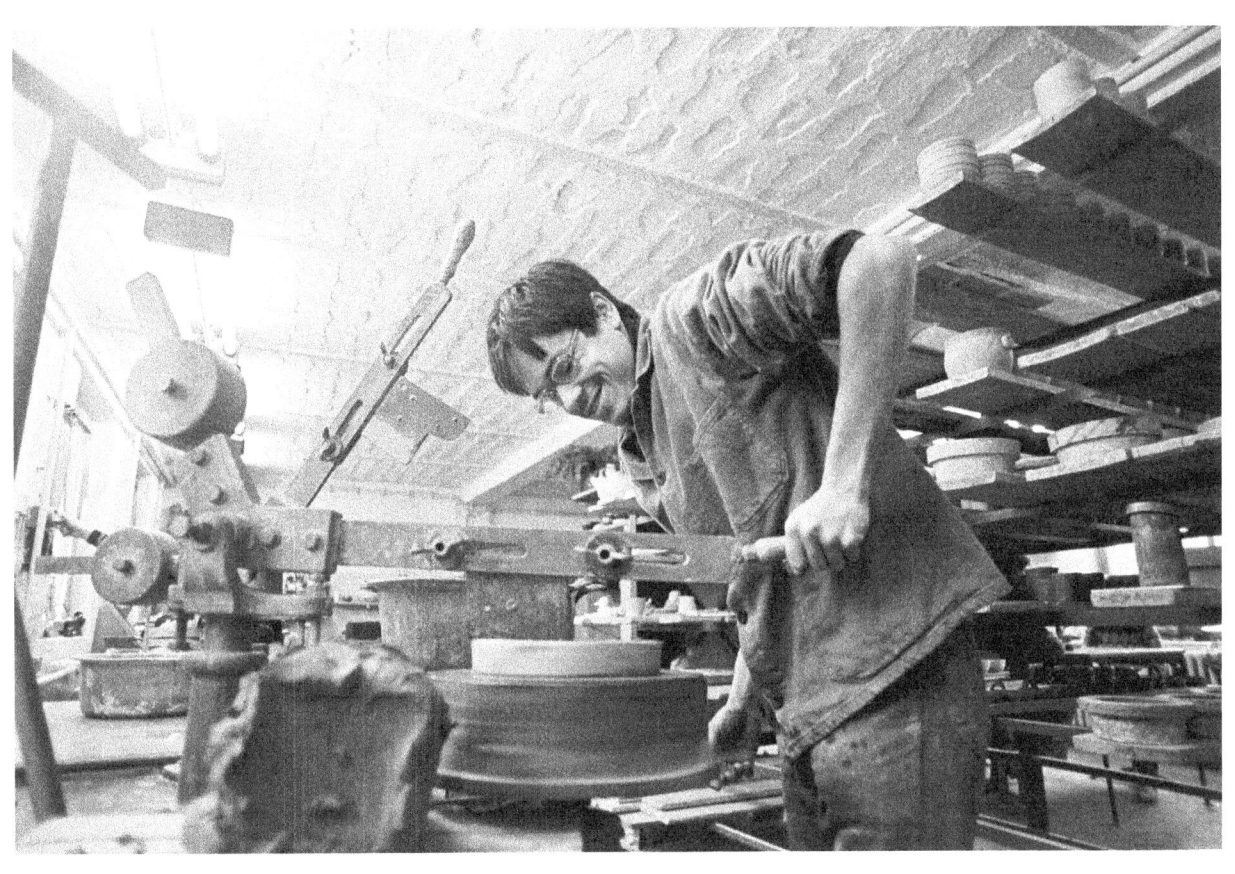

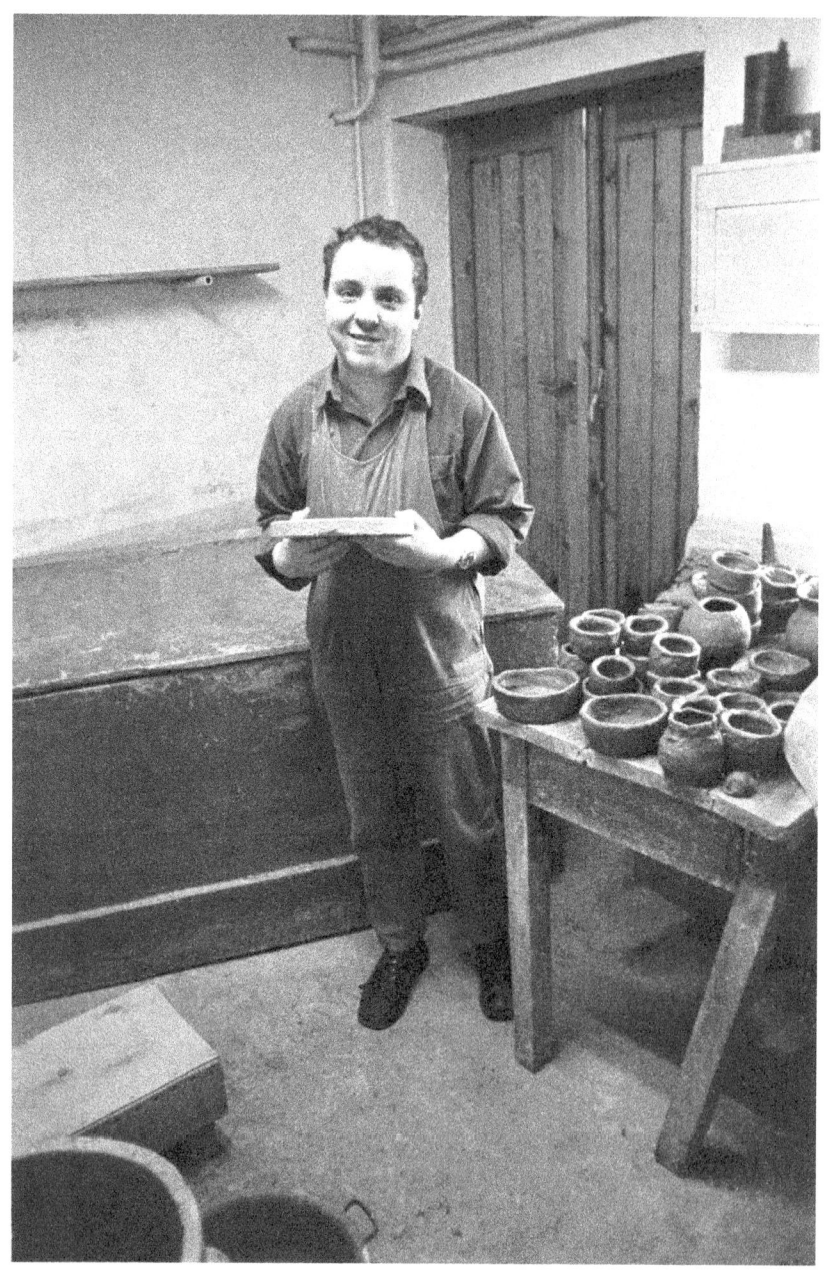

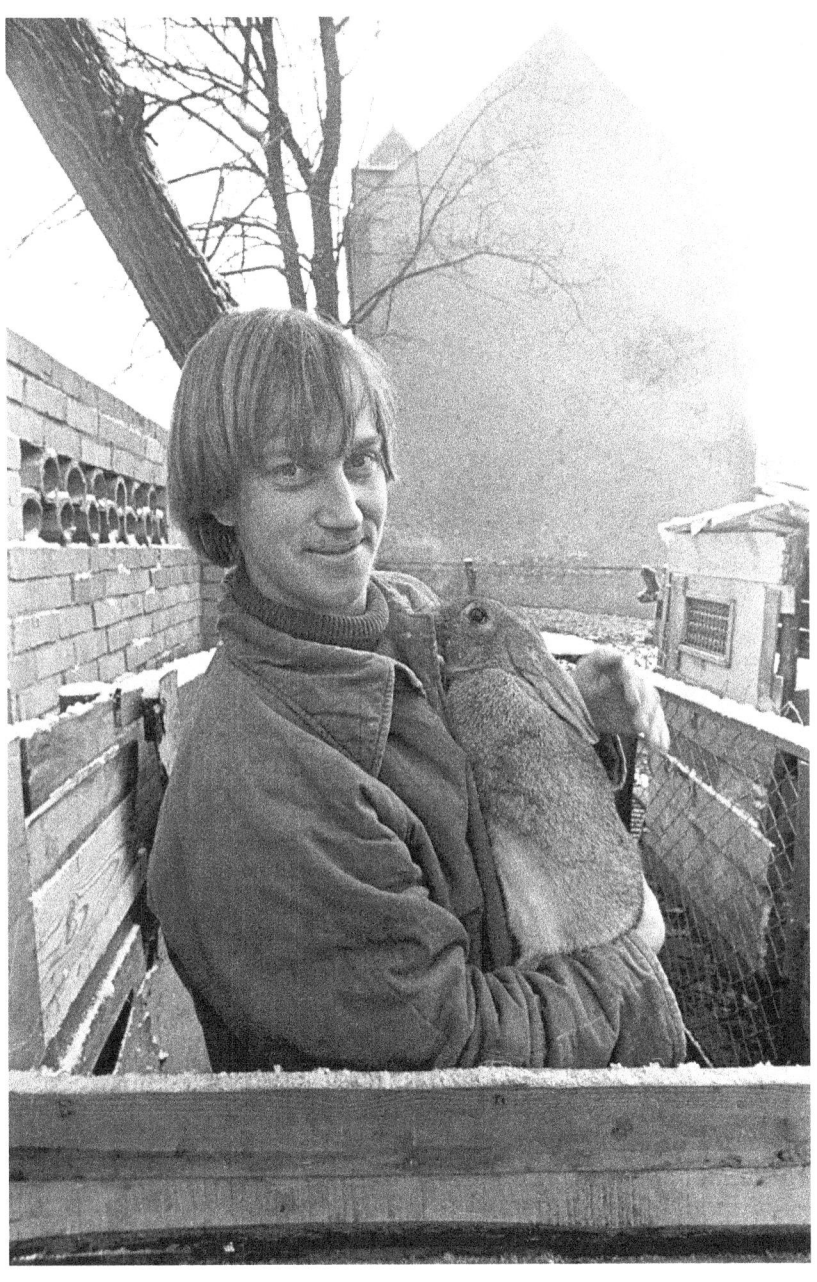

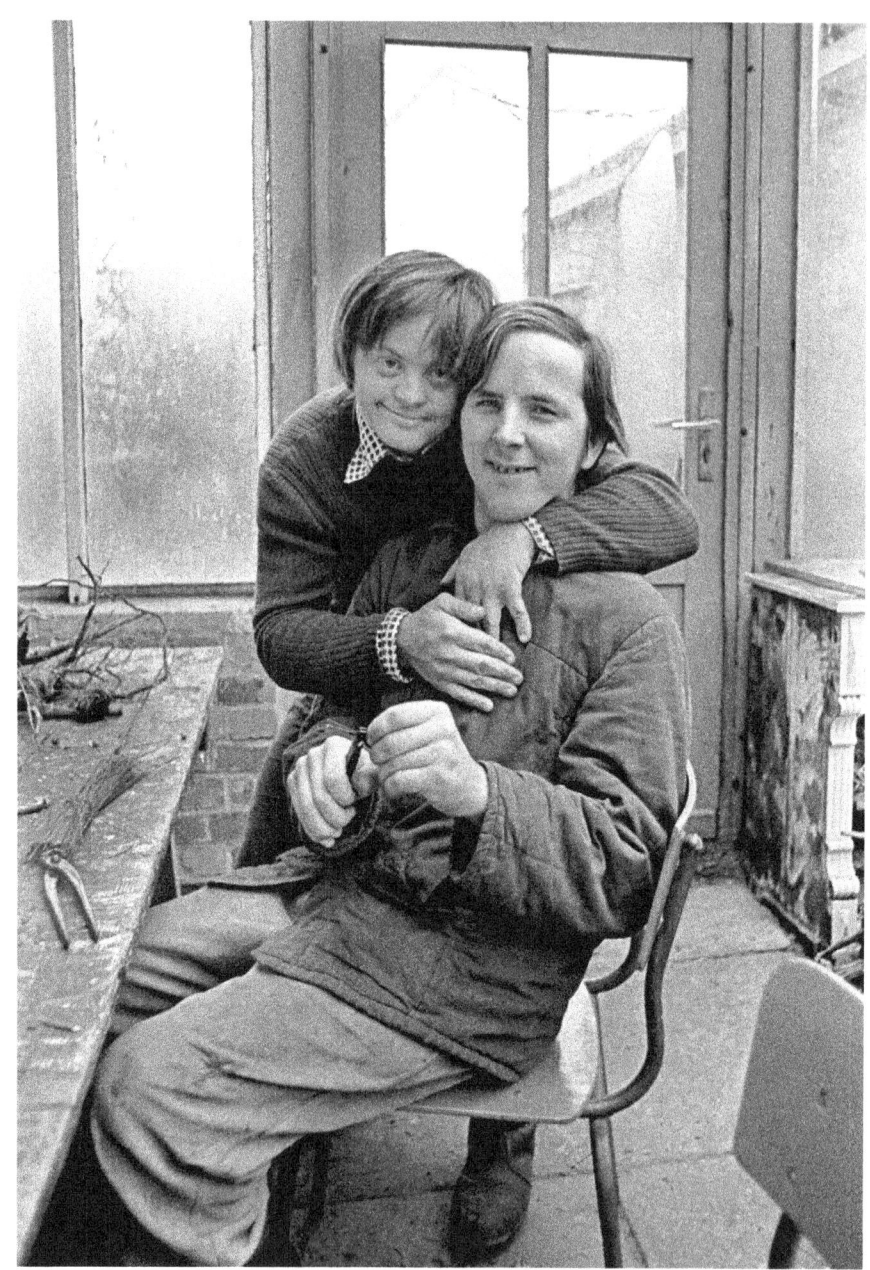

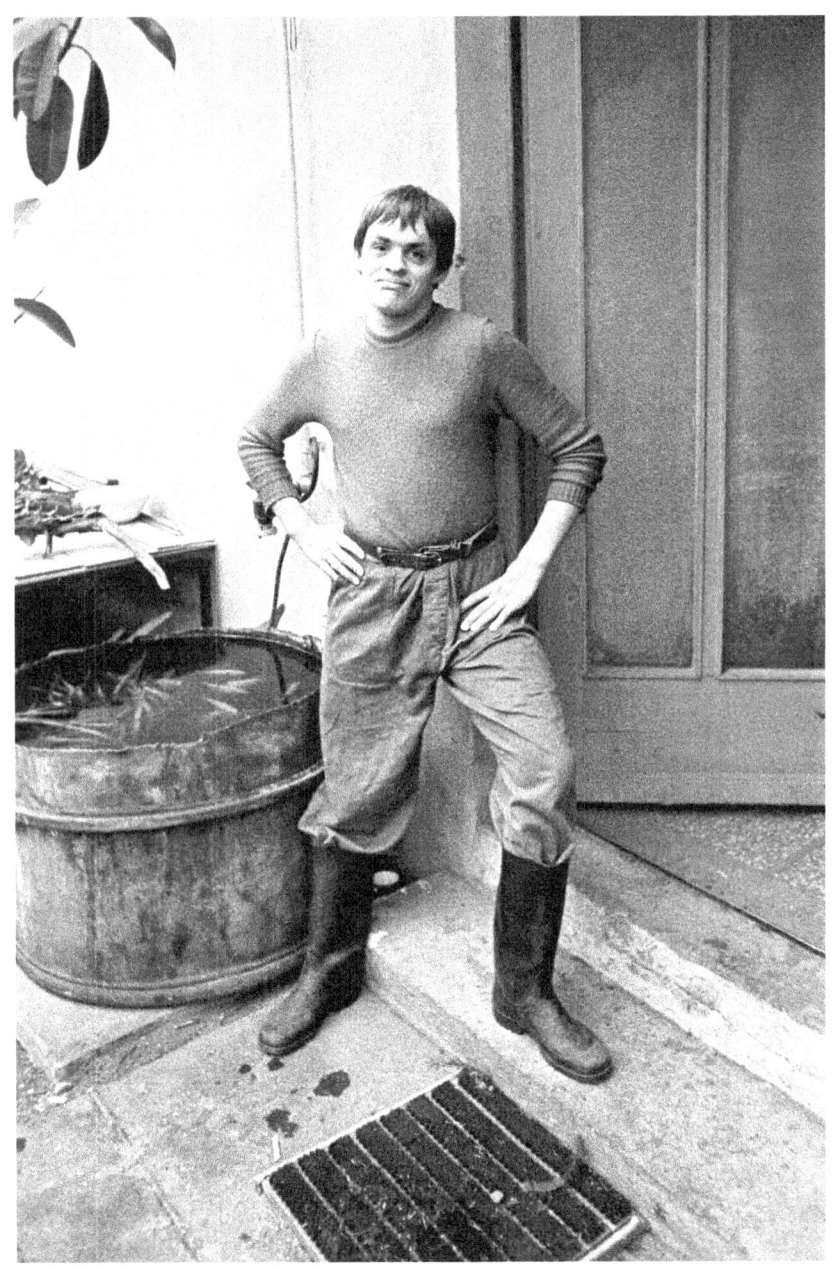

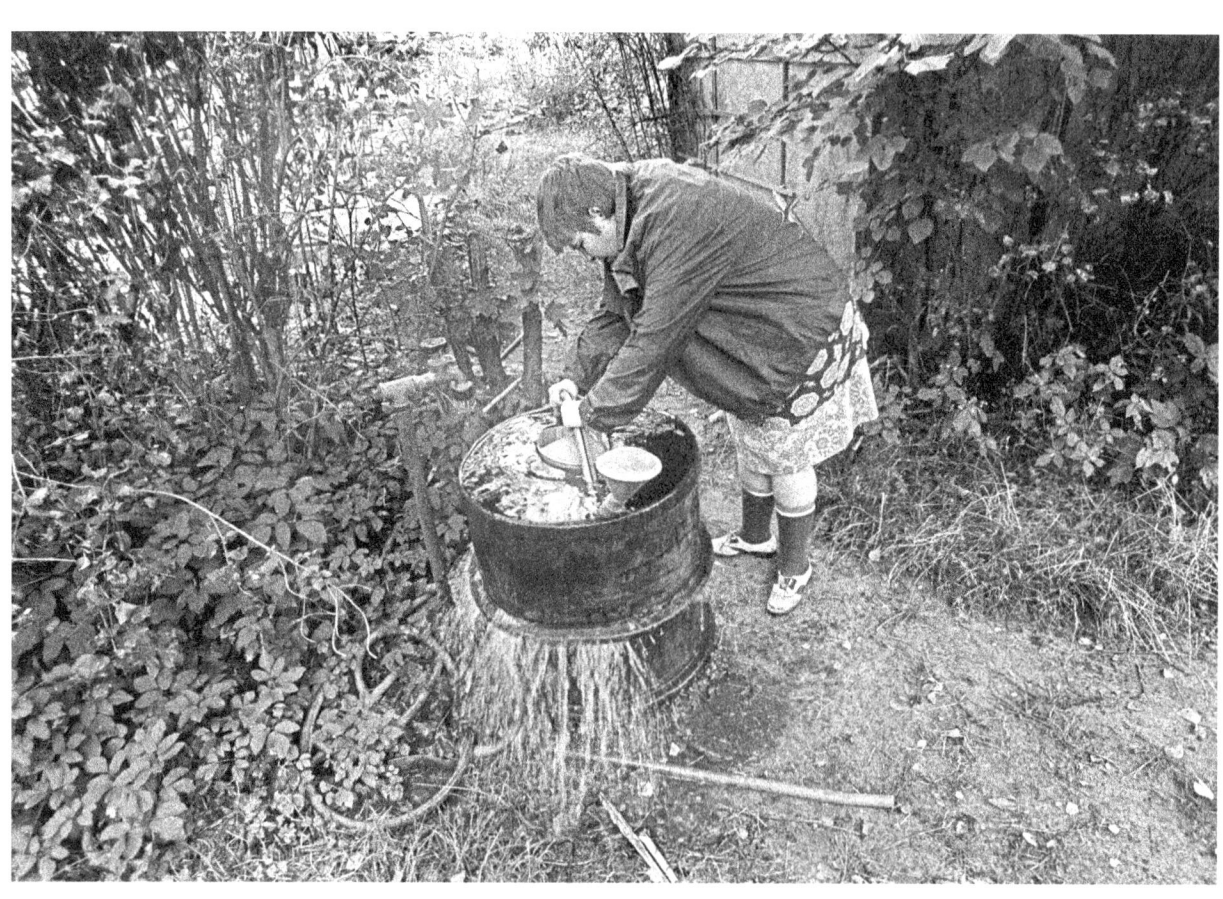

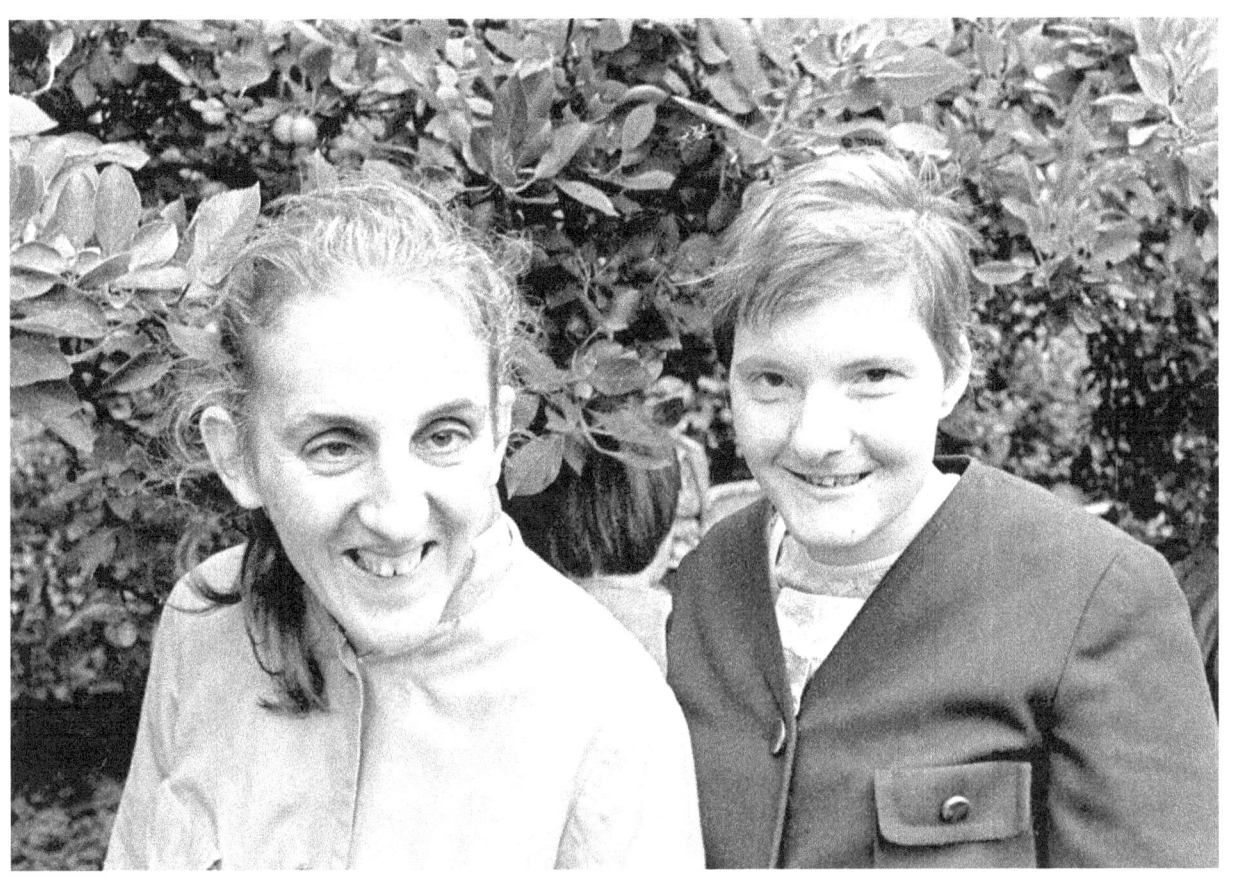

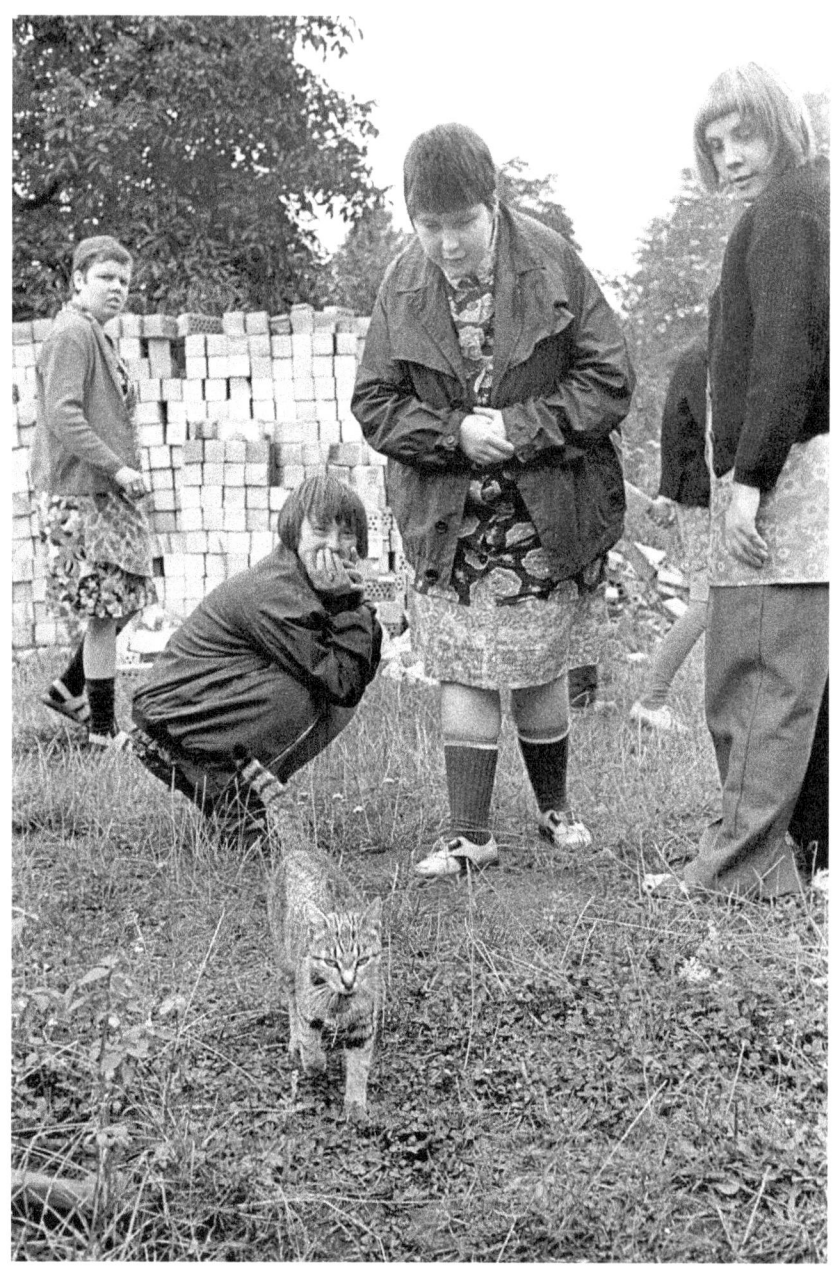

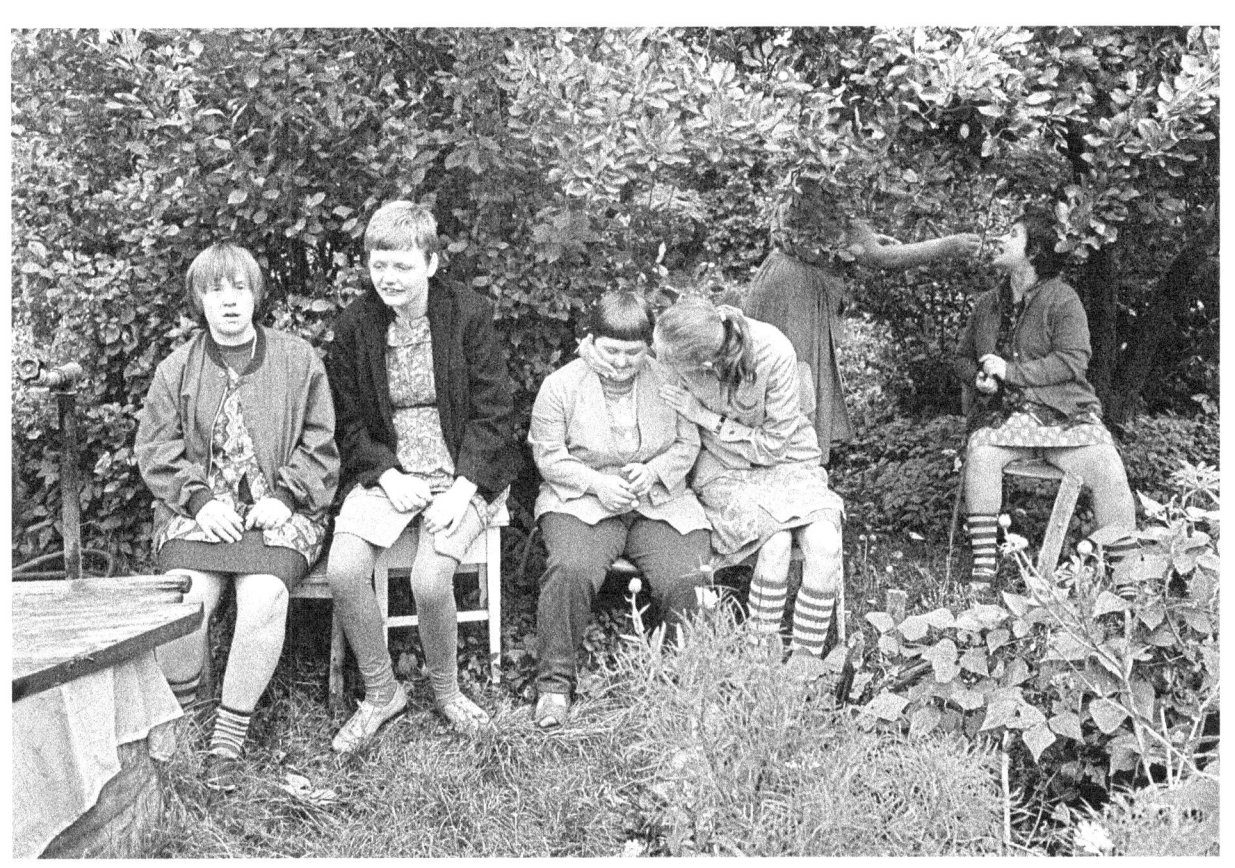

HÖHEPUNKTE DES JAHRES / HIGHLIGHTS OF THE YEAR

Photographs by Dietmar Riemann

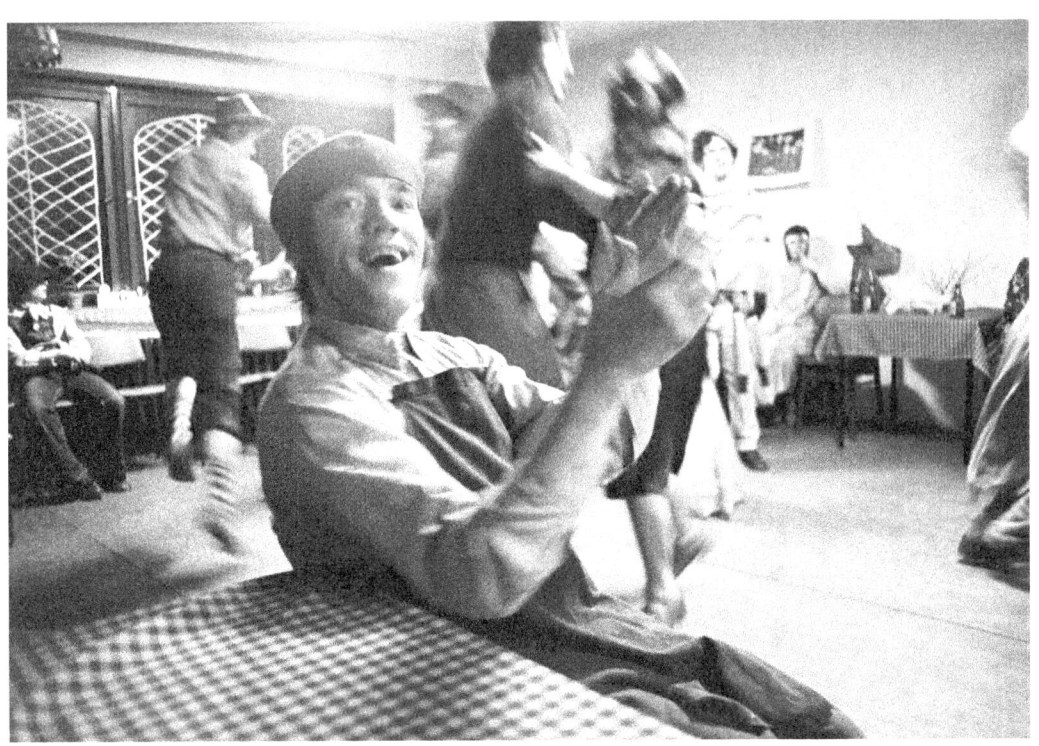

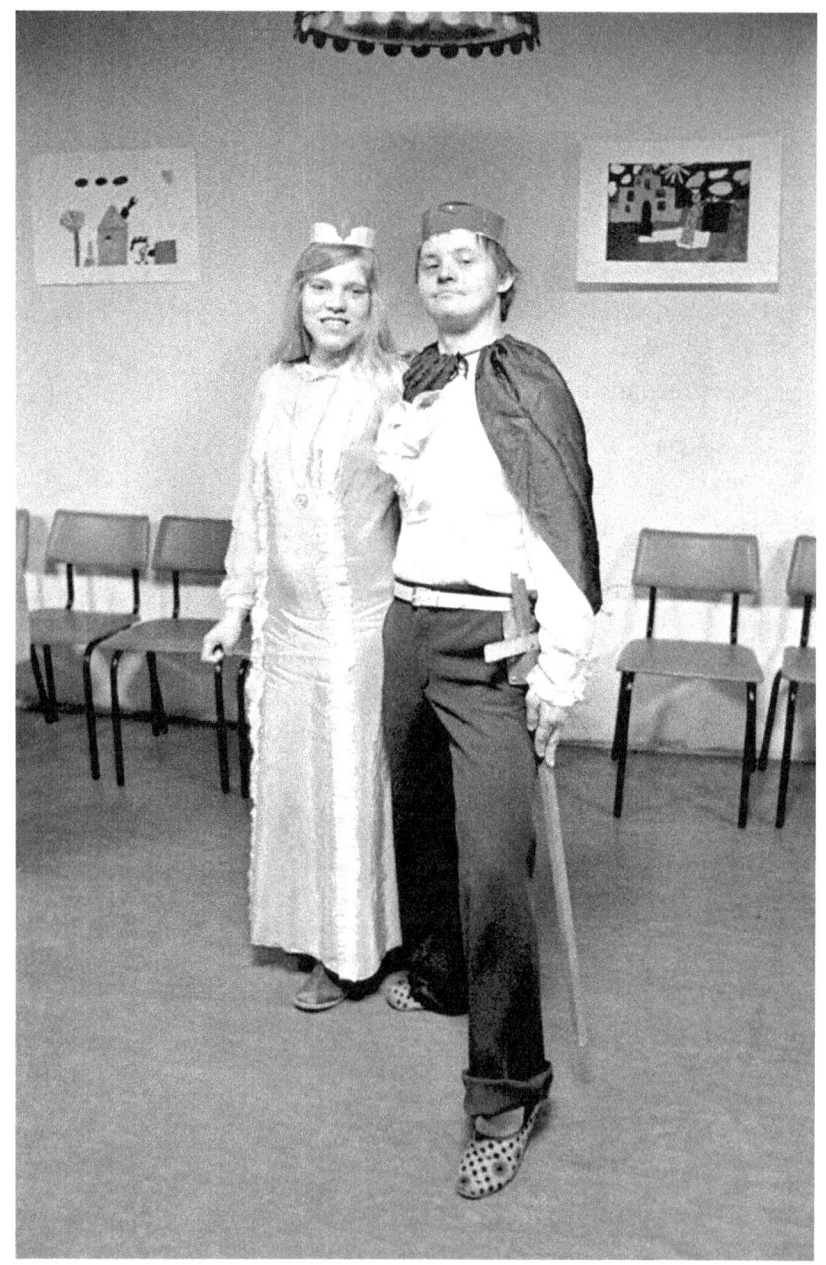

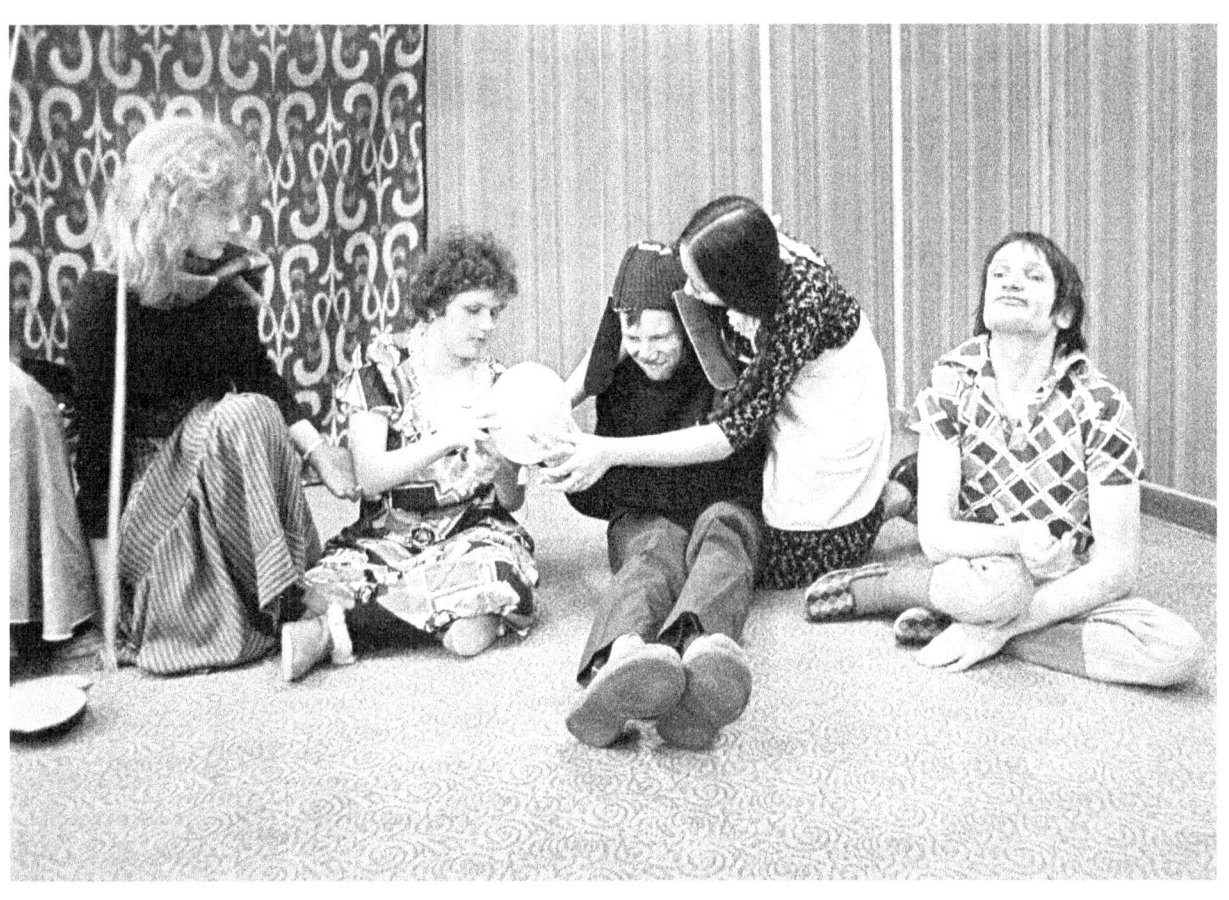

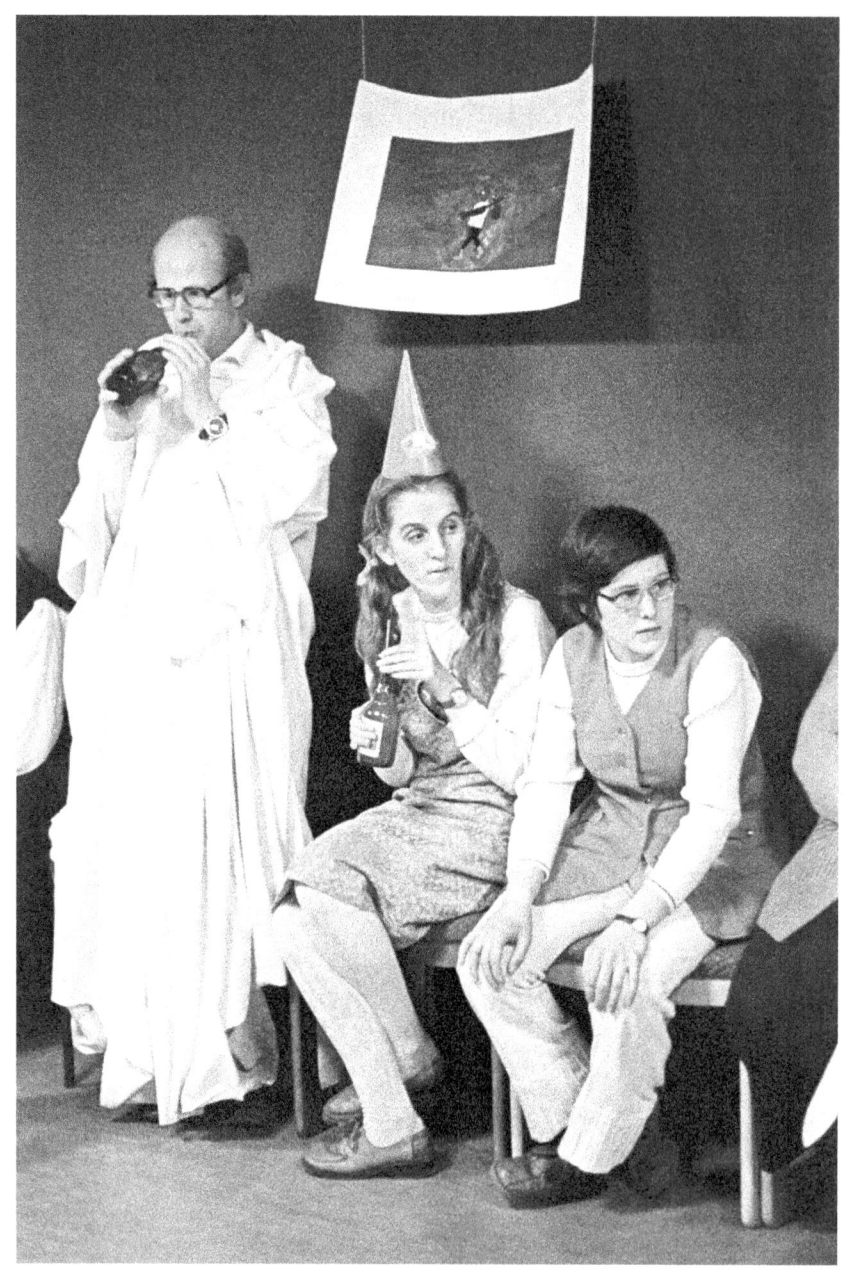

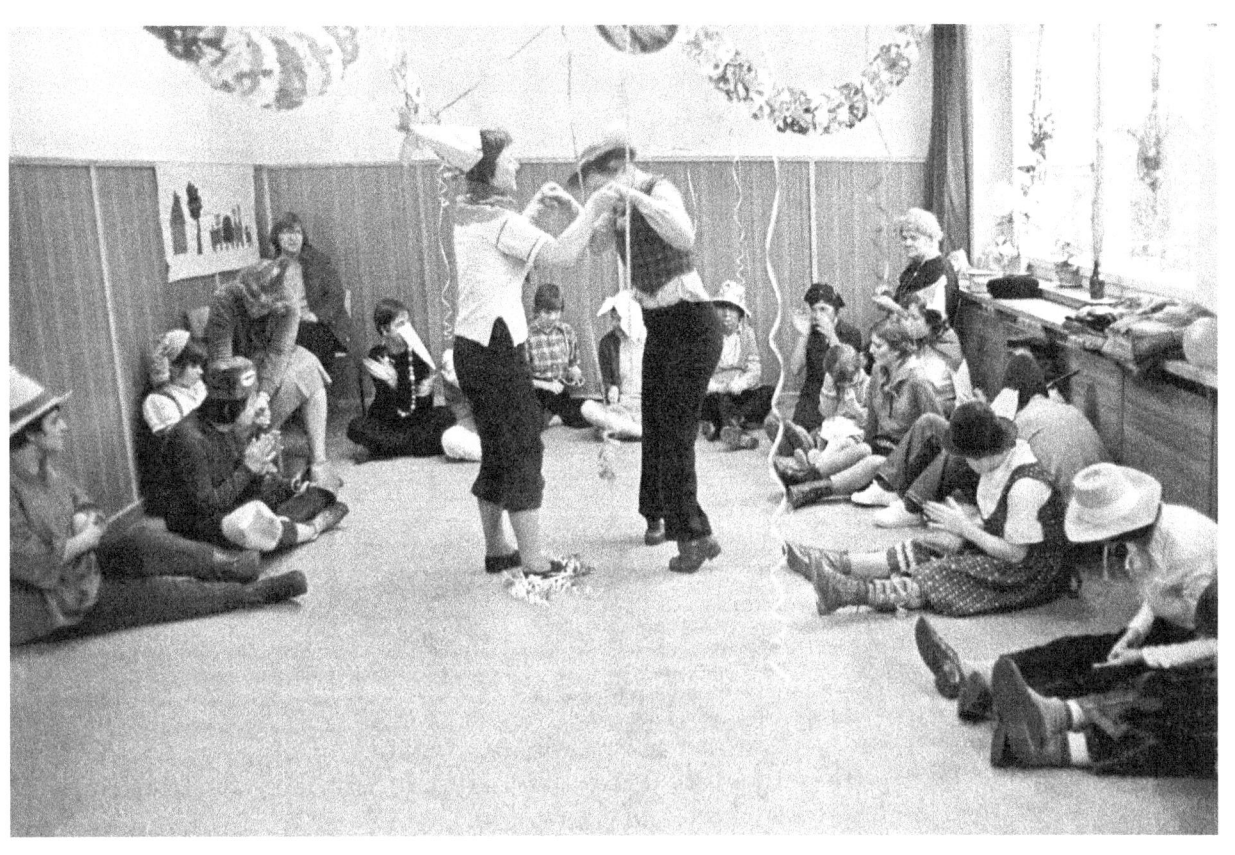

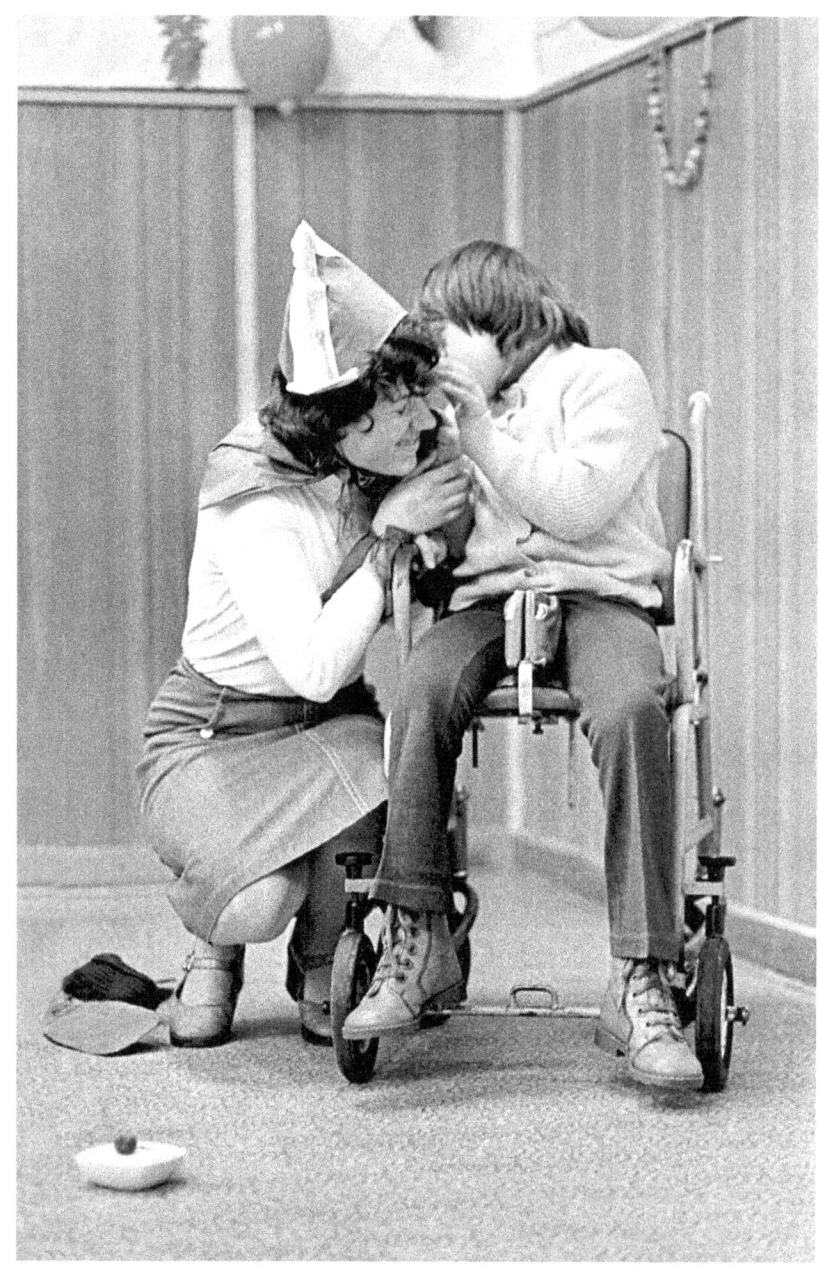

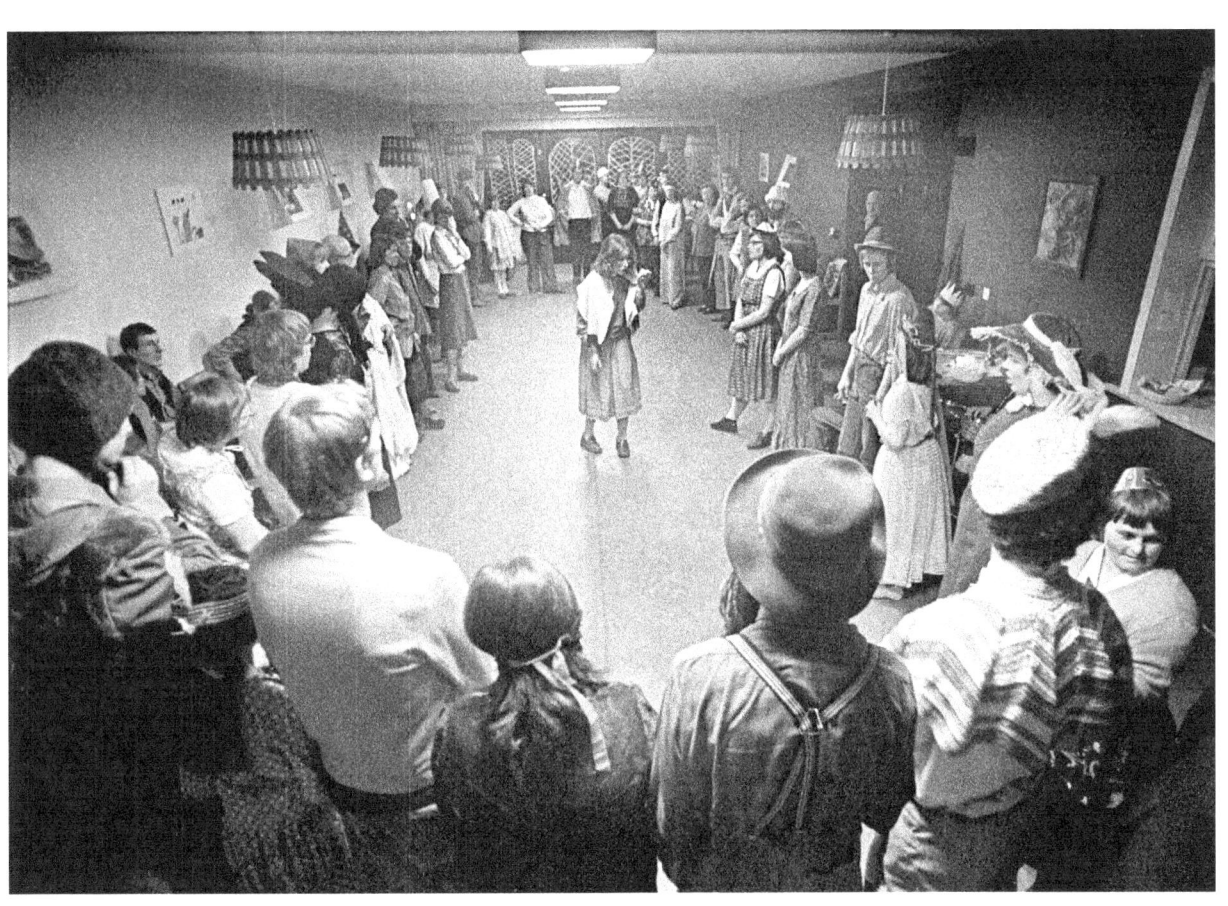

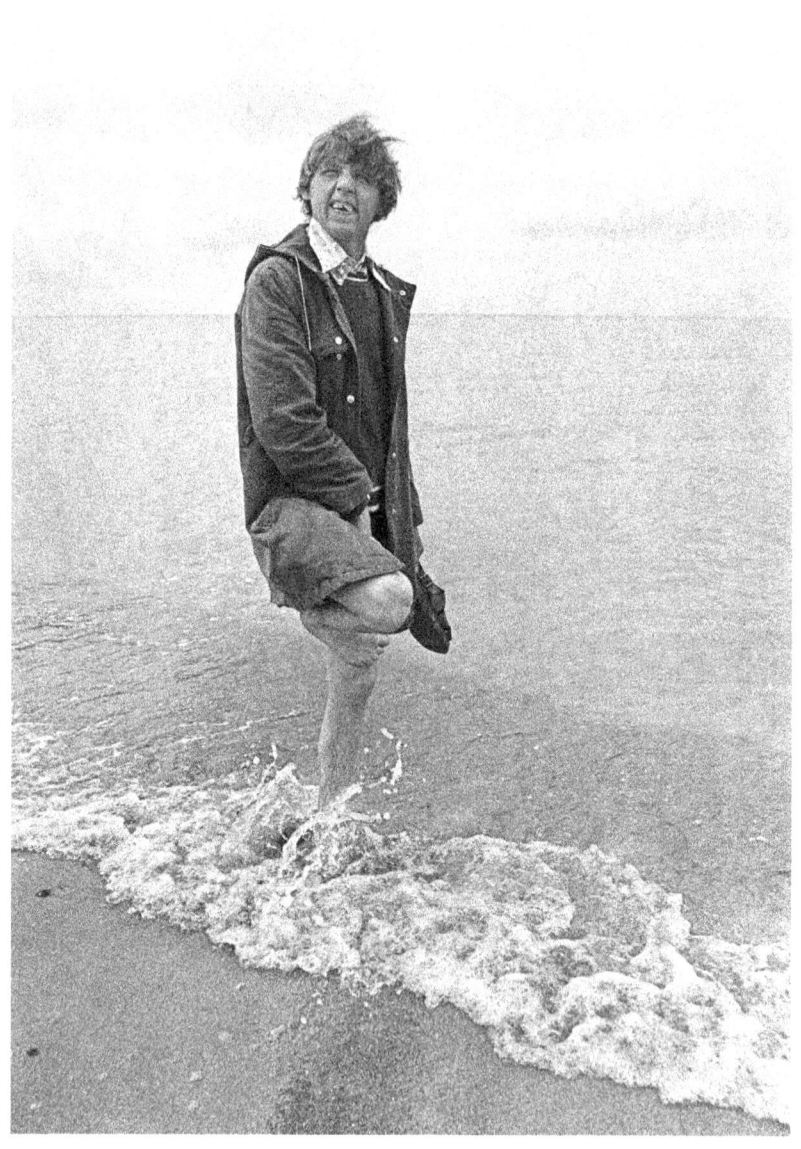

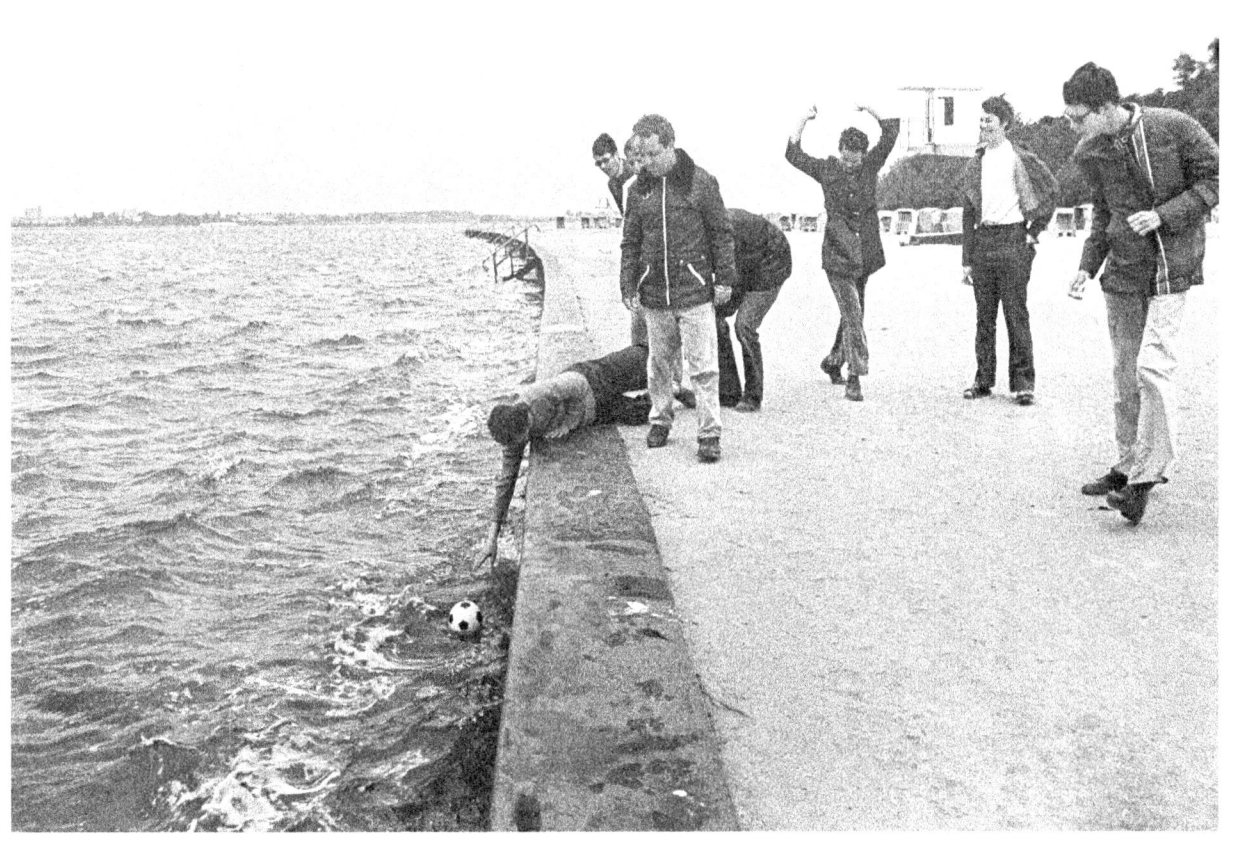

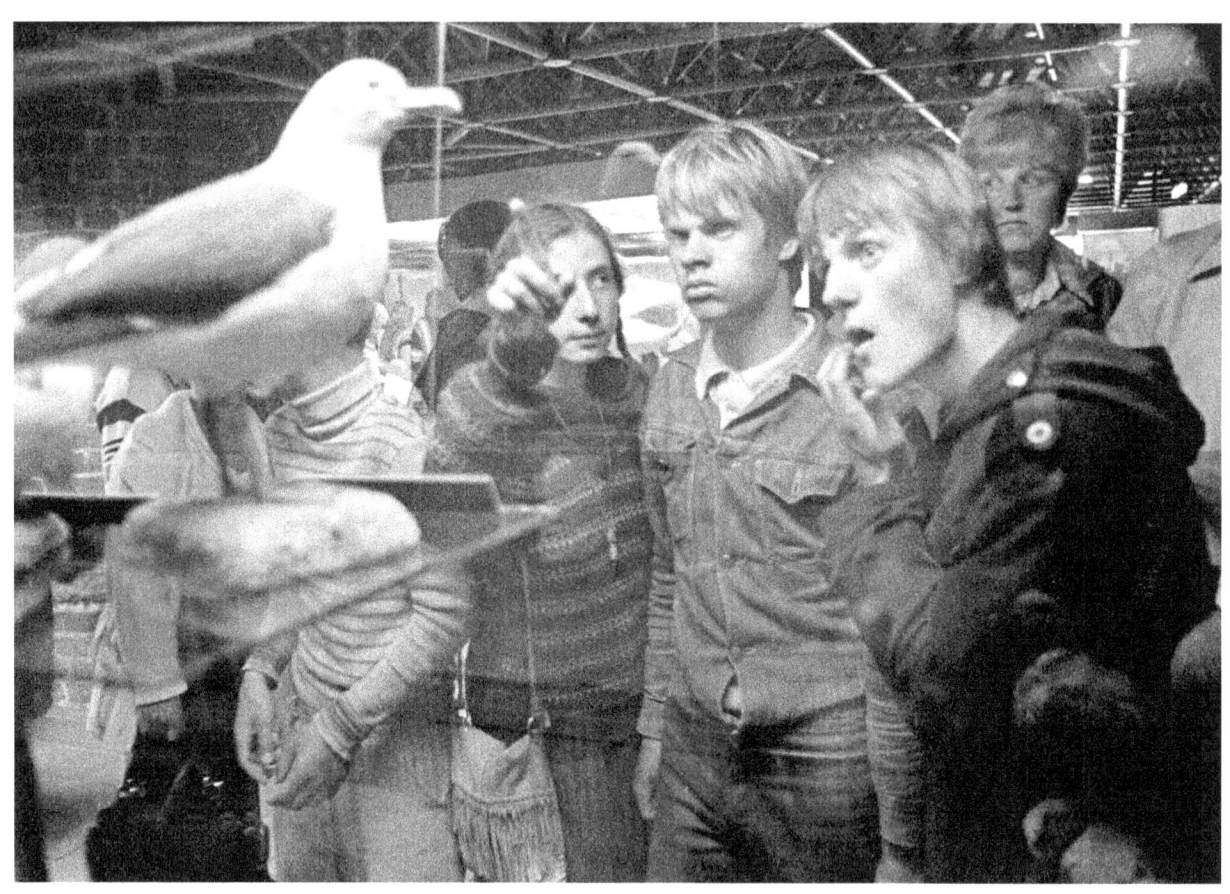

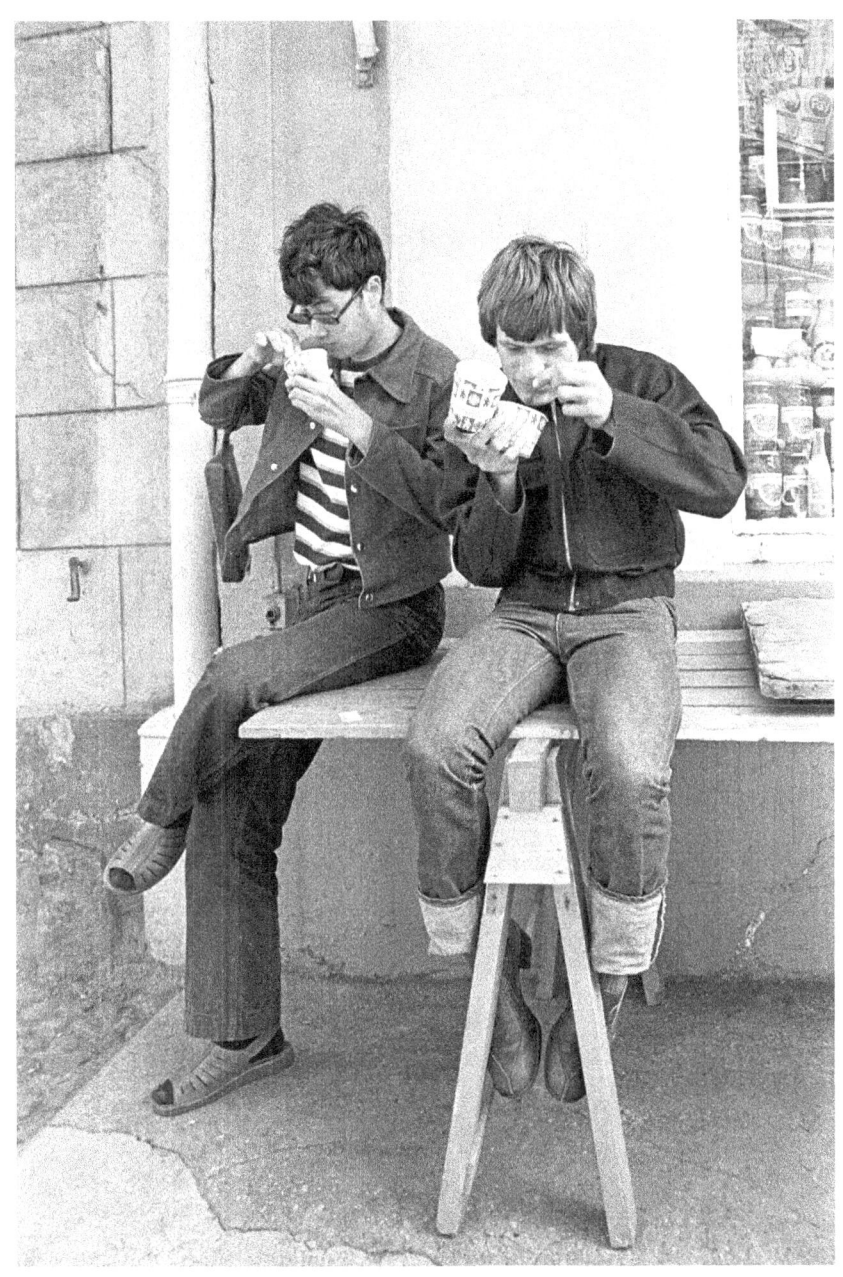

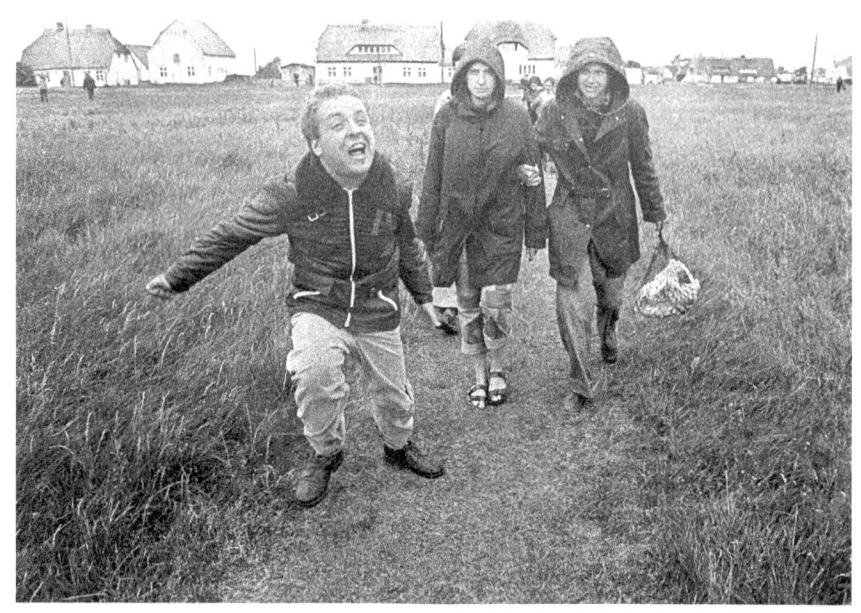

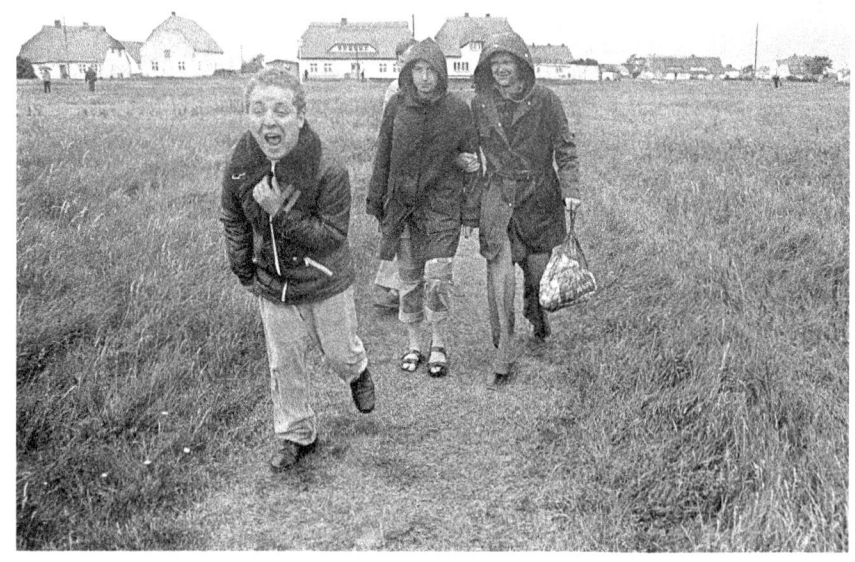

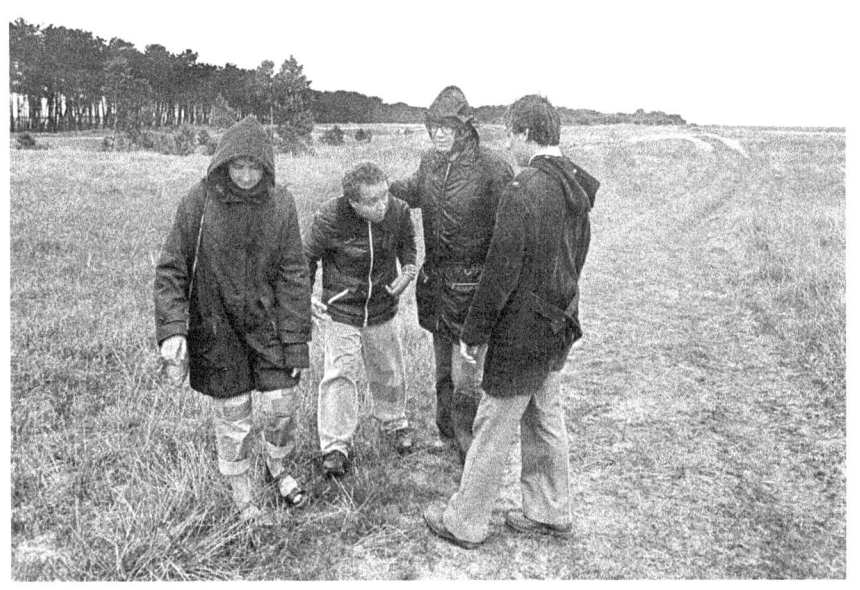

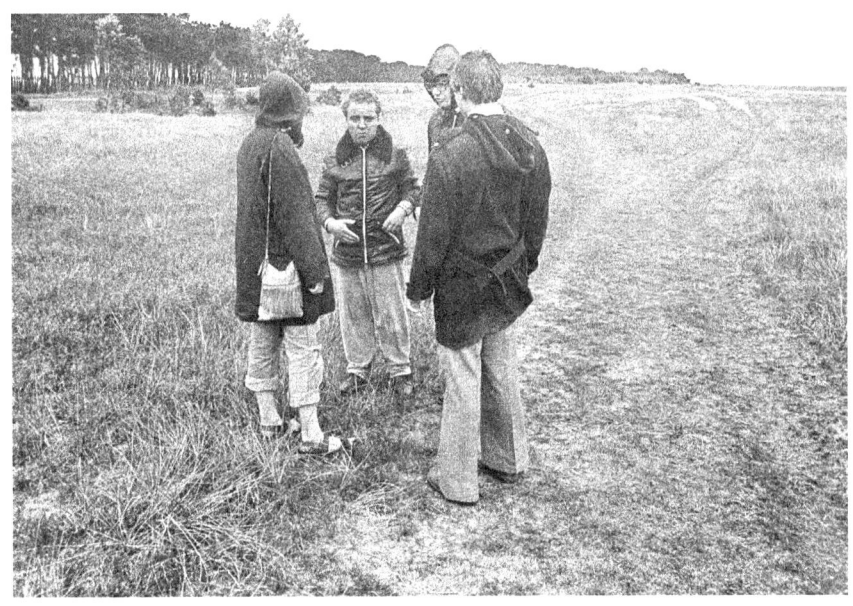

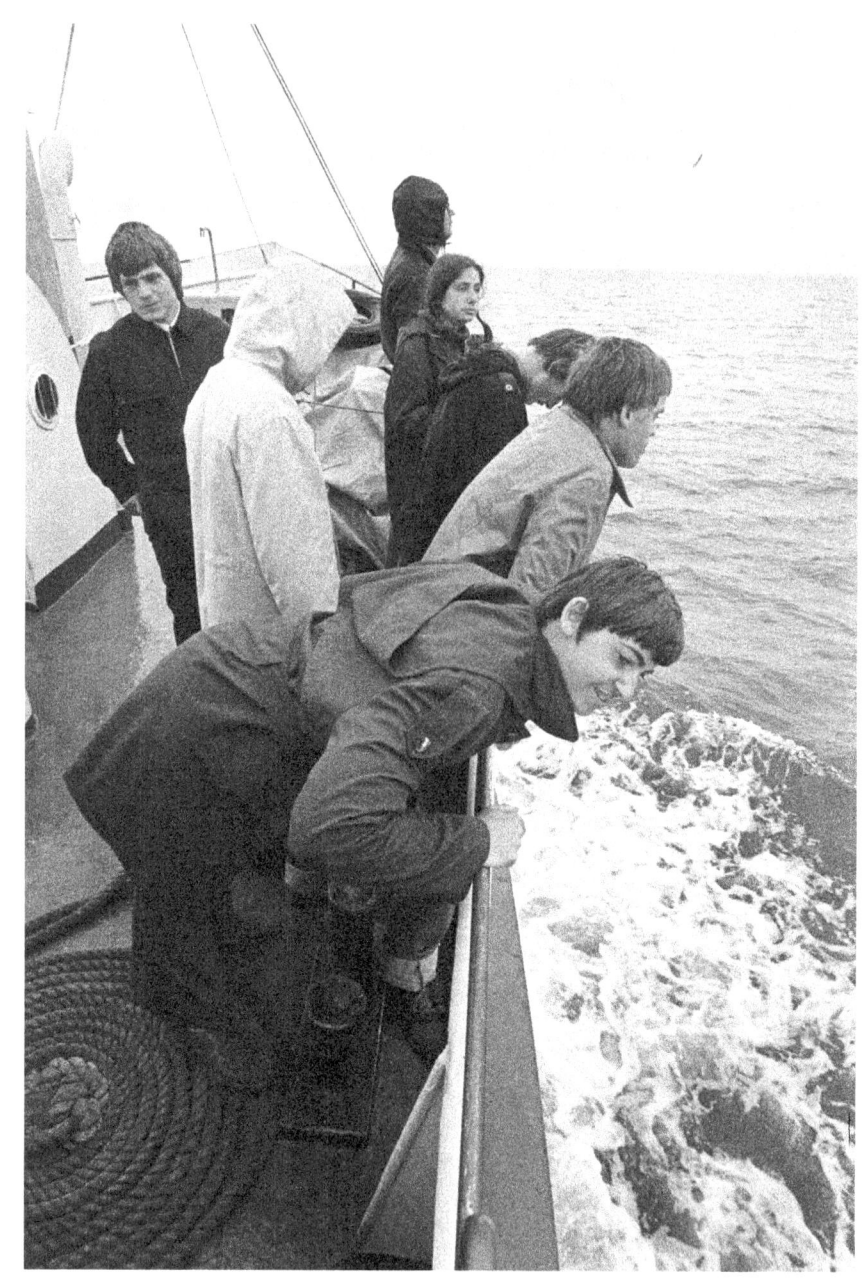

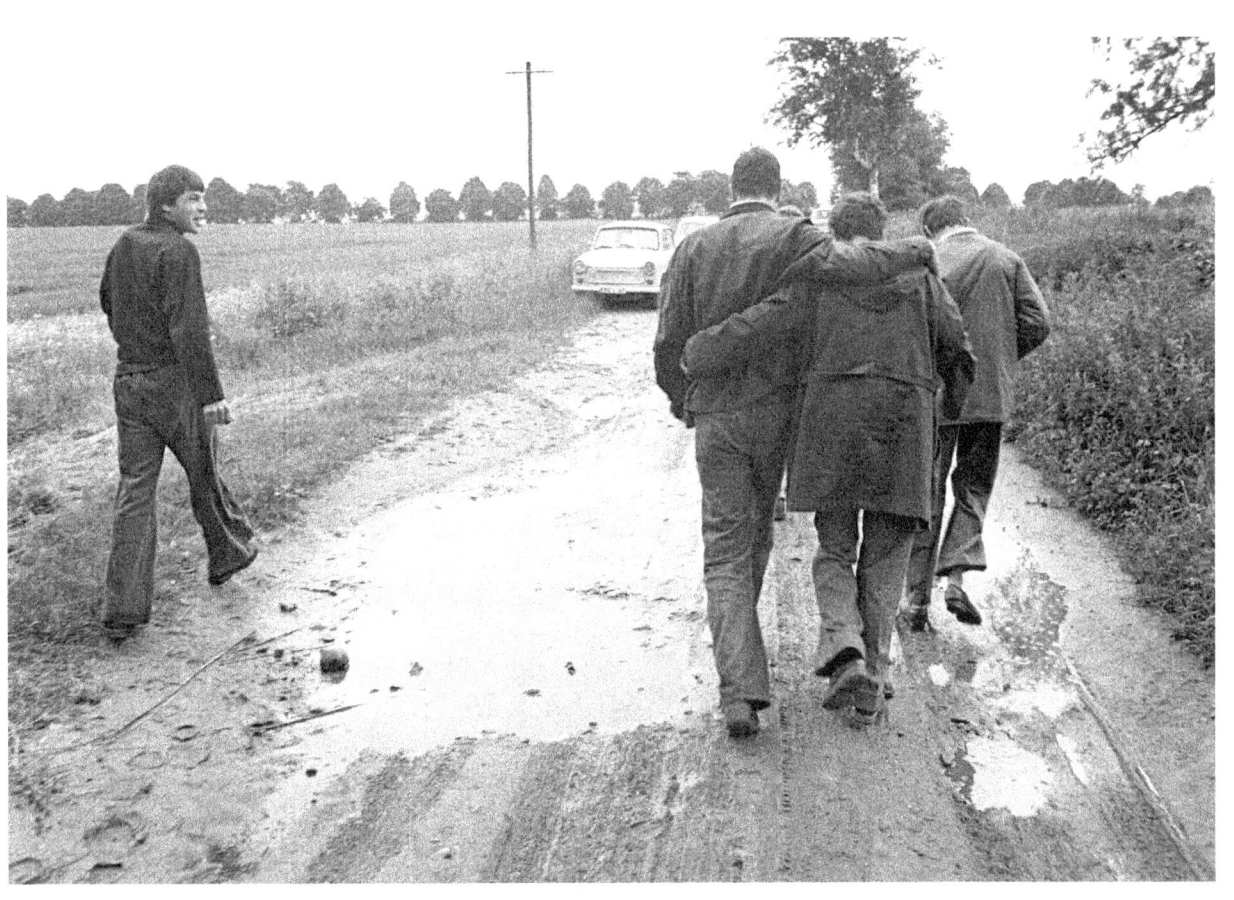

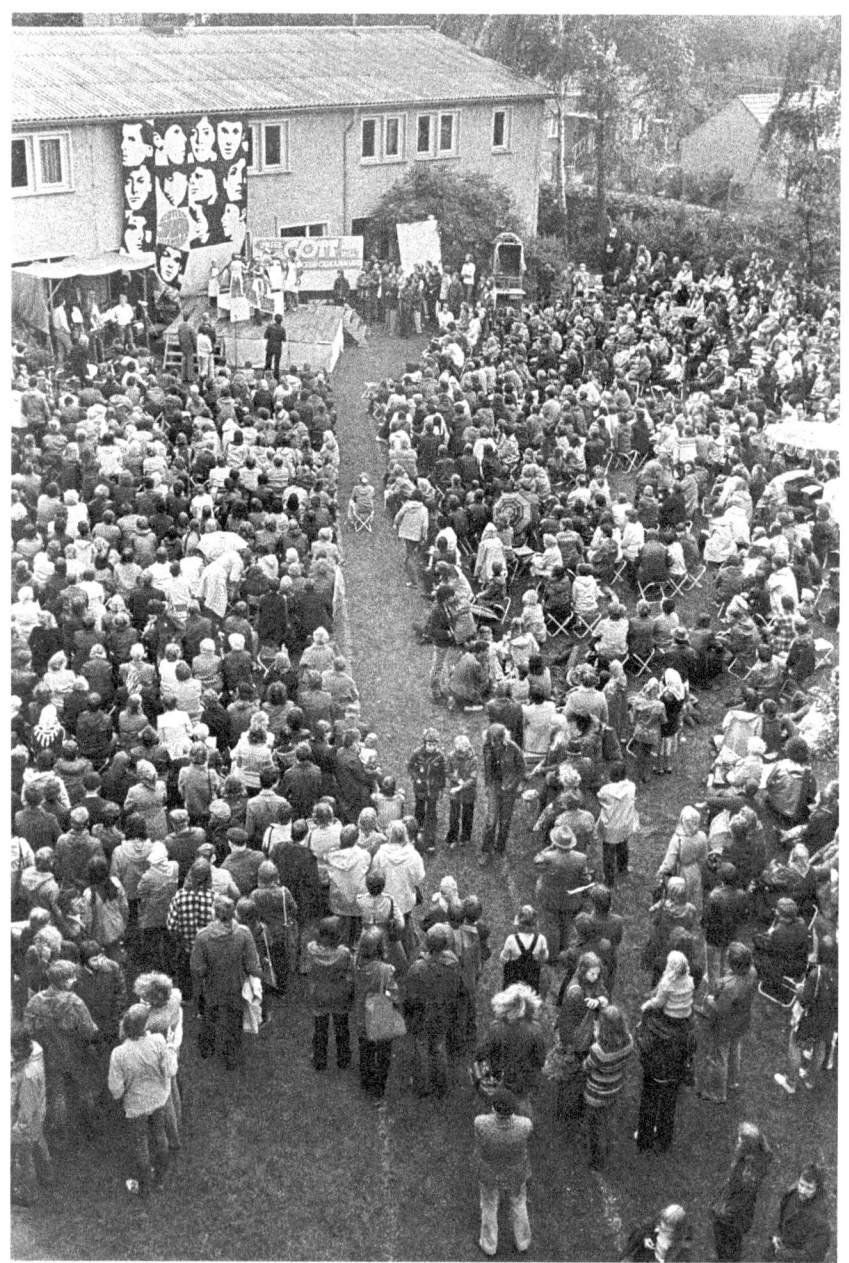

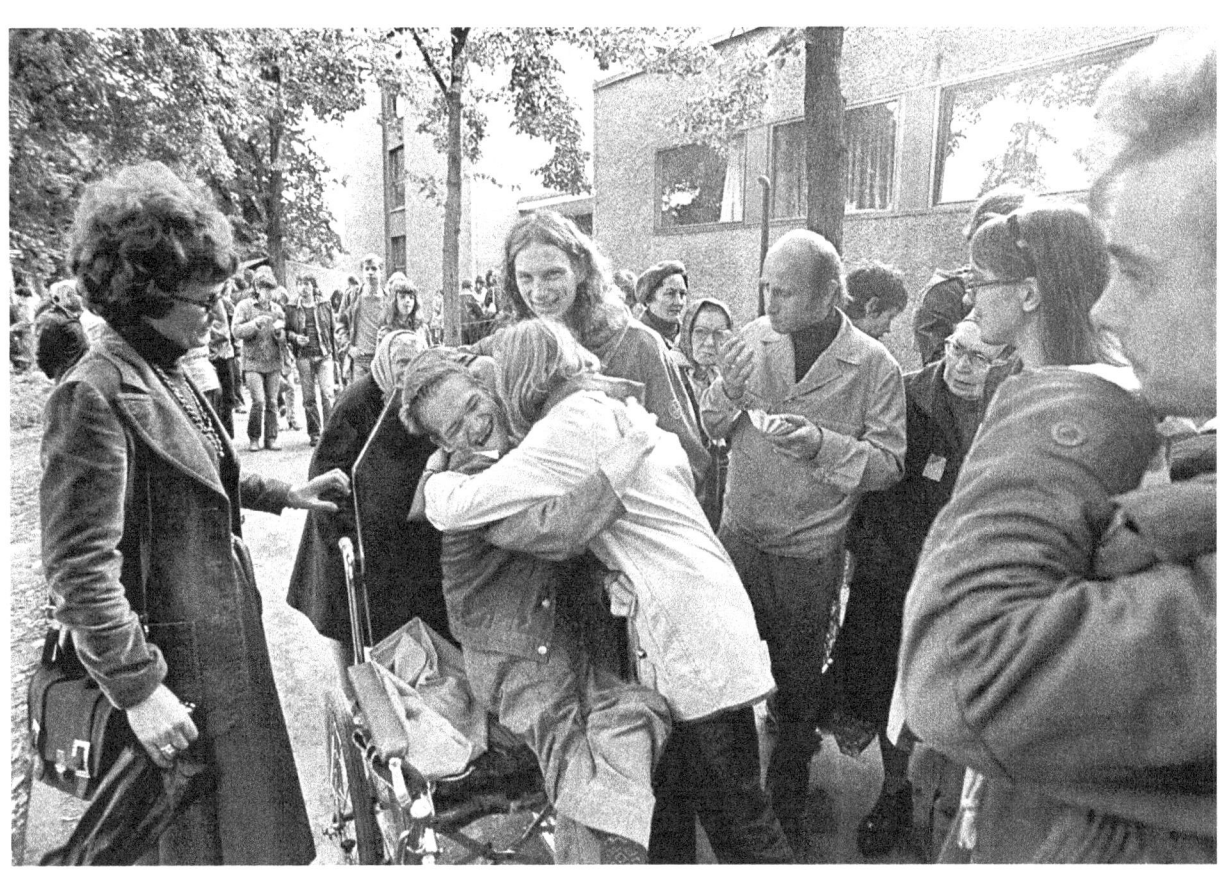

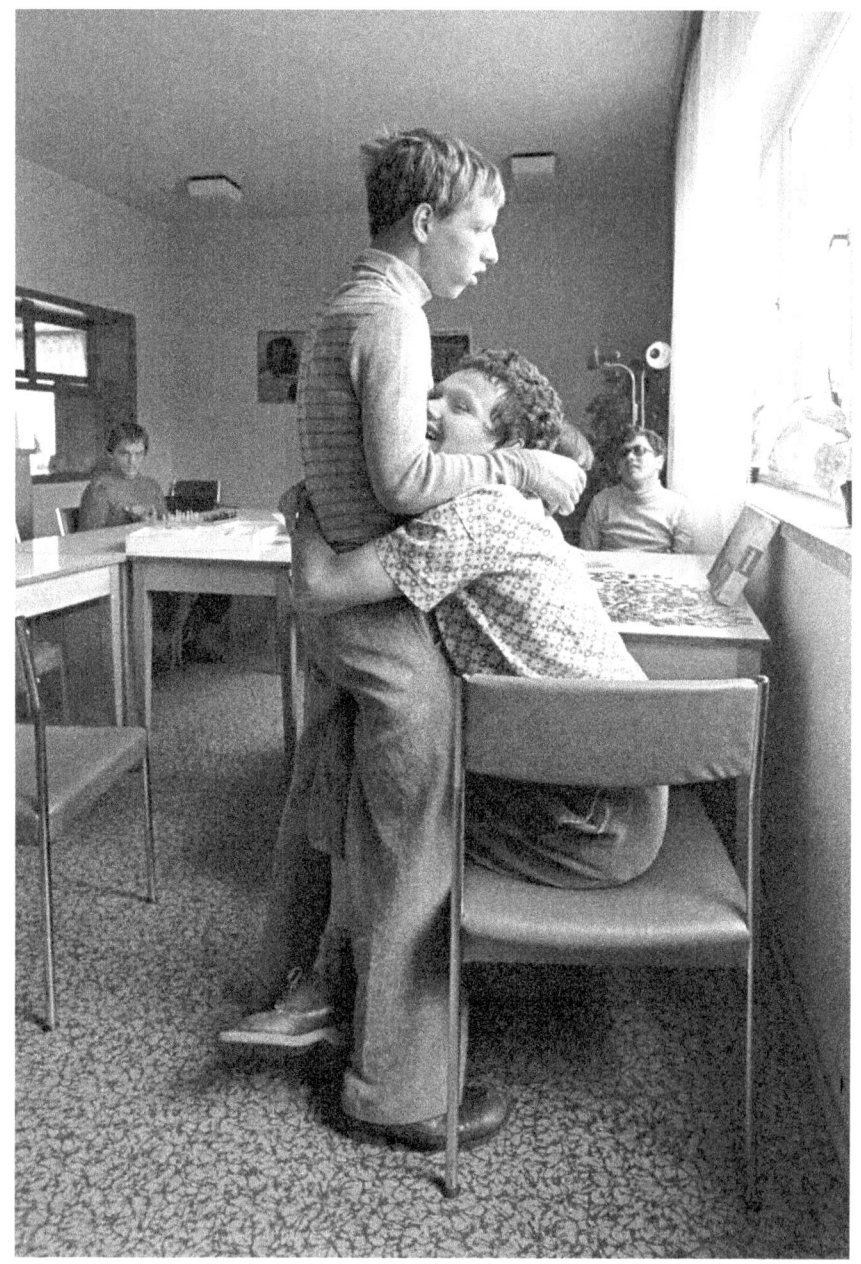

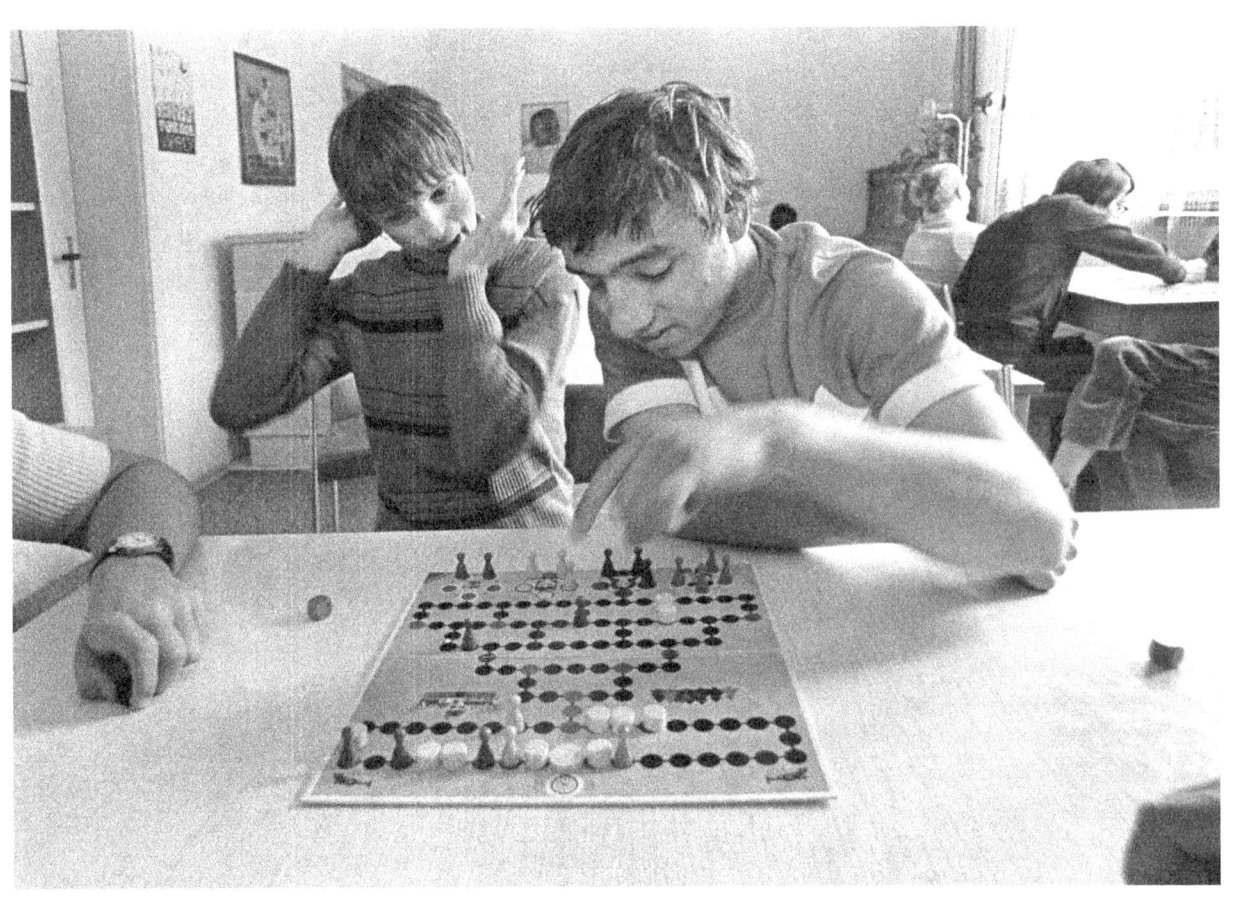

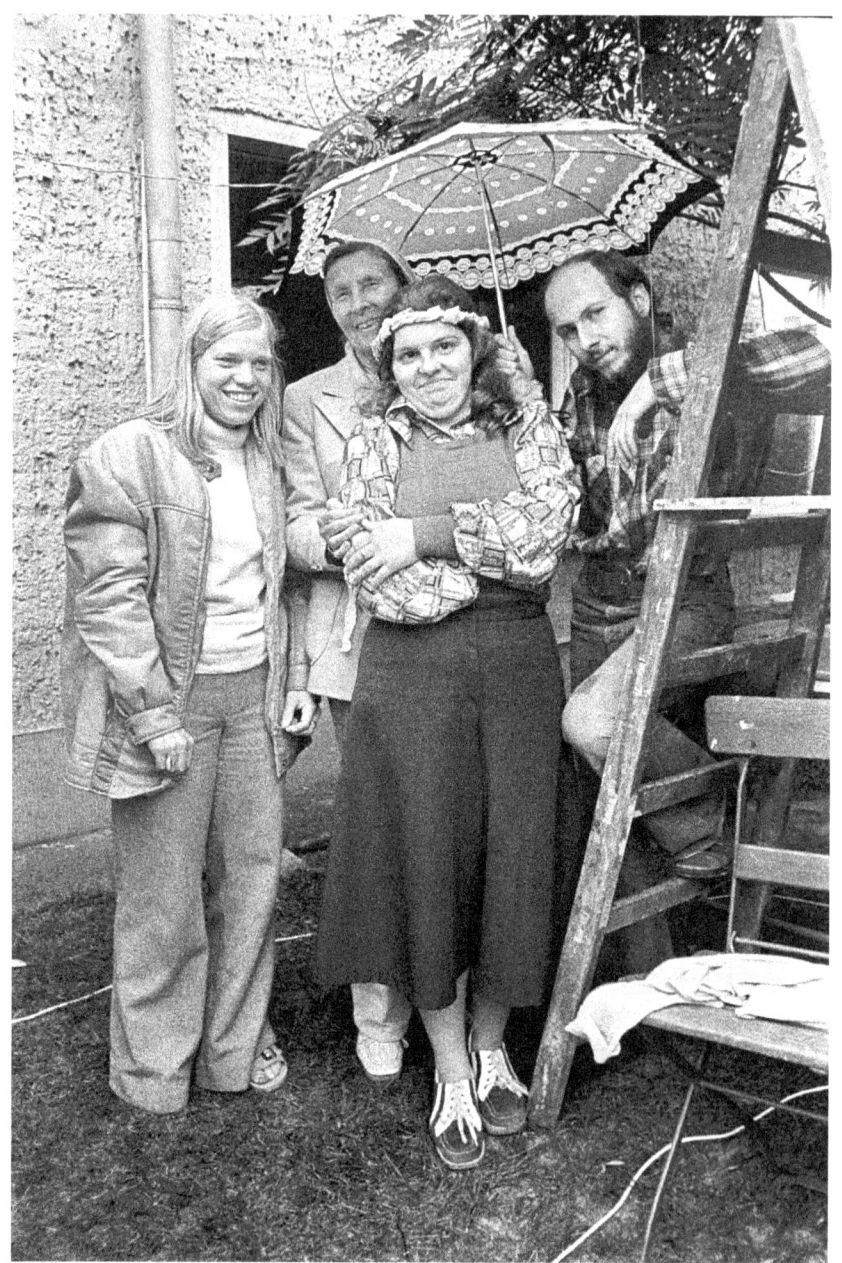

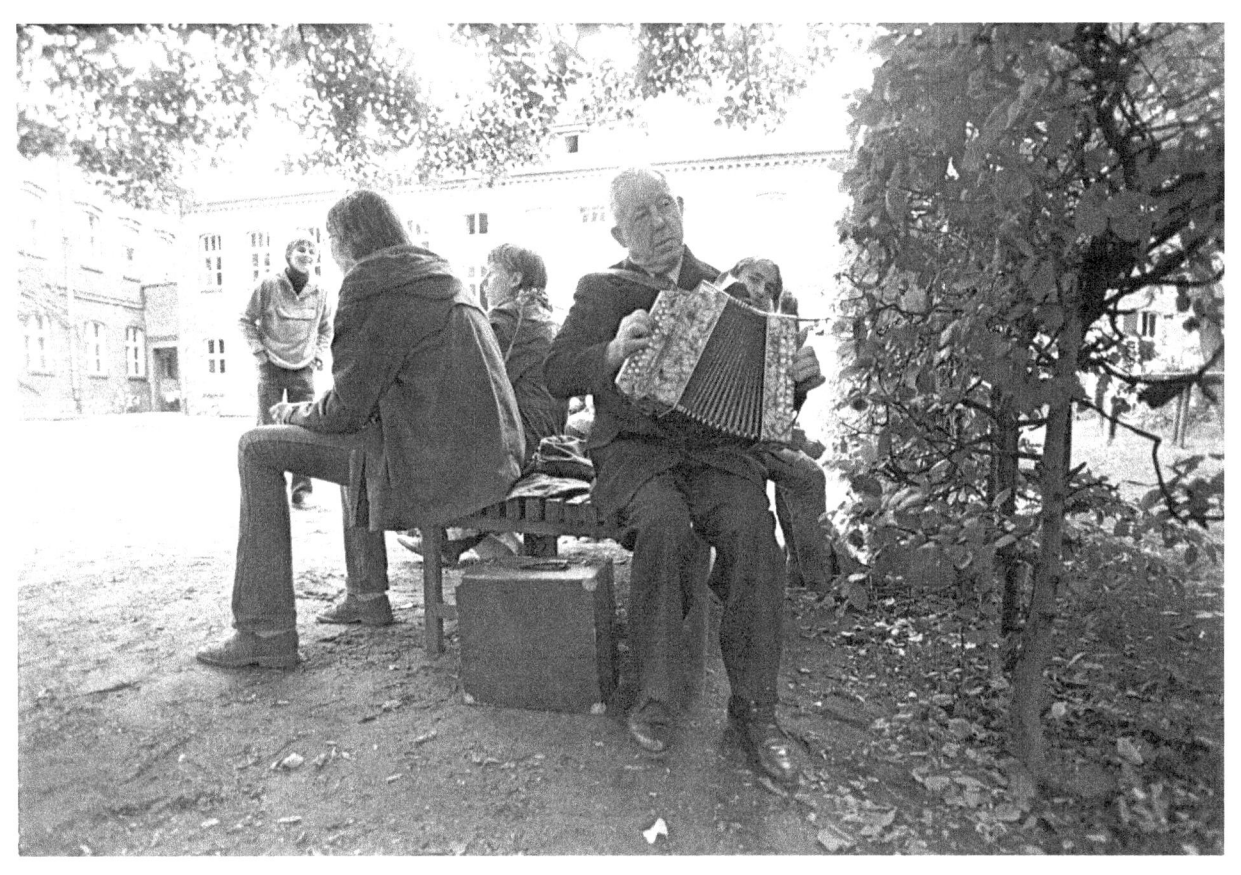

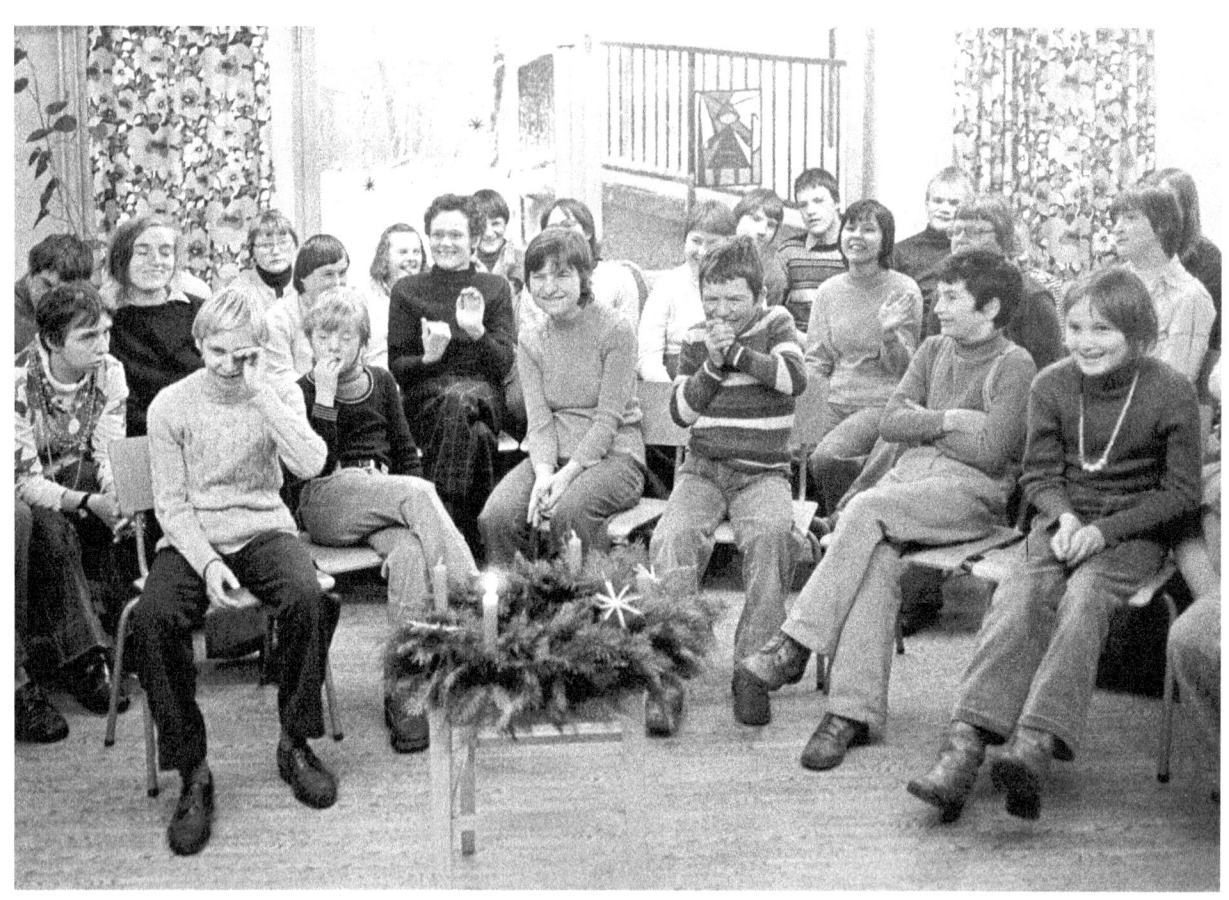

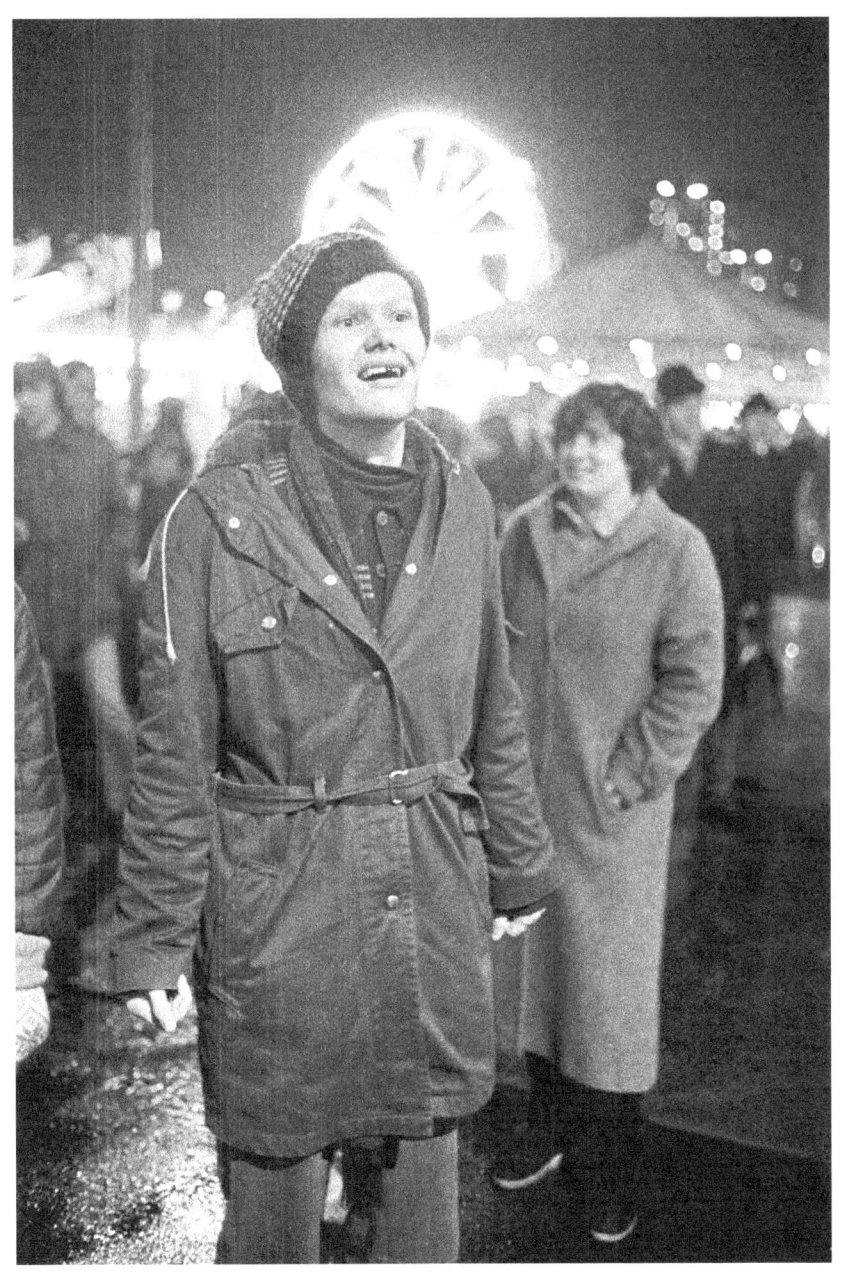

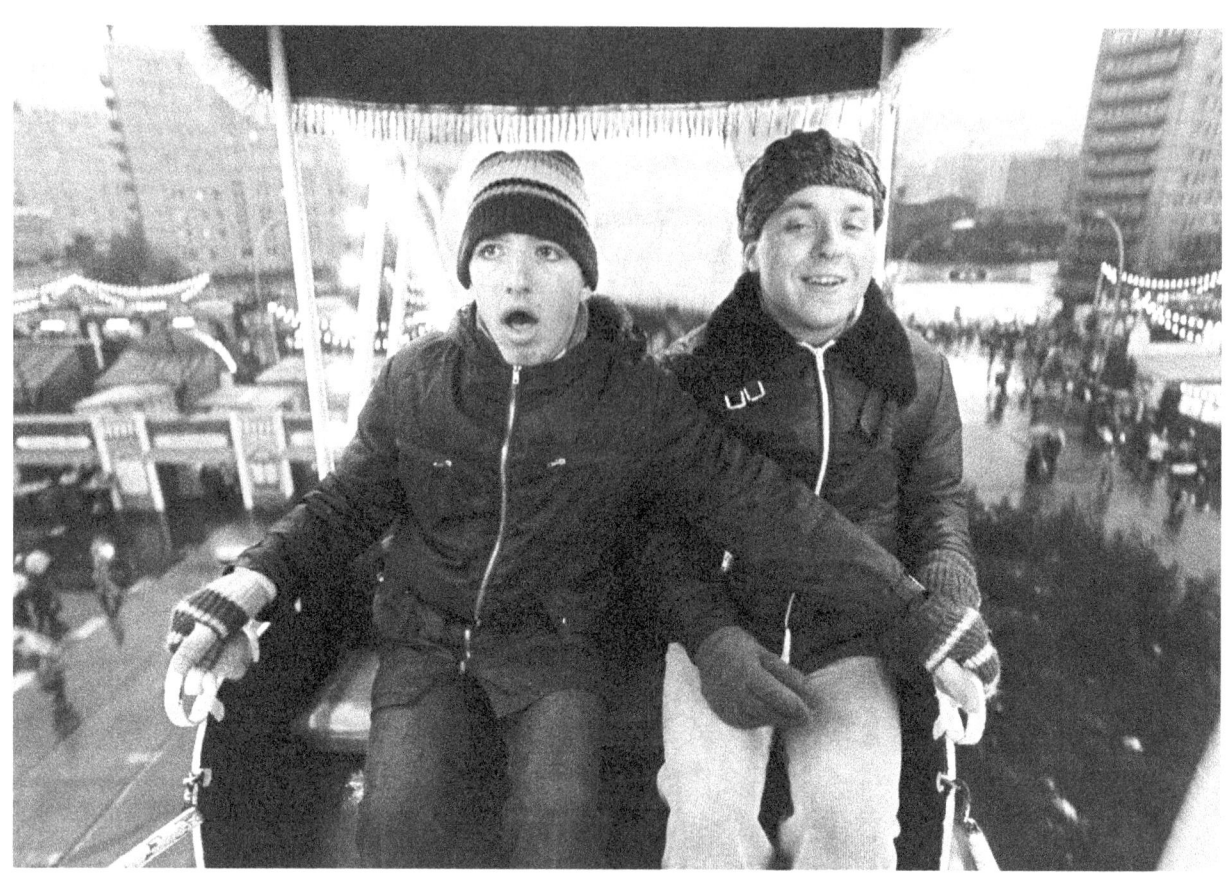

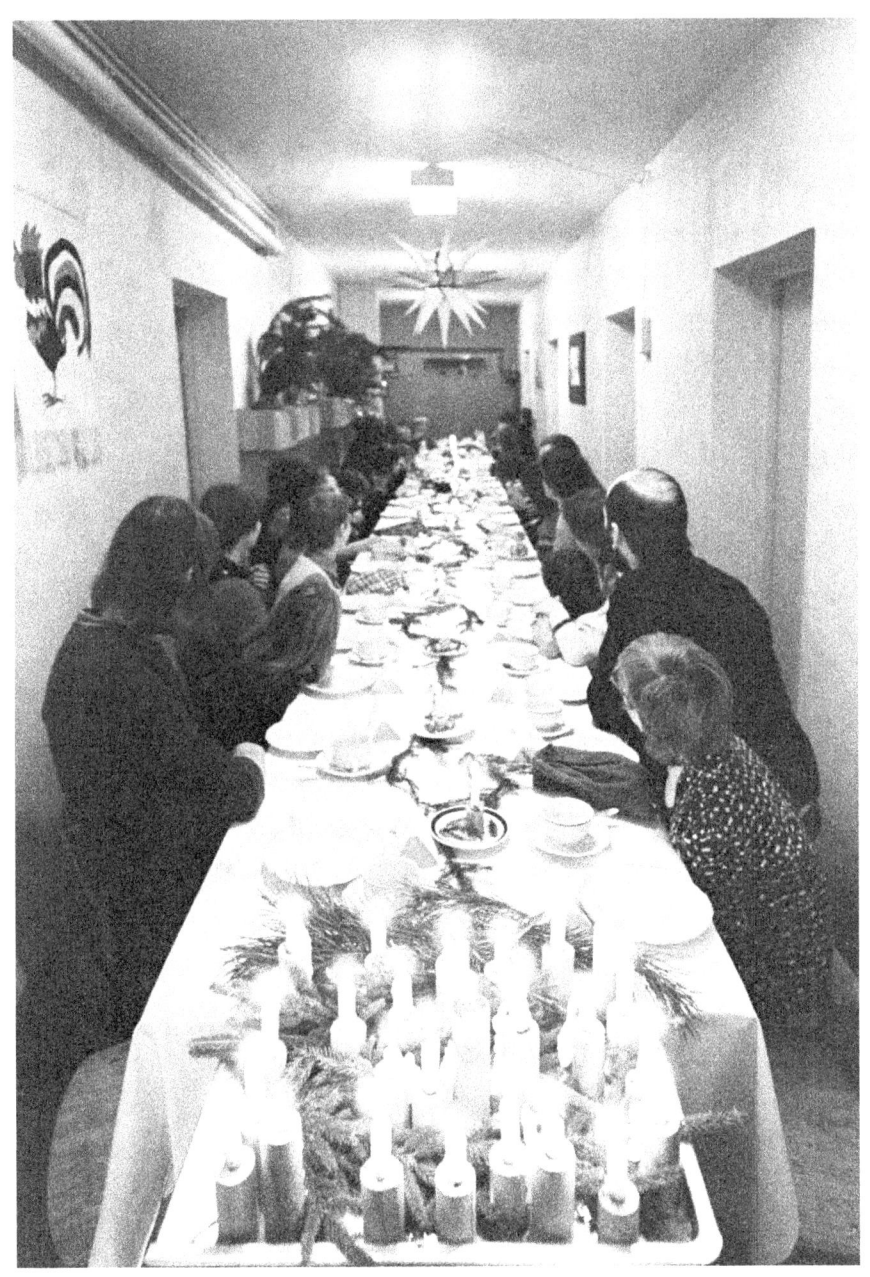

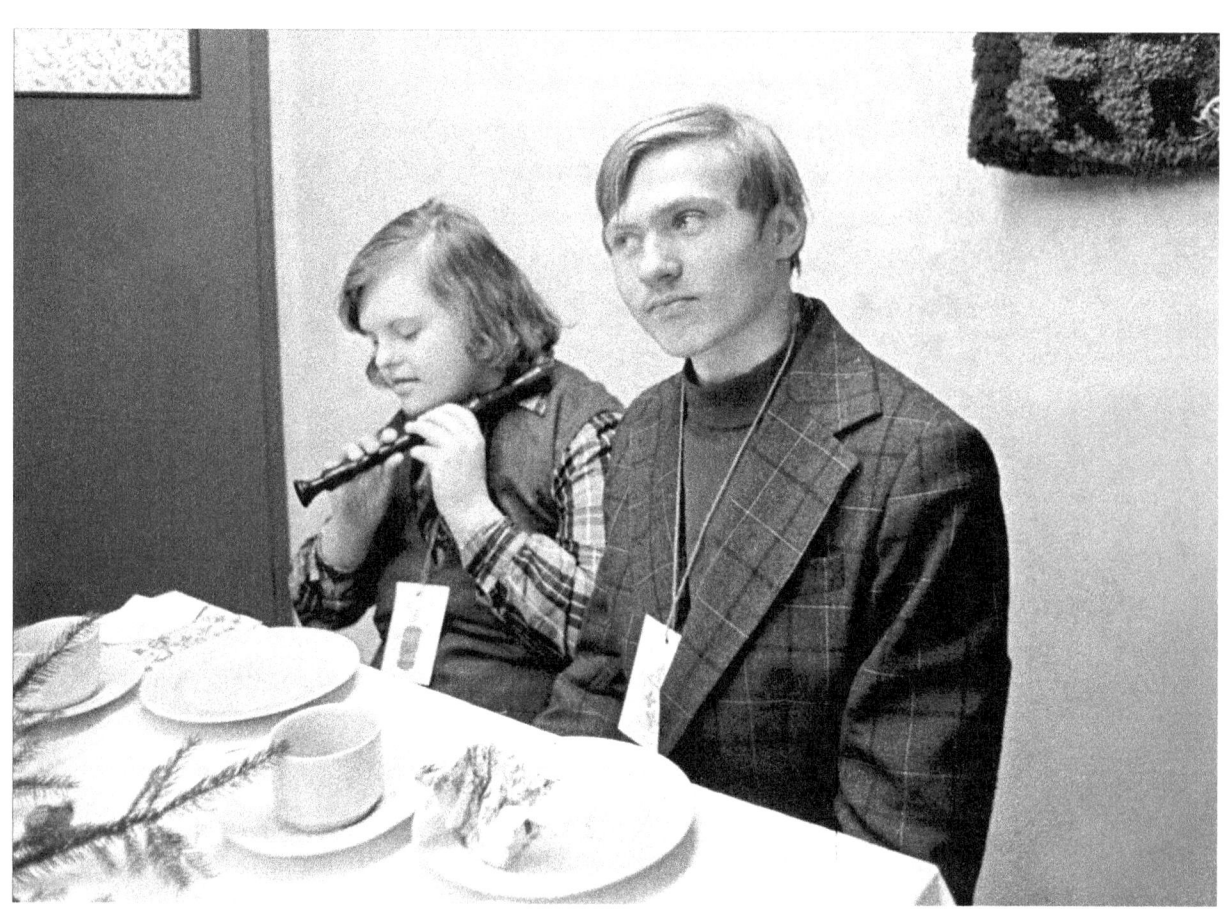

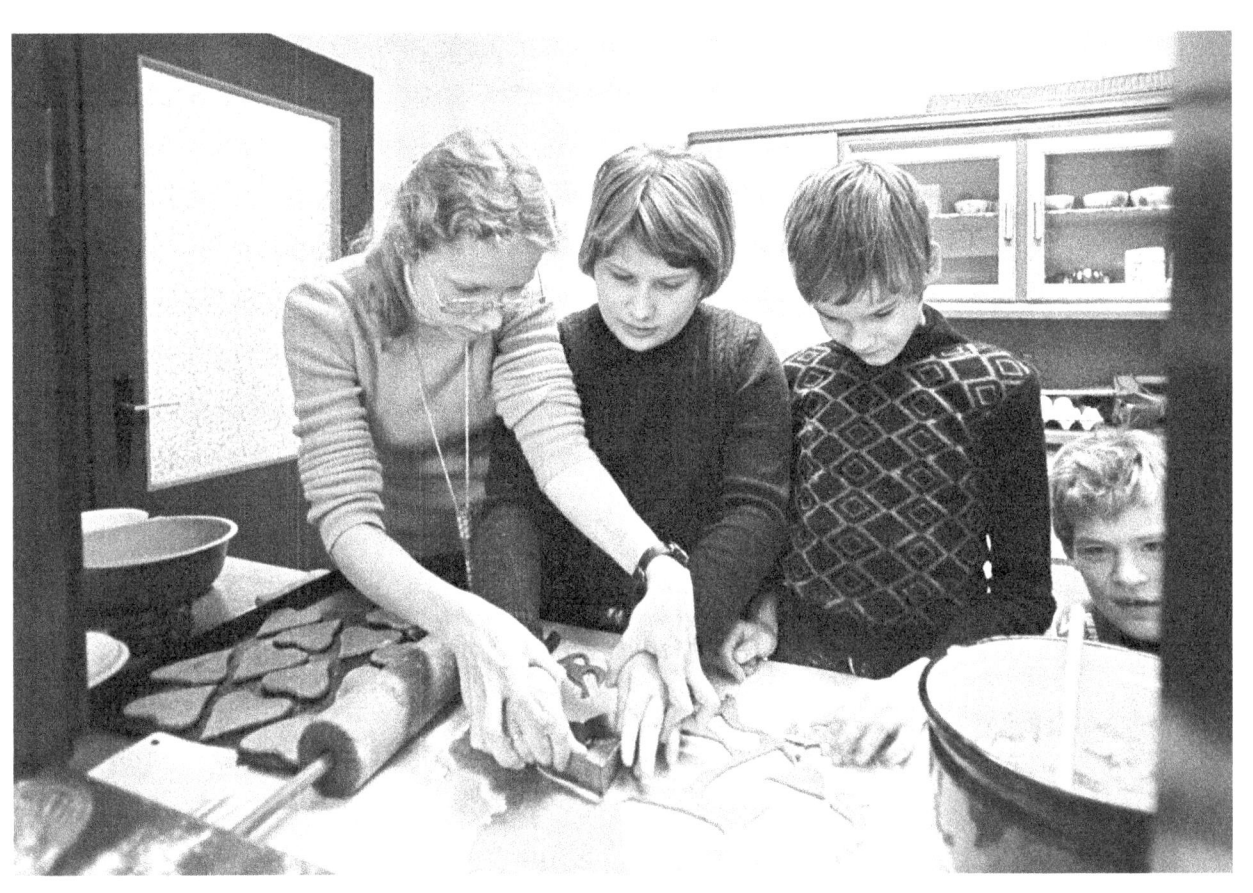

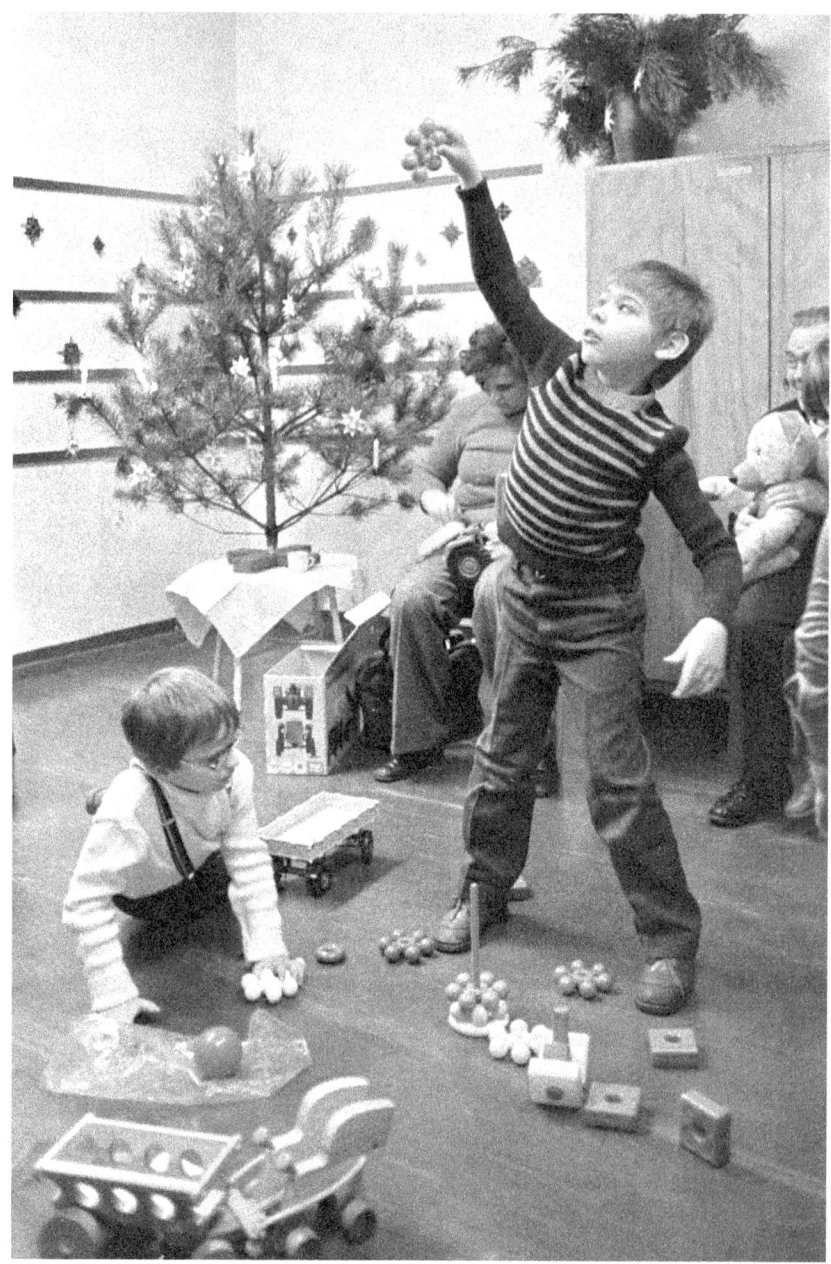

DIE ALTEN / THE ELDERLY

Photographs by Dietmar Riemann

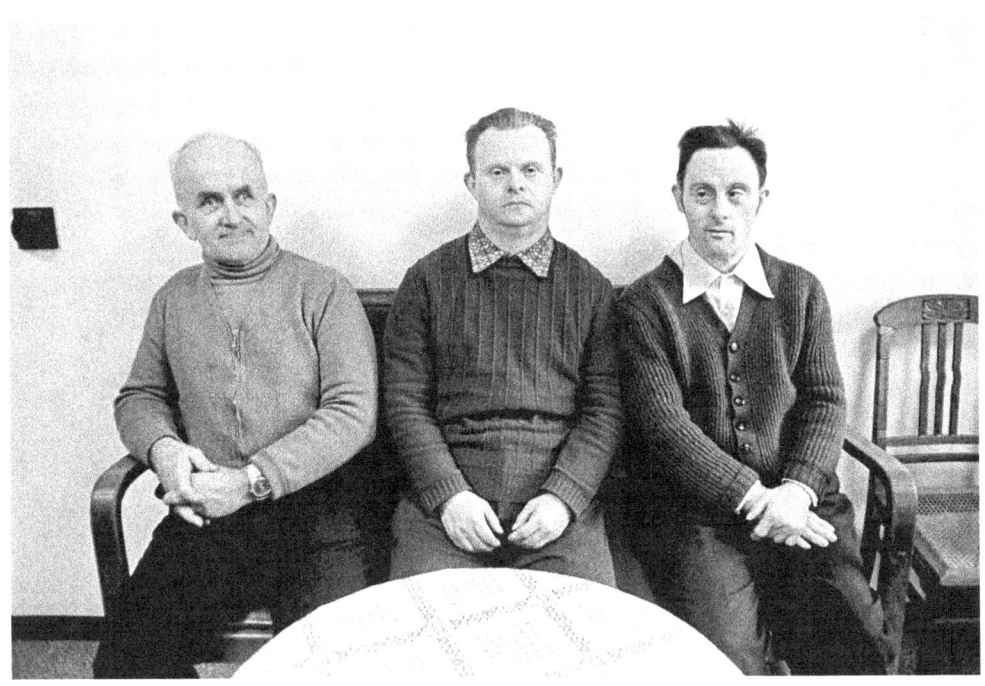

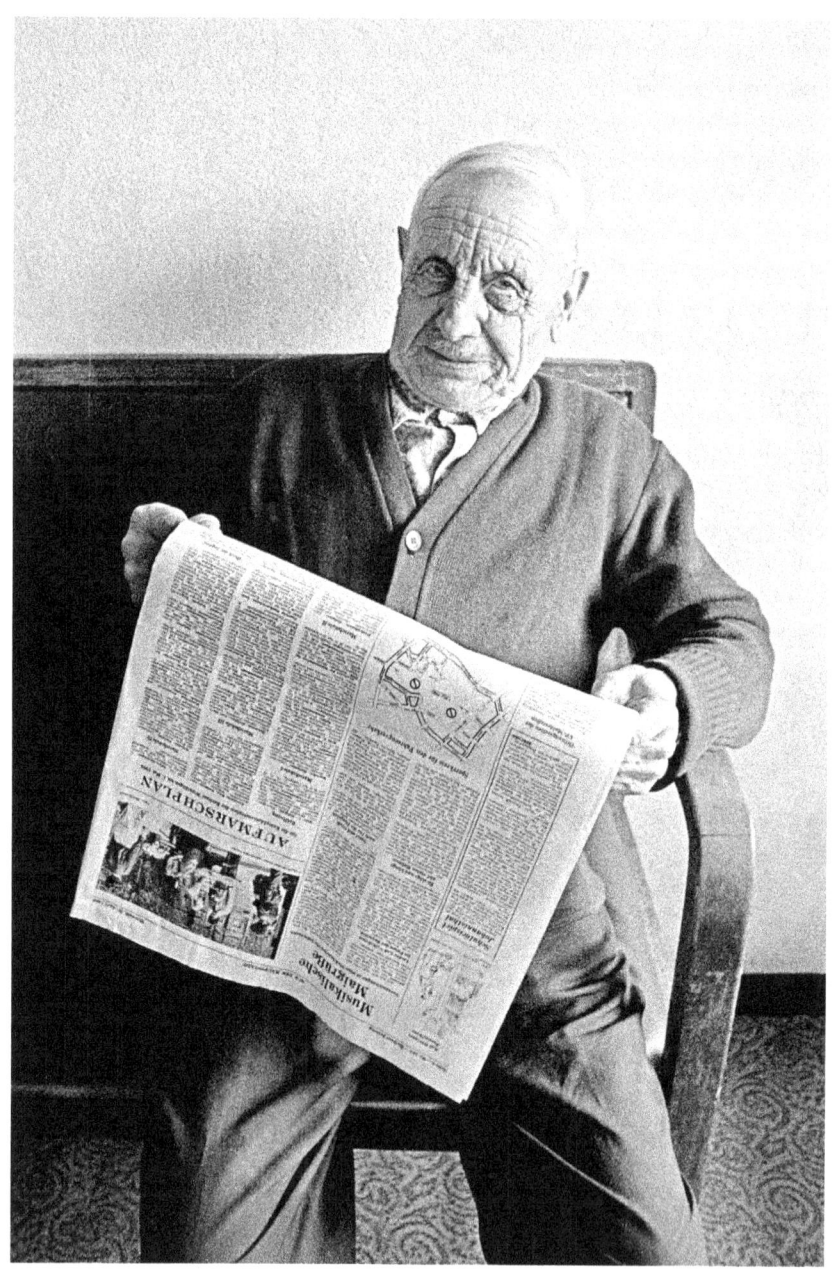

WHAT KIND OF ISLAND IN WHAT KIND OF SEA

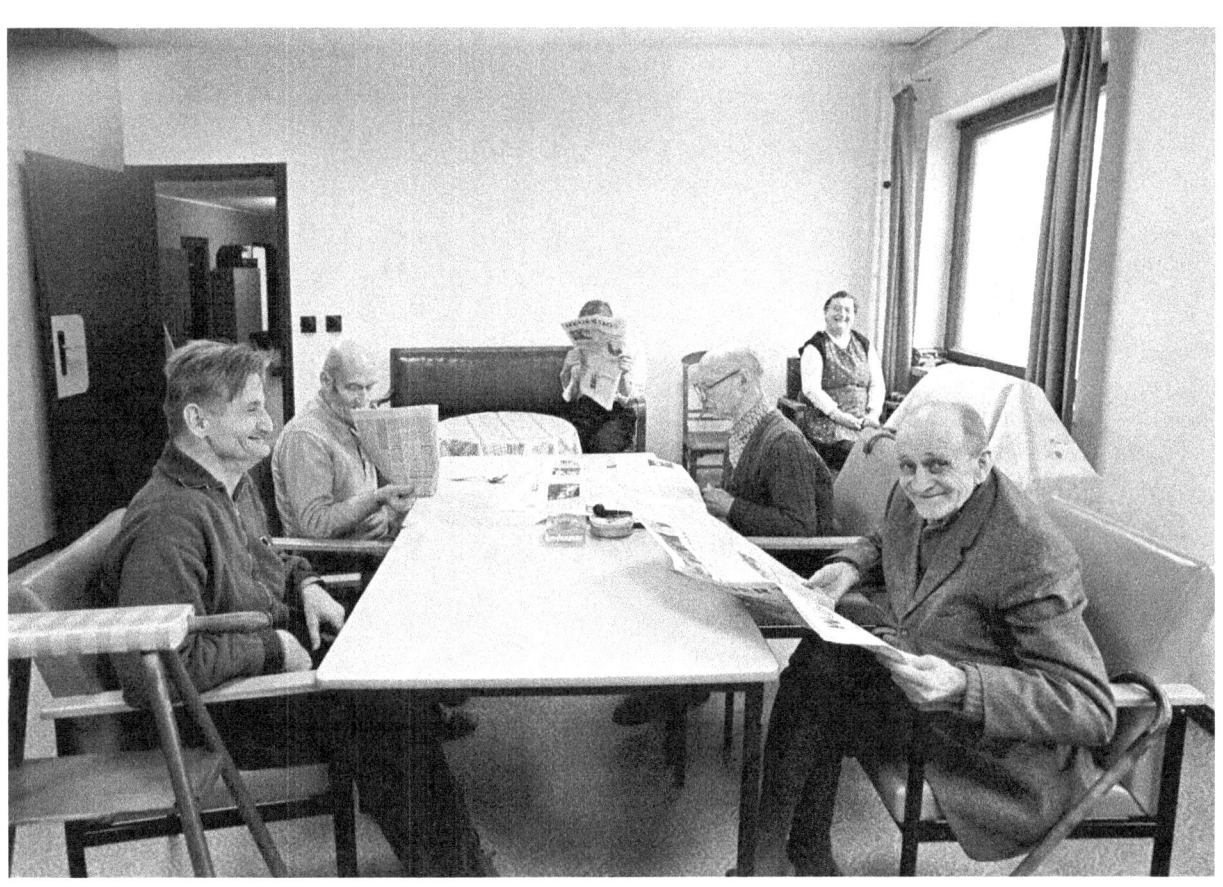

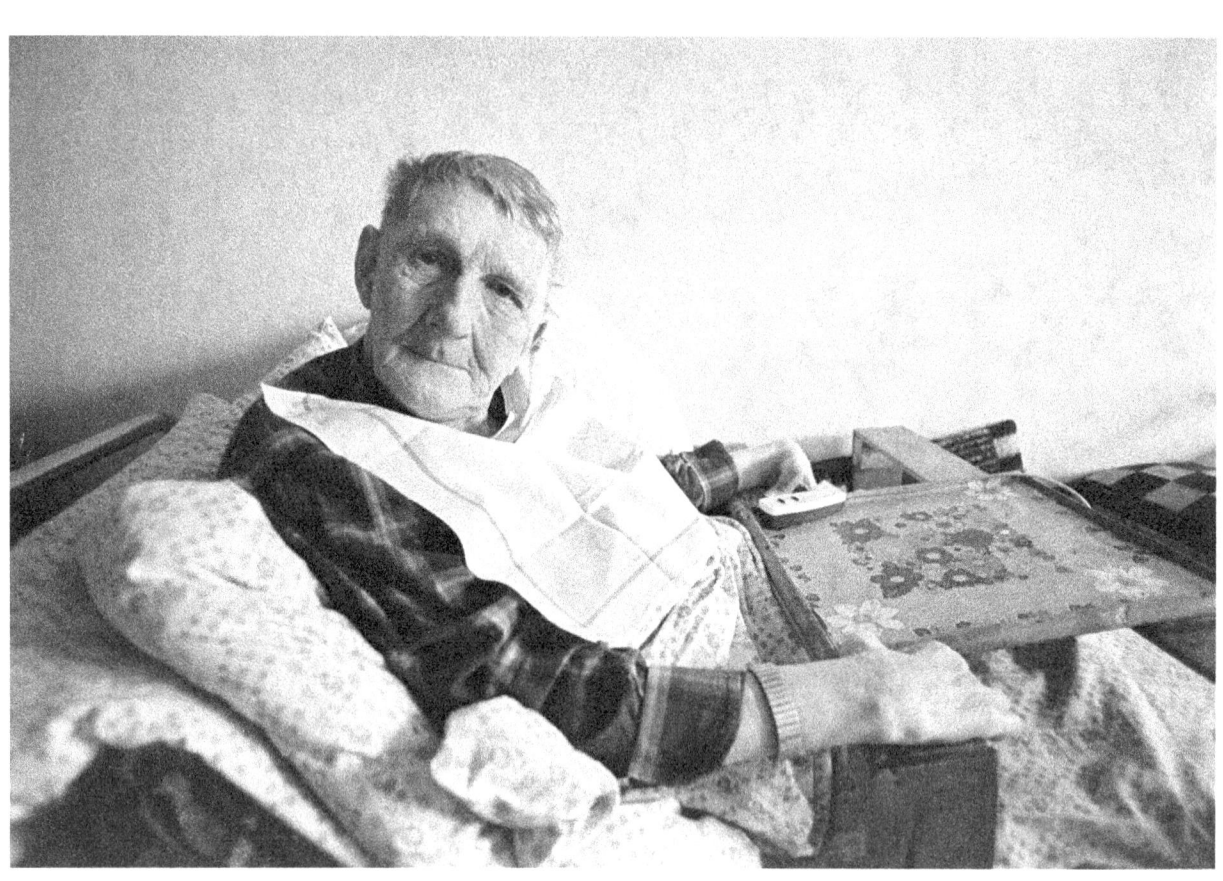

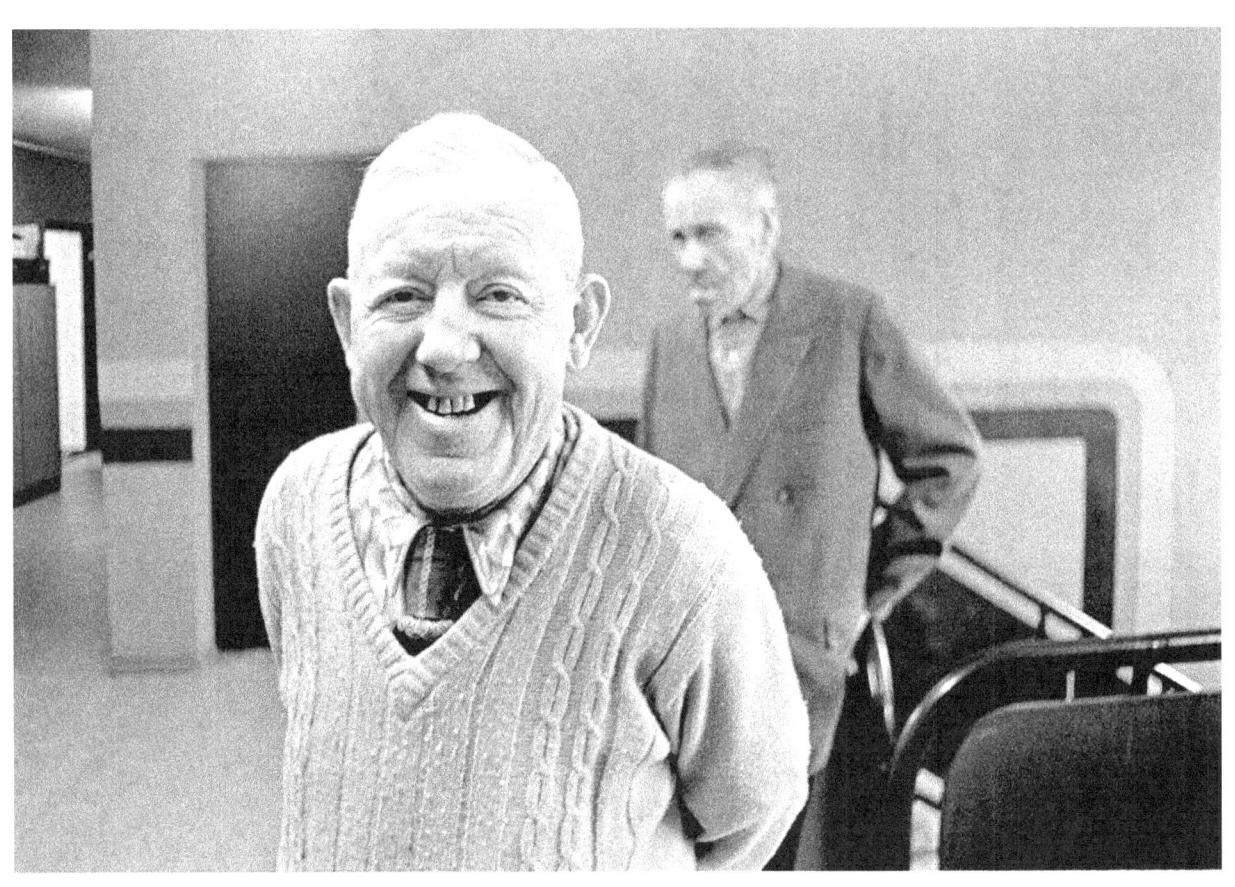

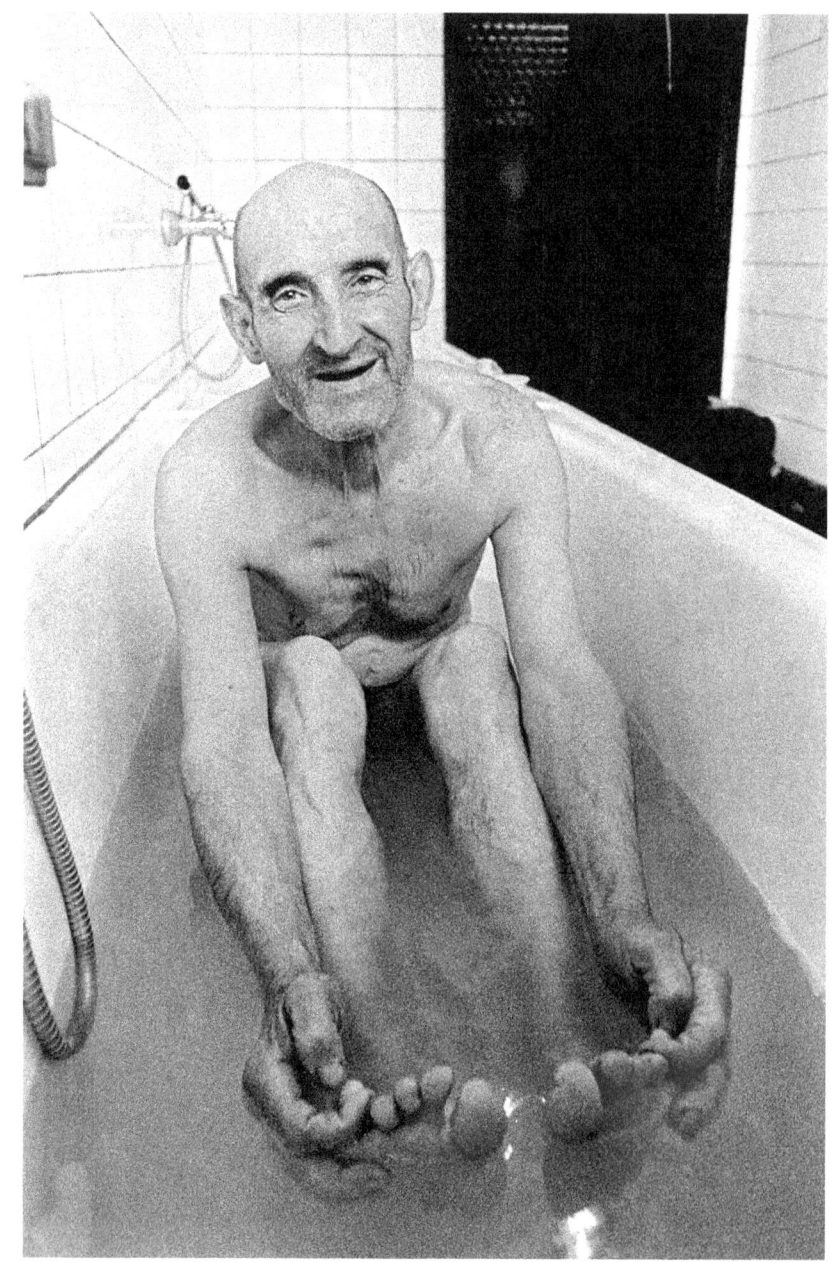

WHAT KIND OF ISLAND IN WHAT KIND OF SEA

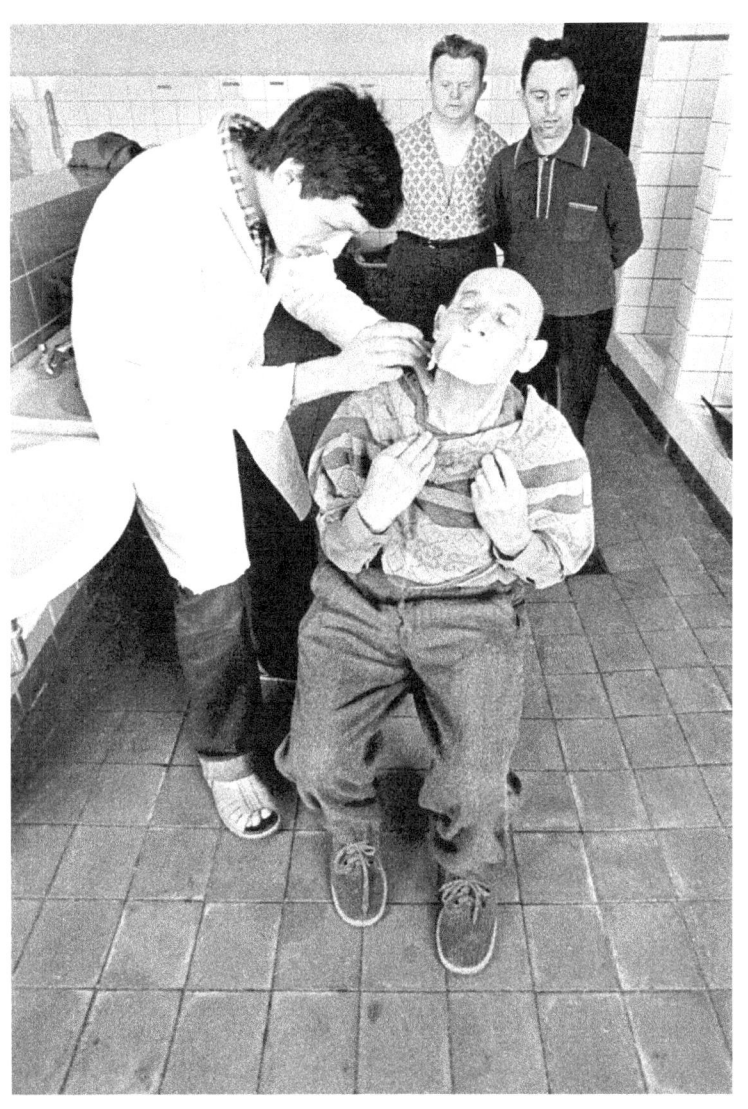

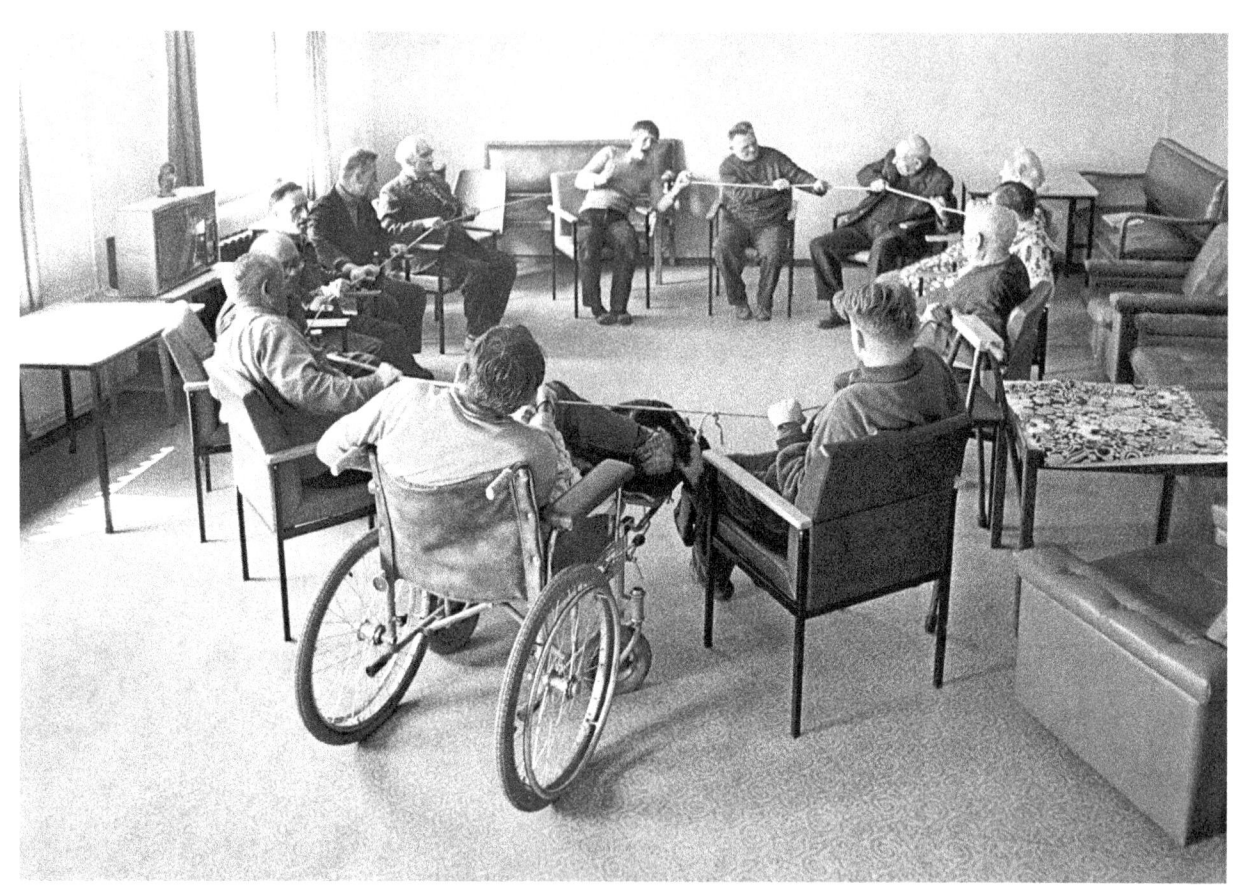

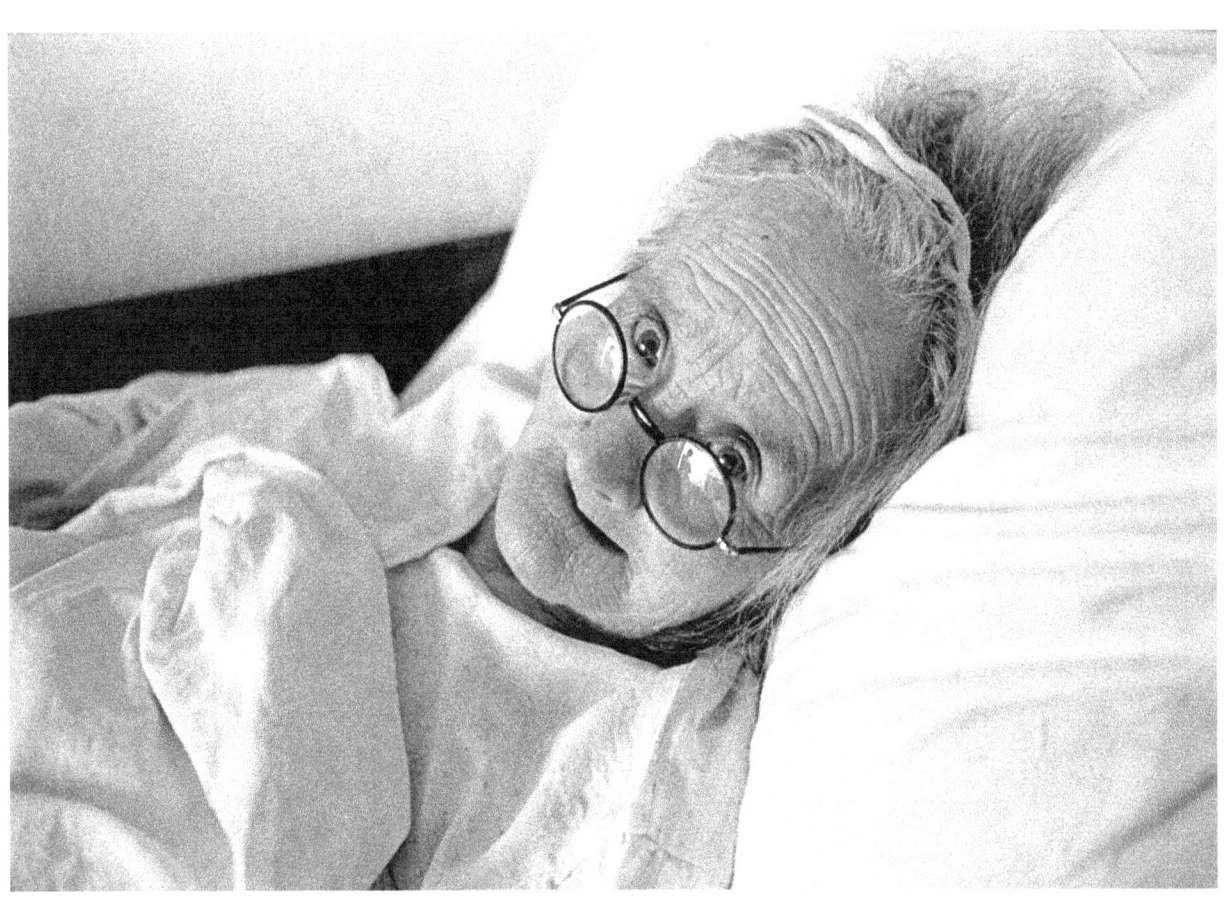

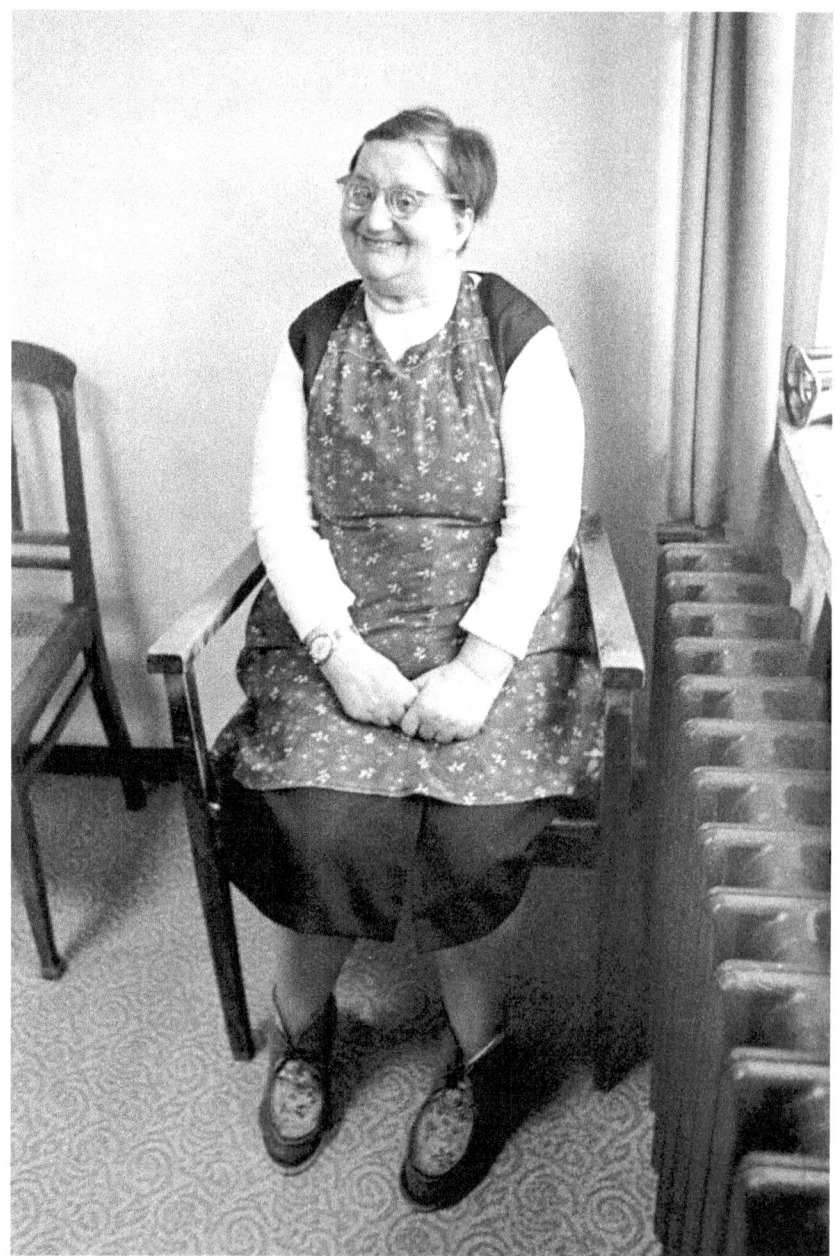

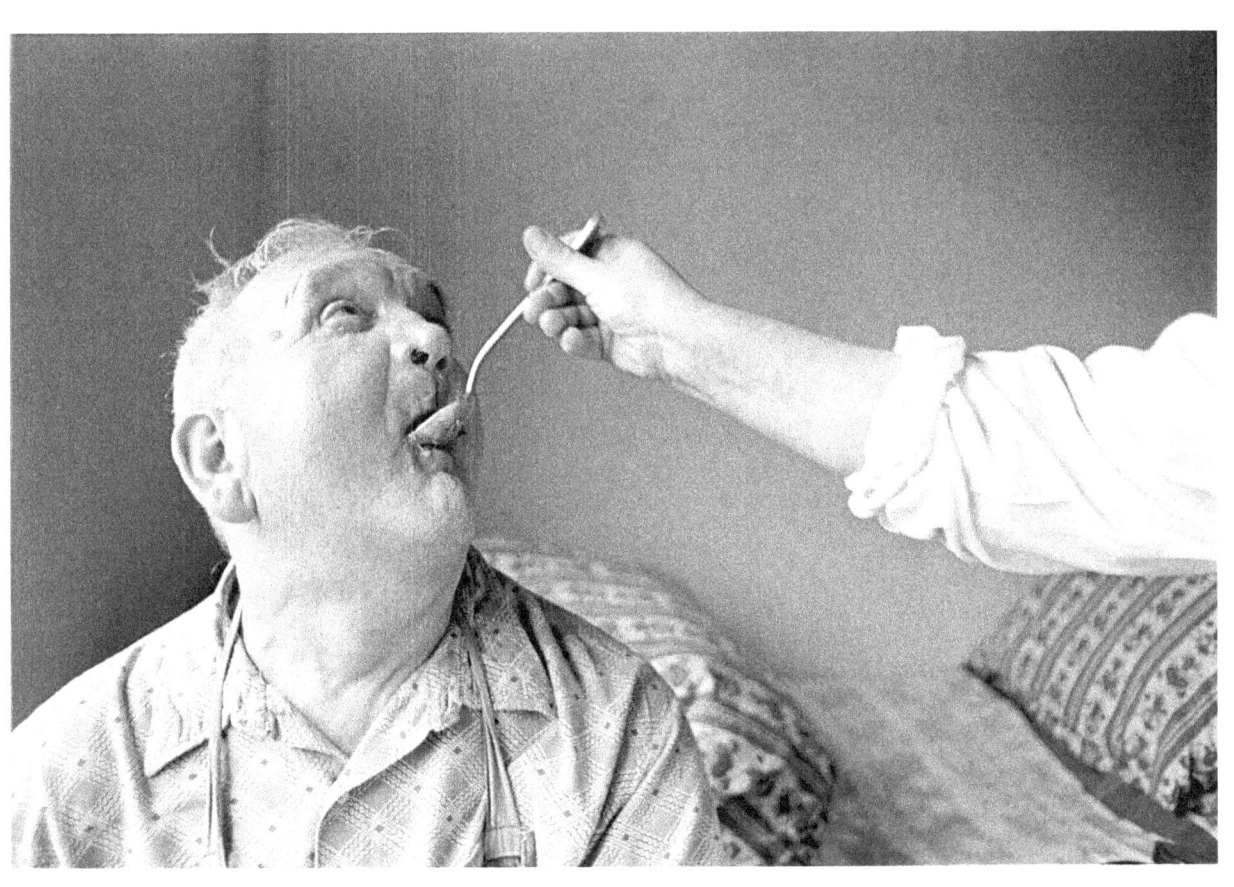

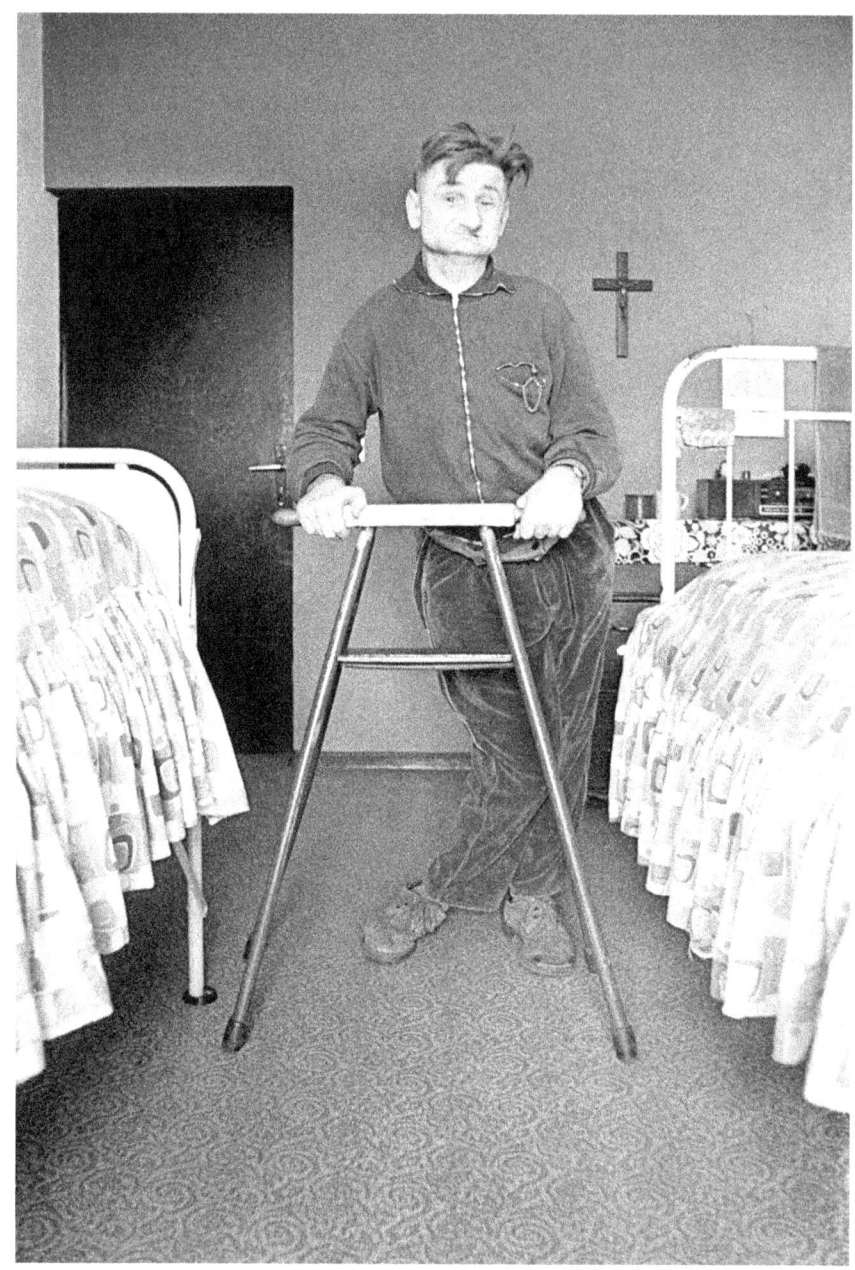

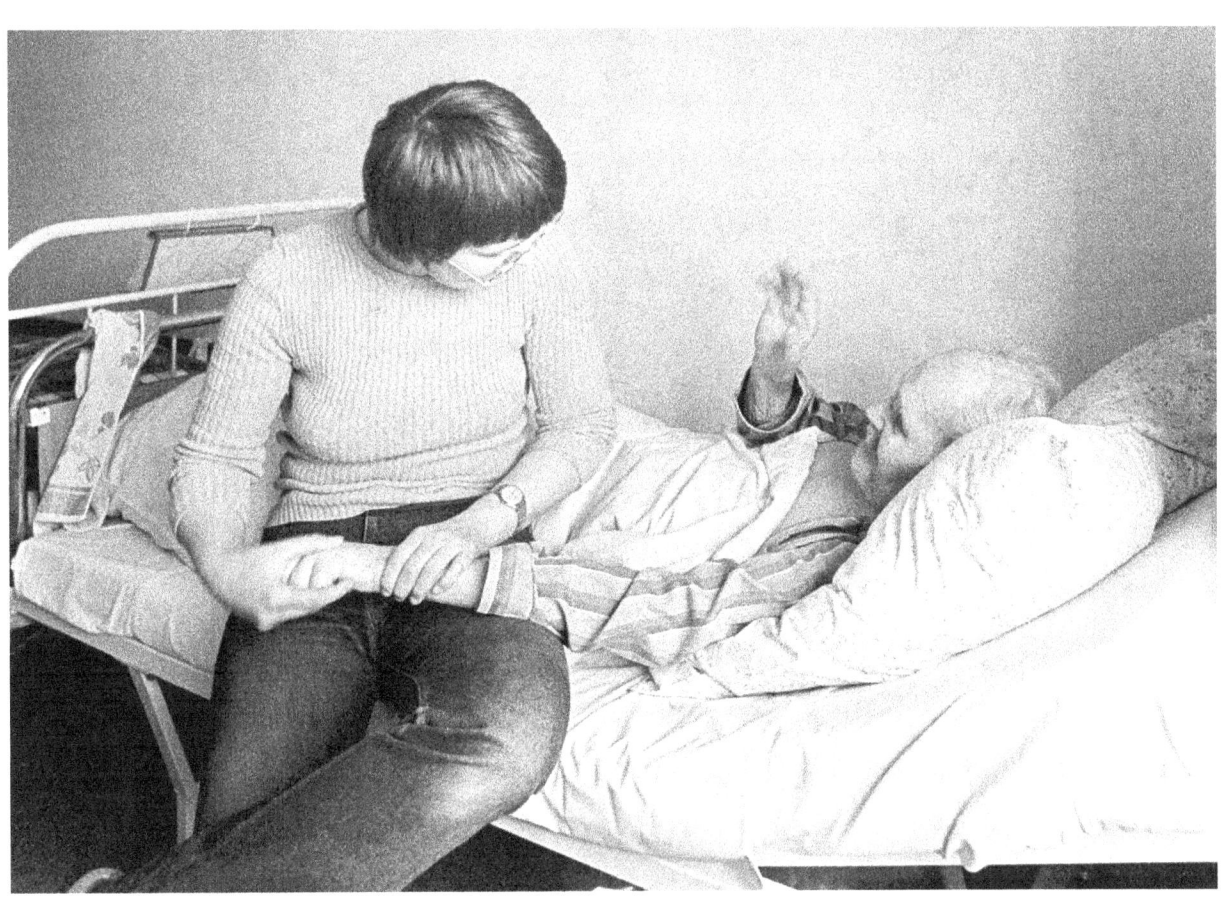

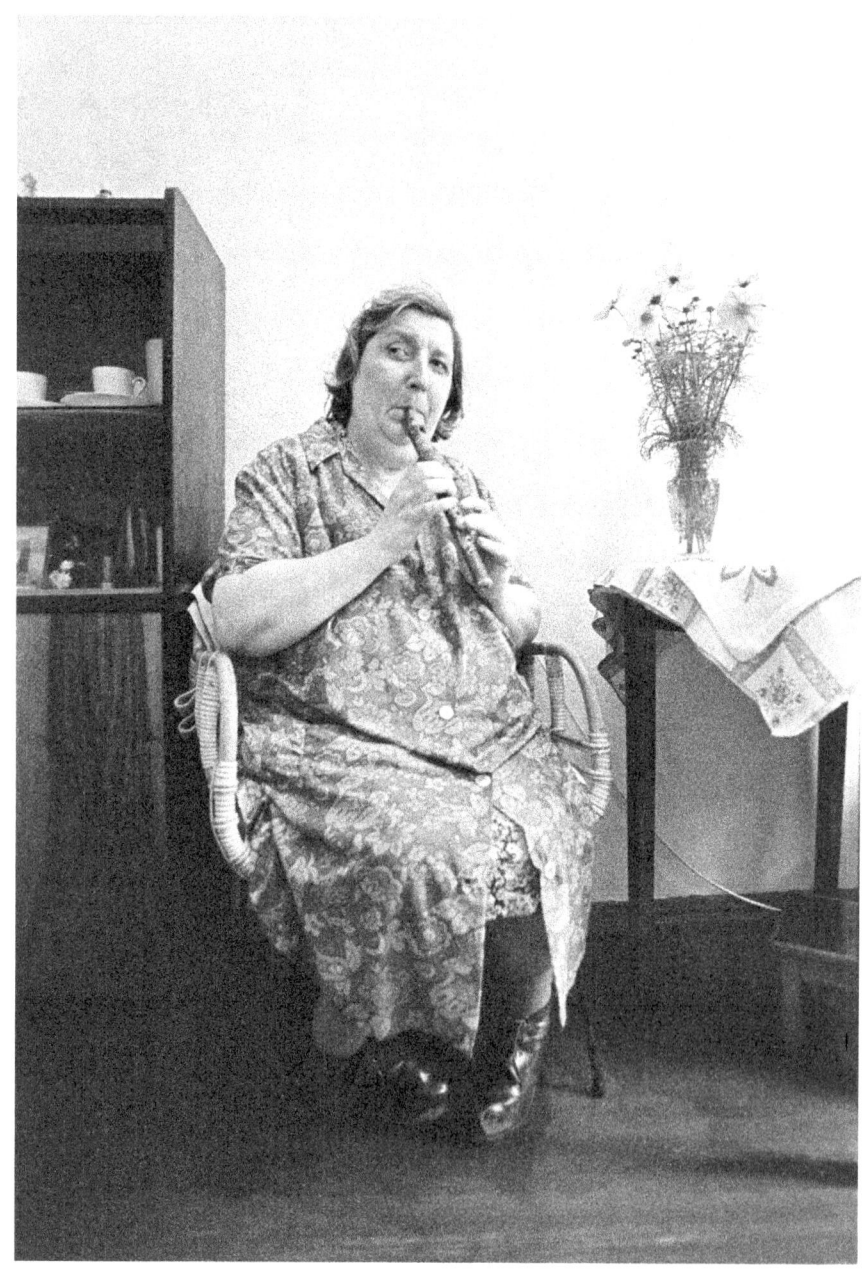

TENDING THE VINE

Personal Reflections on Visiting the Samariteranstalten

Elizabeth C. Hamilton

Was für eine Insel in was für einem Meer is a remarkably moving and eye-opening work. I learned of its existence in 2000 from a friend who had seen it as I was researching literary, cinematic, and cultural images of disability in Germany. I scoured bookstores and libraries in Berlin and Munich but could not locate a copy. Interlibrary loan services back in the United States turned up one copy from which many of the photographs had been cut out with scissors; what images had been taken, by whom, and why? Those left intact were stunning to me, so I presumed that the lost photos were even more moving. Additional weeks brought another copy to Oberlin's Clarence Ward Art Library, confirming my sense of the extraordinary treasure in my hands. While requesting that we purchase this rare book for our own collection, I felt a strong need to ensure that new audiences would have more ready access to Franz Fühmann's words and Dietmar Riemann's photographs of the residents who had made such a difference in their lives and work. I wanted to learn what impact Fühmann and Riemann and their book had had on the residents as well. The nearness that underlay the writing and the pictures must certainly have taken time to develop; how did it come about, and how long did it last? Published research had only partially answered these questions by that time, though more has come out since that gives Fühmann and Riemann the credit they deserve for their groundbreaking work.[1]

My visits to the Samariteranstalten and to the home of Dietmar and Marga Riemann in 2015, and my return to Fürstenwalde in 2017, opened further insights into the making of the book, allowing me to experience firsthand how difficult it is to capture in words and images all that there is to convey about thriving communities of purpose. What follows is an account of an academic inquiry suspended, a personal response to personal stories that affected me deeply and challenged my original notion of audience and purpose. While major themes and histories intersect—representing humanness in word and image, portraying disability, understanding the role of the arts and the church in socialism, testifying to the legacy of National Socialist "euthanasia"—my study is neither a comprehensive history nor literary criticism nor investigative journalism. Better scholars than I will appraise and interpret the complete works of Franz Fühmann and Dietmar Riemann, and better historians, theologians, and social scientists will assess the impact of the Samariteranstalten. My translation, my essay here, and my curating of the images and insights shared with me are efforts to tend a vine. As detailed in the previous pages, the *Insel* book connected disparate individuals in the shared purpose of bearing witness to human dignity. My goal in research became to expand its readership and sustain its good purpose.

In the spring of 2015, I introduced myself by email and described my intention to translate Fühmann's essay to Paul-Gerhard Voget, who was at that time the Theologischer Vorstand of the Samariteranstalten. While my focus was on the East German period in which Fühmann and Riemann had created their book, I wanted as well to understand what place it held in the institution's living memory. Mr. Voget knew of the *Insel* book's significance. He responded to my inquiry with an openness and hospitality that astonished me at the time, yet that I grew to recognize as operating principles there. He emailed and called me by phone to arrange for my visit, making a guest apartment on the premises available to me without cost. On his own initiative, he arranged for Fritz Müller, now living in Berlin, to visit Fürstenwalde to speak with me. Voget introduced me as well to Matthias Fichtmüller, Theologischer Vorstand, and Renate Frost, then a senior director at the Oberlinhaus, a comparable institution in Potsdam where I could learn more about diaconal care for people with disabilities in the region and that, not incidentally, carried my college's namesake.[2]

Dietmar Riemann was equally generous in response to my request to meet, inviting me to speak with him at his home in Mosbach, near Heidelberg. I spent two and a half days learning from him and from his wife, Marga Riemann, herself a professional photographer whose incisive analytical perspective on the complex collaboration enriched my understanding enormously.

It was my great pleasure to meet many residents of the Samariteranstalten, thirteen of whose photographs had appeared in the book thirty years earlier. Their warm hospitality remains strong in my memory.

Paul Voget accompanied me to conversations that I experienced as festive occasions. At each, the residents and I looked at the book together. Sitting with them and talking about their pictures was very much like looking at a family photo album. I asked if anyone wanted to tell me about what they remembered or how they felt about the photographs, or if they had any questions for me. Most did not register that their pictures had been published in a book. They spoke only about the pictures, which naturally evoked memories. They told me more details about what they had been doing in the pictures, and they knew a lot about people who had since moved or died. They spoke very concretely, including about their feelings.

At Lindenhof, a working farm of the Samariteranstalten located in a rural setting, I visited with residents Christine Z., Thomas K., Christa M., Gerda S., and Charlotte M. They made this conversation feel like a party. We spoke at a beautifully set table with flowers on a covered outdoor balcony while rain poured a few feet away. Thomas K. recognized himself right away in the photographs. He knew many others pictured within it and told about what they were doing now. He also raised many questions about other people pictured and wondered aloud what the answers might be. Gerda S. told me that she was seventy-two years old and arrived in Fürstenwalde in 1949. Her family had brought her there when she was six years old, and she never saw them again. Christa M. told me that she was seventy-six but thought she might have mixed up her numbers. Paul Voget thought she meant she was sixty-seven; I also would have guessed her to be younger, but we were both wrong. She showed me her room on the first floor. We took an elevator down from the balcony, since she uses a walker. She had a huge room divided into sleeping and dining areas, with a table and chairs, a stuffed chair, television, desk, bookshelves, lots of posters of cats (over which we bonded), plants, stuffed animals, dolls, knick-knacks, good curtains, pillows, and a rug. Christa M. told me that she liked her space and was proud of it. She gave me a picture that she painted that I still have.

Christine M. asked me a lot of questions about myself: whether I was married (no, but I had a boyfriend); whether we shared a room (yes); whether I slept by the window or by the door (by the window); whether I had children (no, but three cats); what their names were (Xavier, Theo, and Marmalade, pronounced in German with four syllables, which she repeated after me). Charlotte M. didn't say much, but she did look at the pictures. Thomas K. gave me a tour of the common space next to the kitchen, showing me the indoor stove for heat and fire; they were also getting a new outdoor oven for baking bread and making pizza.

I also heard troubling stories: "My parents put me out when I was six. The people from the social welfare agency [*Fürsorge*] picked me up and brought me to Fürstenwalde. I never saw my parents again." Christa M. and Gerda S. told about strict and even cruel deaconesses who made them take cold showers at night when they misbehaved during the day; the deaconesses had been unfriendly, and Christa M. and Gerda S.

liked it better now that they had their own rooms. Mr. Voget listened closely throughout, ensuring that they spoke openly about what they had experienced. He told them in my presence that mistreatment was not acceptable, that telling their stories was important for justice and healing and making sure that no others would be treated badly. In extended conversations with me afterward, he described the ways in which the Samariteranstalten actively engaged in "Aufarbeitung der Geschichte," or processing the past. He acknowledged that the institution's engagement with its own history has been vibrant and self-critical at times—and less so at other times.[3] He pointed out the Stolpersteine, or "stumbling blocks," commemorative plaques placed in the main brick pathway at the Samariteranstalten in memory of those who were killed under National Socialism.[4]

On another day I met with residents at aufwind, a non-profit initiative of the Samariteranstalten and Wichern Diakonie in Frankfurt (on the Oder River, in the state of Brandenburg) that provides support services for adults with cognitive and physical disabilities in their own homes. aufwind's motto is that people with disabilities live like everyone else: "ganz normal und mitten drin" (perfectly normally and right in the middle of it). Assistenznehmer, or recipients of assistance, Rotraud S., Christel O., Kornelia B., Heinz S., and staff members Ms. Diane Krüger, Ms. Dana Tiedge, and Ms. Jenny Baumgärtel welcomed me warmly. We spoke for two and a half hours around a table set with beautiful flowers. They had prepared coffee, water and juice, sandwiches, and cake, and my sense was that they enjoyed the conversation as much as I did. They loved the photos and delighted in recognizing themselves and their friends. They did not remember having their pictures taken, but they remembered the situations in the pictures. Looking at the book was again like any family or group of friends looking at a photo album or yearbook. Their sense of community was very strong and dated back to their childhood experiences together at the Samariteranstalten. All four said that they liked their lives better now that they had their own rooms or apartments. Kornelia B. is married. Christel O. showed me her knitting and crocheting projects, sometimes for sale in fundraisers. She and Ms. Krüger invited me to choose one, and I said I'd like the pair of Eierwärmer, or egg warmers, but might I offer a donation? Although they insisted that I didn't need to, they allowed me to put 2 Euros in their jar. They gave me a festive package of coffee and chocolates. I found it hard to say goodbye.

My German had been horrible that day. But everyone had been very kind and patient as I struggled to find the words.[5] I received excellent questions from the staff members: How did I come upon the Fühmann-Riemann book? What was my interest in writing about the book? How would I incorporate what I learned this week from the residents and recipients of assistance into my study? Neither German nor English words came readily at that point. In retrospect I was grasping for clarity about my project. How would I recognize and honor the people I had met? Since being in Fürstenwalde it was growing clear that my initial plan for scholarship was no longer so meaningful to me.

At a third residence, Wilhelminenhof, on the outskirts of town, I met Margarethe R., Klaus-Dieter S., Gerd F., and Wolfgang F. Their conversation was just as warm and fun as the others had been, though not as long or as intense. We looked at the book together briefly but did not spend much time talking about it. None remembered Dietmar Riemann personally, but they liked his pictures. They knew I would soon meet him and said to pass on their greetings to him. After the group dispersed, I enjoyed a longer conversation with Gerd F. I found him easy to talk to, and he smiled a lot. He had lived there in the Wilhelminenhof for nine years. He offered to show me his room, which was filled with many posters of animals, pictures of his sister and nephew, a large collection of books, a flat-screen television, stereo system, and magazines of all varieties neatly stacked on his bookshelf.

At the end of my visit in Fürstenwalde, I was interviewed by Sonja Jennings from the *Märkische Online Zeitung*. Herr Voget introduced me and simply listened for most of the interview. At the end, he summarized succinctly that meeting the residents had evidently changed my project substantially, that "Behinderung hat Gesichter und Geschichten bekommen" (disability had acquired faces and histories), that would be taken across the ocean to America.[6] I began to see the residents as both my traveling companions and as belonging to the audience for whom I would write. I experienced Fühmann's unease in writing about people he admires—"the vexing crux of my profession"—and began a reflective journey to reassess the techniques, purposes, audiences, ethics, and impact of my academic writing in the field of German studies. Expanded disciplinary perspectives and expanded discourse communities would provide the best possibility for honoring the individuals represented and drawing credible conclusions about this "island" book that proved to be no island. Translation, collaboration, and open access publication became my methods of choice for examining and conveying awe of human dignity of people with cognitive disabilities expressed in this early historical example. While awe alone does not secure their fundamental human rights or adequate conditions for living, awe of human dignity rebuffs discrediting and hostile attitudes that endanger people with cognitive disabilities. Awe of human dignity can motivate the necessary work to advocate for their care, rights, and access to participation in society. And awe, once acknowledged, can be a guiding force for presumably non-disabled or not-yet-disabled people to look for mutually edifying strength, beauty, and value among people long kept out of sight.

In creating *Was für eine Insel in was für einem Mee*r, Franz Fühmann and Dietmar Riemann challenged readers to examine exclusionary cultural attitudes toward cognitive disability through their collaborative, relational, and reflective practices of representation. Their work and working methods are models for new storytelling, art, and scholarship. Let me conclude with one recent example that takes up this model even as the present discussion similarly aspires to enlarge the community of engagement: Paul-Gerhard Voget, residents, and staff members of the Samariteranstalten presented *their* newly published collection of stories, *Was es noch zu sagen gäbe: Geschichten aus den Samariteranstalten anlässlich ihres 125-jährigen Bestehens* (One more thing to say: Stories from the Samaritans' Institutions on the occasion of their 125th year), at an elegant celebration on October 11, 2017, in the cathedral in Fürstenwalde. They had commissioned new music and toasted their book's publication with champagne. Riemann was an invited guest, as was I. Addressing the large audience and the press, Voget underlined that the real lives of the residents and partners were distinctly richer than many might think: "We are people who write books."

Notes

"HERE, THEN, AWE OF HUMAN DIGNITY"

1. Franz Fühmann and Dietmar Riemann, *Was für eine Insel in was für einem Meer* (Rostock: Hinstorff, 1986). Page citations are provided in the text.
2. A Kaufmännischer Vorstand, or executive financial officer, works together with the Theologischer Vorstand in leading the Samaritans' Institution.
3. Carol Poore, *Disability in Twentieth-Century German Culture*, Corporealities: Discourses of Disability (Ann Arbor: University of Michigan Press, 2007), 233.
4. Author Peter Wawerzinek offered his insight in personal correspondence: "Ein zukunftsorientierte Gesellschaft von Arbeiterhelden und Bestarbeitern sparte das Thema aus, dass es geistig und körperliche Behinderte gibt" (A future-oriented society of worker-heroes and best workers neglected to mention that there were cognitively and physically disabled people). Thousands of East Germany's "Bestarbeiter," or "best workers," were celebrated in a regular conference in Berlin.
5. The parable of the Good Samaritan is found in Luke 10:25–37 and elucidates the commandment to "love your neighbor as yourself." In the story, a priest and a Levite both avoid an injured traveler, but a Samaritan stops to care for him.
6. Gisela Helwig, "Handicapped People in the GDR: Cooperation between Church and State," in *Studies in GDR Culture and Society*, ed. Margy Gerber (Lanham, MD: University Press of America, 1987), 7:46.
7. Paul-Gerhard Voget, interview with author, Fürstenwalde, Germany, July 21, 2015.

8. Hans Richter, "Franz Fühmanns Arbeiten für Kinder und Jugendliche," *Literatur für Leser* 2 (1993): 81–93. Unless otherwise noted, all translations are my own.

9. Uwe Kolbe, *Rübezahl in der Garage*. Franz Fühmann in Märkisch-Buchholz und Fürstenwalde 1958–1984, *Frankfurter Buntbücher* 41 (Frankfurt (Oder): Kleist-Museum, 2006).

10. See Dennis Tate, "Franz Fühmann: A Neglected Legacy," in *Socialism and the Literary Imagination: Essays on East German Writers*, ed. Martin Kane (New York: Berg, 1991), 91–105.

11. Copyright Uwe Kolbe, 2007. *Der Stoff des Lebens. Anmerkungen bei Betrachtung von Dietmar Riemanns Photographie der Totenmaske von Franz Fühmann* (The substance of life: Notes on viewing Riemann's photograph of Franz Fühmann's death mask). Printed with accompanying photograph by Dietmar Riemann in program of the exhibit *Geistig behinderte Menschen im Gespräch mit Franz Fühmann über den Basler Totentanz von HAP Grieshaber* (Cognitively disabled people in conversation with Franz Fühmann about the Dance of Death by HAP Grieshaber). Concept and installation by Fritz Müller. On loan from MISSJONARISCH.

12. Dietmar Riemann, interview with author, Mosbach, Germany, July 28, 2015. See also Dietmar Riemann, "Ich wollte nicht mehr mitmachen. Geschichte einer Verweigerung," in *Die Schuld der Mitläufer. Anpassen oder Widerstehen in der DDR*, ed. Roman Grafe (Munich: Pantheon, 2009), 91–100.

13. Dietmar Riemann, "*Was für eine Insel in was für einem Meer*. Die Geschichte eines Bildbandes mit Franz Fühmann," Palmbaum: Literarisches Journal aus Jena 1 (2014): 129, https://www.franz-fuehmann.de/_literatur/documents/Palm_1_14_Fuehmann.pdf.

14. Riemann, "Geschichte eines Bildbandes," 131.

15. Klaus Gubener, correspondence with author, August 11, 2015.

16. Riemann, interview.

17. Klaus Gubener notes, "Mein Vorschlag, Fühmann zu fragen, hielt Riemann für absurd" (Riemann considered my suggestion to ask Fühmann [to write a text to accompany his photographs] absurd). Gubener, correspondence.

18. Riemann, "Geschichte eines Bildbandes," 129.

19. See accompanying image of the note. Image from the personal collection of Klaus Gubener, shared via email with author, August 11, 2015.

20. HAP Grieshaber was Fühmann's close friend and was himself facing death at the time of the exhibition in Fürstenwalde. Fühmann corresponded with Grieshaber and his wife. Personal collection of Klaus Gubener.

21. Klaus Gubener, "Geistig Behinderte Sehen und Deuten: HAP Grieshabers Totentanz von Basel. Franz Fühmanns Tonbandabschrift," personal collection, 2000.

22. See Riemann's essay on the creation of the volume ("Geschichte eines Bildbandes," 137) and a passage from Riemann's website: "Eine Ausstellung der Behinderten-Bilder in der Galerie eines Berliner Kulturhauses (heute 'Brotfabrik') wird zwangsweise abgehängt, die Galeristin entlassen, das ganze Haus vorerst geschlossen. Das bedeutete de facto Ausstellungsverbot in staatlichen Einrichtungen," https://www.ddr-fotografie-riemann.de.

23. Riemann, "Geschichte eines Bildbandes," 135.

24. Riemann, interview.

25. Riemann, "Geschichte eines Bildbandes," 135.

26. See Poore, *Disability*, 234. An unattributed 2012 article in the online newspaper *Neues Deutschland* also notes: "Fühmann gäbe sich immer mehr mit Geisteskranken ab, so dass er bereits deren Verhaltensweisen annehme, notierte der Staatssekretär im DDR-Kulturministerium Kurt Löffler in einem Bericht an das MfS" ("Kinder des Olymp: Sibylle Bergemann fotografierte das Berliner Theater RambaZamba," *Neues Deutschland. Sozialistische Zeitung*, January 13, 2012, https://www.nd-aktuell.de/artikel/215439.kinder-des-olymp.html). See as well Riemann, "Geschichte eines Bildbandes," 138: "Genosse [geschwärzte Stelle, sie meint den Staatssekretär] schätzt ein, dass früher oder später eine Einweisung von Fühmann in eine psychiatrische Anstalt nicht zu umgehen sei und dann eine politische Wertung seitens feindlicher Kräfte zu erwarten ist" (Comrade [expurgated text, referring to the undersecretary] predicts that sooner or later it will be unavoidable that Fühmann is committed to a psychiatric institution and then we should expect a political assessment from enemy forces).

27. Riemann, "Geschichte eines Bildbandes," 136; and Riemann, interview.

28. Radio host Peter Liebert interviewed Dietmar Riemann on January 17, 1987. Recording from the personal collection of Dietmar Riemann.

29. Gudrun Klatt, "Franz Fühmann, Dietmar Riemann: Was für eine Insel in was für einem Meer," *Weimarer Beiträge: Zeitschrift für Literaturwissenschaft, Ästhetik und Kulturwissenschaften* 34, no. 4 (1988): 641–649.

30. While Riemann's extensive writings on the topic of his departure from East Germany to some degree exceed the scope of this essay, I include here his conviction that "die friedliche Revolution," or "peaceful revolution," did not fully acknowledge the dissidents who paid great personal costs in their efforts to leave the country. Riemann believes that "die Wende," or "the turn" or "change," is an inappropriate term for the transition period of the opening of the East and West border. He favors more pointed terminology signaling the collapse of East Germany.

31. Riemann, interview.

32. Poore, *Disability*, 246.

33. Peter Wawerzinek, in-person conversation and email with author, February 21, 2014.

34. Carol Poore identified only one literary work to thematize Nazi "euthanasia" that had been published by this time: East German author Christoph Hein's novel *Horns Ende* (Horn's end) appeared in 1985. West German author Franz Xaver Kroetz's novel *Der Mondscheinknecht* (The moonlight servant) would follow in 1988. Poore, *Disability*, 242.

35. Andreas Hechler, "Diagnosen von Gewicht. Innerfamiliäre Folgen der Ermordung meiner als 'lebensunwert' diagnostizierten Urgroßmutter," in *Gegendiagnose. Beiträge zur radikalen Kritik an Psychiatrie und Psychologie*, Psycho_Gesundheitspolitik im Kapitalismus, vol. 1 (Münster: edition assemblage, August 2015), 174.

TENDING THE VINE

1. See Carol Poore, *Disability in Twentieth-Century German Culture*, Corporealities: Discourses of Disability (Ann Arbor: University Michigan Press, 2007). See also Peter Braun and Martin Straub, *Ins Innere Annäherungen an*

Franz Fühmann (Göttingen: Wallstein, 2016), which includes Dietmar Riemann's own essay in the volume: "Aus dem Zyklus 'Leben mit Geistig Behinderten' in den Samariteranstalten Fürstenwalde" (194–203); and Uwe Kolbe, *Rübezahl in der Garage. Franz Fühmann in Märkisch-Buchholz und Fürstenwalde 1958–1984*, Frankfurter Buntbücher 41 (Frankfurt (Oder): Kleist-Museum, 2006).

2. I had long been interested in J.F. Oberlin and wrote a short piece for the Oberlin College web site about his life's work, seen through the lens of German literature and education: "Fact or Fiction: Oberlin's Passion for Social Justice Begins in German." https://inside.oberlin.edu/facultyexperts/german/prof-elizabeth-c-hamilton.shtml.

3. The Samariteranstalten publish a magazine, *Unterwegs*, "En route" or "On the way," which regularly includes reflection on a topical question or period in history. Residents, staff members, and guest authors contribute prose and artwork. Special issues have been dedicated to anniversary years and to the process of remembering the past. My own visit to Fürstenwalde was featured in the second issue of 2015.

4. The international stumbling block movement that began in the early 1990s is significant for its own complicated history and is not without detractors. Some object to the invitation to walk on the memorials of those who suffered degradation leading to death. Criticism from another angle contends that, as with other memorializing initiatives, disabled people were among the last to be included.

5. I have long perceived that disability and second-language learning have much in common, at least with respect to the experience of and fear of being presumed to be incompetent.

6. Conversation during interview for the *Märkische Online Zeitung*, Fürstenwalde, July 24, 2015.

Bibliography

Braun, Peter, and Martin Straub, eds. *Ins Innere. Annäherungen an Franz Fühmann*. Göttingen: Wallstein, 2016.

Dinter, Ingrid. *Unvollendete Trauerarbeit in der DDR-Literatur. Ein Studium der Vergangenheitsbewältigung*. DDR-Studien/East German Studies 7. New York: Peter Lang, 1994.

Franze, Jens C., and Paul-Gerhardt Voget, eds. *Die Samariteranstalten Fürstenwalde. Eine diakonische Stiftung zwischen Kaiserreich und Bundesrepublik*. Berlin-Brandenburg: be.bra wissenschaft, 2012.

Fühmann, Franz. *Essays, Gespräche, Aufsätze 1964–1981*. Rostock: Hinstorff, 1983.

———. *Works*. 8 vols. Rostock: Hinstorff, 1993.

Fühmann, Franz, and Dietmar Riemann. *Was für eine Insel in was für einem Meer*. Rostock: Hinstorff, 1986.

Gubener, Klaus. "Geistig Behinderte Sehen und Deuten: HAP Grieshabers Totentanz von Basel. Franz Fühmanns Tonbandabschrift." Personal collection, 2000.

Hamilton, Elizabeth C. "Fact or Fiction: Oberlin's Passion for Social Justice Begins in German." https://inside.oberlin.edu/facultyexperts/german/prof-elizabeth-c-hamilton.shtml.

Hechler, Andreas. "Diagnosen von Gewicht. Innerfamiliäre Folgen der Ermordung meiner als 'lebensunwert' diagnostizierten Urgroßmutter." In *Gegendiagnose. Beiträge zur radikalen Kritik an Psychiatrie und Psychologie*, 143–193. Psycho_Gesundheitspolitik im Kapitalismus, vol. 1. Münster: edition assemblage, August 2015.

———. "Diagnoses That Matter: My Great-Grandmother's Murder as One Deemed 'Unworthy of Living' and Its Impact on Our Family." Translated by Elizabeth C. Hamilton and Leo R. Kalkbrenner. *Disability Studies Quarterly* 37, no. 2 (2017). https://doi.org/10.18061/dsq.v37i2.5573.

Helwig, Gisela. "Handicapped People in the GDR: Cooperation between Church and State." In *Studies in GDR Culture and Society*, edited by Margy Gerber, 7:43–54. Lanham, MD: University Press of America, 1987.

Jenning, Sonja. "Auf Spurensuchen in den Samariteranstalten." *Märkische Online Zeitung*, July 24, 2015. https://www.moz.de/lokales/fuerstenwalde/auf-spurensuche-in-den-samariteranstalten-48571364.html.

Jun, Gerda. *Kinder, die anders sind.* 1981. Treffbuch 16. Bonn: Psychiatrie-Verlag, 1989.

Kiefer-Hofmann, Angela. *Die Jacke des Herrn A. Erzählungen aus den Samariteranstalten.* Berlin: Wichern-Verlag, 2012.

"Kinder des Olymp: Sibylle Bergemann fotografierte das Berliner Theater RambaZamba." *Neues Deutschland. Sozialistische Zeitung*, January 13, 2012. https://www.nd-aktuell.de/artikel/215439.kinder-des-olymp.html.

Klatt, Gudrun. "Franz Fühmann, Dietmar Riemann: Was für eine Insel in was für einem Meer." *Weimarer Beiträge: Zeitschrift für Literaturwissenschaft, Ästhetik und Kulturwissenschaften* 34, no. 4 (1988): 641–649.

Kolbe, Uwe. "Der Stoff des Lebens. Einige Bemerkungen bei Betrachtung von Dietmar Riemanns Fotografie der Totenmaske Franz Fühmanns." In *Vinetas Archive. Annäherungen an Gründe.* Göttingen: Wallstein, 2011.

———. *Rübezahl in der Garage. Franz Fühmann in Märkisch-Buchholz und Fürstenwalde 1958–1984.* Frankfurter Buntbücher 41. Frankfurt (Oder): Kleist-Museum, 2006.

"100 Jahre Samariteranstalten. Insel im Meer oder Teil der Stadt?" Edited by Jürgen Schreiter and Friedrich Stachat. Fürstenwalde: Samariteranstalten, 1992.

Poore, Carol. *Disability in Twentieth-Century German Culture.* Corporealities: Discourses of Disability. Ann Arbor: University of Michigan Press, 2007.

———. "Illness and the Socialist Personality: Philosophical Debates and Literary Images in the GDR." In *Studies in GDR Culture and Society*, edited by Margy Gerber, 6:123–135. Lanham, MD: University Press of America, 1986.

Richter, Hans. "Franz Fühmanns Arbeiten für Kinder und Jugendliche." *Literatur für Leser* 2 (1993): 81–93.

Riemann, Dietmar. "Aus dem Zyklus 'Leben mit Geistig Behinderten' in den Samariteranstalten Fürstenwalde." In *Ins Innere. Annäherungen an Franz Fühmann*, edited by Peter Braun and Martin Straub, 194–203. Göttingen: Wallstein, 2016.

———. DDR-Fotografie Riemann. https://www.ddr-fotografie-riemann.de.

———. "Ich wollte nicht mehr mitmachen. Geschichte einer Verweigerung." In *Die Schuld der Mitläufer. Anpassen oder Widerstehen in der DDR*, edited by Roman Grafe, 91–100. Munich: Pantheon, 2009.

———. *Laufzettel. Tagebuch einer Ausreise.* Göttingen: Vandenhoek & Ruprecht, 2005.

———. "Posthumer Besuch bei Franz Fühmann in Märkisch-Buchholz im September 1984." In "Die Stelle des Hofnarren fiel dem Rotstift zum Opfer," edited by Jürgen Krätzer. Special issue, *Die Horen. Zeitschrift für Literatur, Kunst und Kritik* 256, no. 59 (2014): 10–22.

———. Radio interview with Peter Liebert. *Kulturmagazin*, "Dialog," January 17, 1987. Radio DDR 2. Audio file from the collection of Dietmar Riemann.

———. *"Was für eine Insel in was für einem Meer.* Die Geschichte eines Bildbandes mit Franz Fühmann." *Literarisches Journal aus Jena* 1 (2014): 128–138.
https://www.franz-fuehmann.de/_literatur/documents/Palm_1_14_Fuehmann.pdf.

———. *"Was für eine Insel in was für einem Meer.* Erfahrungen mit Franz Fühmann." In *Ins Innere. Annäherungen an Franz Fühmann*, edited by Peter Braun and Martin Straub, 204–220. Göttingen: Wallstein, 2016.

Robinson, Benjamin. "One Iota of Difference: Remembering GDR Literature as Socialist Literature." In *Twenty Years On: Competing Memories of the GDR in Postunification German Culture*, edited by Renate Rechtian and Dennis Tate, 217–231. Studies in German Literature Linguistics and Culture. Rochester, NY: Camden House, 2011.

Schreiber, Kerstin. "Zu Gast in den Samariteranstalten." *Unterwegs* 2 (2015): 20–21.

Tate, Dennis. "Franz Fühmann: A Neglected Legacy." In *Socialism and the Literary Imagination: Essays on East German Writers*, edited by Martin Kane, 91–105. New York: Berg, 1991.

———. *Franz Fühmann Innovation and Authenticity: A Study of His Prose-Writing.* Amsterdam: Rodopi, 1995.

———. "The Sufferings of 'Kamerad Fühmann': A Case of Distorted Reception in Both German States." In *German Literature at a Time of Change, 1989-1990*, edited by Arthur Williams, Stuart Parkes, and Roland Smith, 285–298. Bern: Peter Lang, 1991.

Voget, Paul-Gerhardt, ed., with illustrations from Harald Birck. *Was es noch zu sagen gäbe. Geschichten aus den Samariteranstalten anlässlich ihres 125-jährigen Bestehens.* Fürstenwalde: Samariteranstalten, 2017.

Winter, Bettina. "NS-'Euthanasie'-Verbrechen. Verdrängen—Erinnern—Aufarbeiten. Die Gedenkstätte Hadamar." In *Medizingeschichte und Gesellschaftskritik. Festschrift für Gerhard Baader*, edited by Michael Hubenstorf, Ragnhild Münch, Heinz-Peter Schmiedebach, and Sigrid Stöckel, 470–490. Husum: Matthiesen, 1997.